Thinking for primary writing

**Improving
children's writing
through creative thinking**

Acknowledgements

Behind this book are the five years of PhD study and all of the thinking, shaping, developing, crying, laughing, writing, deleting and writing again that go along with it. None of this would have been possible without some significant contributions from some great people.

First, to Suzanne Ashton, Nicola Bunday and the brilliant staff and pupils at Boundary Primary School, Blackpool. You kindly let me come in and facilitate creative thinking and writing workshops with your classes which I absolutely loved doing. The staff who took part in the research were honest, open and so helpful and the children were fantastic. The insights gained and framework created was largely because of you all. Thank you.

Second, to Professor Sally Elton-Chalcraft, Dr Karen Lockney and Dr Alison Jackson. Over the years of doing my PhD, you, as my supervisory team, challenged my thinking, widened the parameters of my reading, developed my writing and supported me so fiercely along the road. Your feedback was always so timely and helpful.

Third, to my PhD external examiners, Professor David Waugh and Professor Teresa Cremin. Your helpful critique and supportive encouragement to publish my research in this way was the boost I needed to not put my thesis on the shelf but do something positive with it.

Fourth, to my colleagues and students at University of Cumbria. To the English team who let me shoehorn my ideas into some of our modules and run with it. To my brilliant PGCE primary students whose work has inspired some of the case studies in the book and whose feedback has helped move my thinking on.

And finally, to the fabulous Lily Harrison at Critical Publishing. Thank you for your timely feedback, encouragement and support. I promise I will one day get the capitalisation right on 'Key Stage'!

To order our books please go to our website www.criticalpublishing.com or contact our distributor Ingram Publisher Services, telephone 01752 202301 or email IPSUK.orders@ingramcontent.com. Details of bulk order discounts can be found at www.criticalpublishing.com/delivery-information.

Our titles are also available in electronic format: for individual use via our website and for libraries and other institutions from all the major ebook platforms.

Thinking for primary writing

Improving children's writing through creative thinking

Adrian Copping

First published in 2024 by Critical Publishing Ltd

All rights reserved. No part of this publication may be reproduced, stored in a retrieval system, or transmitted in any form or by any means, electronic, mechanical, photocopying, recording or otherwise, without prior permission in writing from the publisher.

The author has made every effort to ensure the accuracy of information contained in this publication, but assumes no responsibility for any errors, inaccuracies, inconsistencies and omissions. Likewise, every effort has been made to contact copyright holders. If any copyright material has been reproduced unwittingly and without permission the Publisher will gladly receive information enabling them to rectify any error or omission in subsequent editions.

Copyright © 2024 Adrian Copping

British Library Cataloguing in Publication Data
A CIP record for this book is available from the British Library

ISBN: 978-1-915713-21-6

This book is also available in the following e-book formats:

EPUB ISBN: 978-1-915713-22-3
Adobe e-book ISBN: 978-1-915713-23-0

The right of Adrian Copping to be identified as the Author of this work have been asserted by him in accordance with the Copyright, Design and Patents Act 1988.

Text design by Greensplash
Cover design by Out of House Limited
Project management by Newgen Publishing UK

Critical Publishing
3 Connaught Road
St Albans
AL3 5RX

www.criticalpublishing.com

Printed on FSC accredited paper

Contents

	About the author	vi
	Introduction: thinking for writing – what? where? why? how?	1
1	The architect's brief: what is so hard about writing?	15
2	Choosing the tools: creative thinking skills to develop writing	29
3	Laying the foundations	43
4	The building blocks	57
5	The importance of cement: connecting the blocks	71
6	Working within the gaps	85
7	Call the scaffolders: the role of the task	97
8	Here comes the building inspector: assessment and learning	111
9	The big reveal: what they said	127
10	Changing the landscape	141
	References	155
	Index	169

About the author

Adrian Copping

Adrian Copping has worked within primary education for over 25 years, as a teacher, subject leader, senior leader and teacher educator. He taught in two contrasting primary schools and currently leads the University of Cumbria's Primary PGCE where he has been involved in researching and writing on primary English for over ten years. He completed a PhD in creative thinking and children's writing, which has formed part of the research and framework for this book.

Introduction: thinking for writing – what? where? why? how?

It's not the destination, but the adventure along the way.

(Travis Rice, nd)

This book is the story of my research adventure into what has been learned through bringing together the fields of creative thinking and primary writing. Both fields have been extensively researched; however, there is a paucity of research that I have found exploring how one influences the other, Wang (2012) being the only piece of empirical work that my literature searches discovered. This book looks to bring you, the reader, on my adventure of bringing together these two varied areas of study and exploring practically the concepts, challenges and discoveries that happened. The quotation at the beginning suggests that the destination is not important, but for me it is. However, the process, the adventure, is just as important, and the destination, where this book ends, may well be the beginning of a whole new adventure. This Introduction, as the heading suggests, provides some context to the research I undertook by answering the questions 'what?', 'where?', 'why?' and 'how?' in relation to my *'thinking for writing'* primary framework.

What was the research?

The research I undertook, from which this book stems, sought to explore the following three questions.

1. From teachers' and children's perspectives, to what extent do opportunities to think creatively during the writing process influence children's work?
2. From their viewpoint, to what extent do teachers' perspectives, personal experience and external factors such as school policy influence their writing pedagogy and the development of children's creative thinking?
3. From the teachers' and children's perspectives, how is creative thinking evidenced and how does this evidence influence writing process and product?

The research was undertaken using a case study approach. This approach was chosen because my concern was how individuals interpret their reality and socially construct their interpretations to achieve a shared reality within their context. Stark and Torrance (2005, p 33) state that case study *'stresses social interaction and the social construction of meaning in situ'*. Case study is an approach that focuses on process and as Stark and Torrance (2005, p 33) go on to add, *'Case study assumes that social reality is created through social interaction ... seeking to identify and describe'* the reality within the context that it takes place. A case study approach to this research was appropriate because it did not aim to discover any objective reality or solve a problem. Instead, my research aimed to describe or interpret a situation, looking in depth at a phenomenon and from a variety of angles (Thomas, 2011). Case study provided me as researcher a vehicle to *'provide a highly detailed, contextualised analysis of an instance in action'* (MacDonald and Walker, 1975, p 182 in Van Wynsberghe and Khan, 2007, p 83). In summary, through the approach of case study, my aim was not to discover objective reality or general cause-and-effect linkages but to identify and interpret socially constructed knowledge relating to creative thinking and writing in my participants' context. It follows, therefore, that the case study approach is also rooted in providing *'concrete case knowledge'* (Flyvbjerg, 2013, p 173). The context case for my research was bounded by a particular primary school in the north-west of England. Savin-Baden and Howell-Major (2013) citing Creswell (2003) provide suggestions for how a case could be bound: by time and place, time and activity, and definition and context. In the context of my research, most of these suggestions could have been applied. One school was chosen to provide the first boundary for the case because my aim was to interpret meaning within a context so as to develop theory (Savin-Baden and Howell-Major, 2013).

The case study consisted of the planning and facilitation of six full-day writing workshops, with six different classes over a two-year period. The research evolved over time and the findings from evidence collected during each event informed the design of the subsequent workshops. The way the case study was designed is shown in Figure 0.1 below.

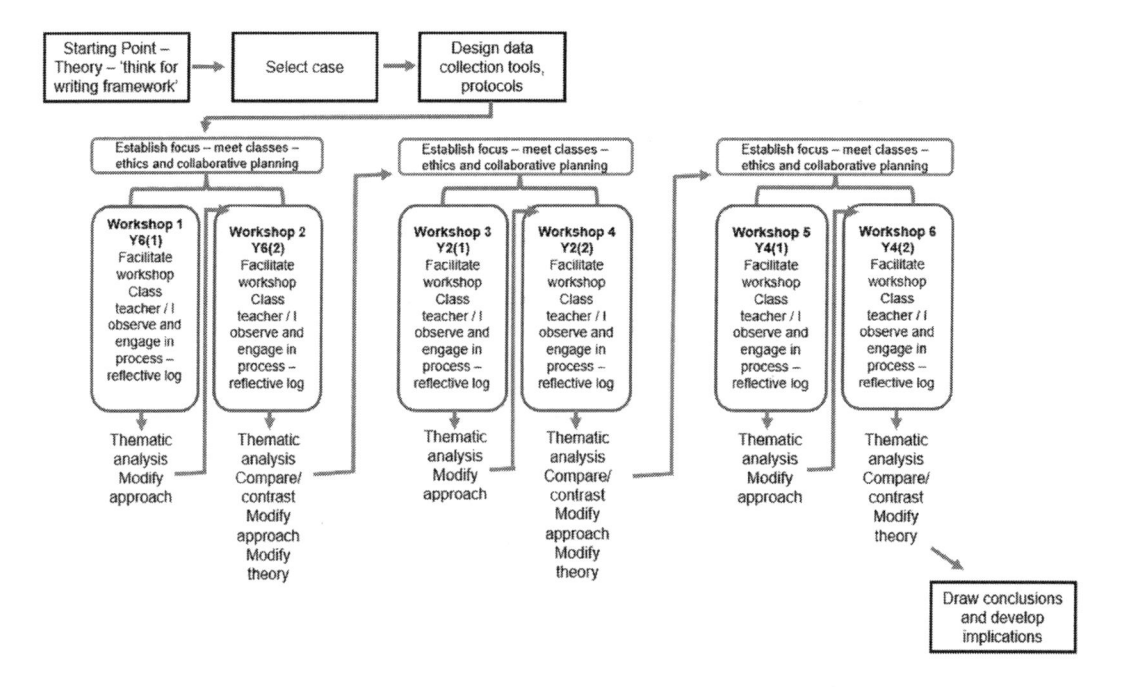

Figure 0.1 *My case study research design*

Each workshop had a focus selected by the school, and some of the case studies you will read in this book are extrapolations of the writing workshops undertaken. I planned and facilitated the workshops, which centred around creative thinking techniques such as simulations, collaborative writing, embracing pretence through writing in role and visualisation. Each workshop was structured so that children would engage with the writing process and build towards a purposeful product. Part of this process involved providing the children with a lot of autonomy in their writing. You may have noticed I used the term *'facilitation'* rather than *'teaching'*. This is a purposeful use of language, as facilitation suggests enabling learning rather than just direct instruction. As part of the workshops, there was some direct instruction, but the main approach was to facilitate learning through scaffolded activity and a coaching approach.

Where did this research take place?

The school, Parklands primary school (pseudonym), was chosen because it is a school that is of interest to me. Over a period of several years, I had been asked by teaching staff members, in my capacity as senior lecturer in primary education, to support them in their early career teaching years. These staff members had previously been students on the teacher education programme that I lead. I had also, in my capacity as a historical re-enactor, been invited to provide experiential *'English Civil War'* days of learning and activities for two of the classes. I was therefore known to the school and had an existing professional relationship with them. Parklands primary school was also chosen because of the socio-economic demographic it has. The school serves the community of Manor Park estate (pseudonym). Manor Park is a socially deprived area. It is the largest council populated area per head of local population in England. It was suffering high rates of crime and disorder. At the time of my research, crime had been significantly reduced but the police were regular visitors to Parklands primary. Hanscombe et al (2011) posit that this chaos in the lives of children living on the estate, most attending Parklands, has a direct correlation to poor performance in school. Shared environmental factors, such as those affecting Manor Park estate, according to Hanscombe et al's (2011) study accounts for 63 per cent of the correlation. This chaos and trauma as a result of these environmental factors could arguably expose the children living there to adverse childhood experiences (ACEs) (Bethell et al, 2014) which include crime, social discrimination and deprivation. Dahlitz (2017) discusses the nature of the impact of these ACEs on brain development, especially the prefrontal cortex part of the brain, responsible for creative thinking, reasoning and concentration, amongst other functions. Dahlitz (2017) assigns reduced interconnections between lobes within the prefrontal cortex to early trauma. Therefore, the choice of Parklands primary for my case study at this time was very important. Exploring the influence of creative thinking on writing pedagogy with children who, due to early trauma experienced because of where they live which may have impaired creative thinking as part of their brain architecture, could certainly develop my understanding of that phenomenon and its influence upon writing.

Why did this research take place?

Educational and political context

In January 2015, Secretary of State for Education Nicky Morgan endorsed a knowledge-based curriculum in a speech published on the Department for Education (DfE) website. This speech reflected the changes made to the national curriculum in 2013, which is still statutory, including knowledge-based changes made to the 2019 SATs. *(nb 2019 is the year the majority of my research took place.)* These changes gave English more focus on technical aspects of writing such as grammar, punctuation and spelling. This presented implications for teachers' pedagogical knowledge of the contribution these aspects make to effective writing (Myhill et al, 2013). As a result, writing pedagogy has shifted to teaching from the national curriculum grammar and punctuation appendices with an emphasis on learning key terms. This leaves limited time available for developing understanding of how these grammatical features can effectively contribute to quality writing. It is probably worth noting here, as Boyd (2022) states, drawing on the work of Wyse and Torgerson (2017) that a single Randomised Controlled Trial (RCT) heavily influenced the inclusion of more formalised grammar instruction in the primary curriculum. This single trial, Boyd (2022) states, took place in a secondary school and no checks were in place on the dependability of the intervention. This is one example of the problematic evidence base upon which such a significant national pedagogic decision is made.

During May each year, eligible children will sit SATs papers. Papers are delivered to maintained schools and must be locked away until the prescribed testing dates. For 2019, the grammar, punctuation and spelling test was made optional for Key Stage 1. The tests are marked by school staff and teachers can use this test as part of evidence over the year to make overall writing attainment judgements against the DfE's Teacher Assessment Frameworks.

Key Stage 2 SATs have an increased statutory focus on spelling, grammar and punctuation with two tests and one on reading. These are sent away and marked externally. As for Key Stage 1 writing, teacher assessment judgements should be using the interim Teacher Assessment Frameworks when making their judgements.

The increased focus on the more technical aspects of writing – spelling, grammar and punctuation – in the national curriculum (DfE, 2013) and the government's belief in a knowledge-based curriculum is evidenced in the statutory assessment that children complete and schools report to inform their league table position. This gives the results high stakes for each school, keen to increase their league table position and to be seen in the school marketplace as a high-quality site of learning for children. More children on roll means more money for the school, as a school's funding is allocated per child. It is therefore within this context of a culture of teaching to a test which values knowledge of a wide variety of the technical aspects of writing, including key terms and high anxiety (Connor, 2003), caused by high-stakes testing that my research takes place.

The implications of the educational context as laid out above are significant. The pressure on teachers to cover a demanding curriculum and deliver high scores on tests has reduced the focus of teaching writing to produce pieces with grammatical features identified in the DfE exemplification. High-stakes testing has distorted practice, reduced the curriculum and given children a narrower range of opportunity (Polesel et al, 2014). However, the majority of research into effective writing pedagogy over the last 30 years is rooted in a process model (Graves, 1983; Graham et al, 2012; Cremin, 2015). This model purports that learning takes place through the process of writing and that it is context-situated (Kellogg, 1999). Writing is about composition, effect and intent as the author and the grammatical features of the writing are tools for the writer to use to create pictures, evoke emotion and weave their intent. It is a creative endeavour. My research, therefore, sought to '*meddle in the middle*' (McWilliam, 2009) and explore the process of writing, a pedagogy of process that the literature endorses, rather than the quantifiable, product-based writing that political policy demands.

Another implication of high-stakes testing is a focus on curriculum coverage rather than on securing understanding. This has led to the marketisation of learning with published schemes and resources readily available ensuring curriculum coverage, and therefore the assumption that children are then prepared for the tests. These tests are designed to align with the curriculum and test recall of the knowledge the curriculum contains, but do they support the development of understanding? Kellogg (1999) contends that the process of writing can lead to a growth in understanding, and this is why my research was worthwhile. My research looked to develop a model that can support teachers to develop children's understanding through the process of writing. Within that process is understanding that writing is a creative endeavour and therefore involves creative thinking. This research was worthwhile in that it looked to develop a model to support teachers in developing a pedagogy of understanding, not just knowledge, to help children understand the grammatical and structural tools in composing writing and use them for their own purposes. Bereiter and Scardamalia (1993) contend that it is not more constructs that are required but an understanding of the nature and functions of the writing process and the knowledge to apply this to writing tasks.

In summary, this research was undertaken to explore alternative approaches that a teacher can use to achieve high-quality writing. It stems from a growing dissatisfaction with a formulaic approach to teaching writing I have witnessed in schools, often driven by well-meaning published schemes and plans. This research aimed to arm teachers and children with a variety of tools to pick up and use when the need arises, coming from a base of thinking, writing intentionally and communicating meaning effectively, using grammatical tools and conventions purposefully.

How did this research take place?

If you have started the Introduction to this book at the beginning, my hope is that you will already have some ideas in your mind as to how this research took place, as I have laid a few clues for you in the preceding sections. However, in this section, I take you through some of my thinking processes in developing the writing workshops, but also some of the headline findings following each pair of workshops and how that influenced the evolution of my thinking for primary writing model.

Workshops 1 and 2: Year 6 – creating a simulation

I must admit that to be given the science fiction genre by the school did not fill me with immediate joy. However, it turned out to be exciting and motivating for me to plan and facilitate. It was felt that my whole-day writing workshop would provide a good introduction to the genre for the children and engage them with it. A whole day was also chosen, rather than a more traditional one-hour English lesson per day over a week, as less time would elapse between each phase of the writing process and facilitate connection-making between phase elements (Fink et al, 2007), an important characteristic of creative thinking. '*Galactic Defence*' was designed to provide a context within which to facilitate the cognitive attitude of problem-solving (Meadows, 2006). You can read more about this in detail in Maariya's case study in Chapter 4. The workshop design was also informed by a piece of my own empirical research (Copping, 2018). This research emphasised the importance of creating an environment for thinking, placing value on the writing process, not just the product, providing a clear purpose for writing and setting high expectations for writing and thinking. The problem-solving context began with a simulation, to engage the participants and, as Cremin (2009, p 98) states, '*the lived experience of drama becomes a natural writing frame that is charged with the emotions and experiences of the imagined world*'. A simulation therefore can allow children to become fully immersed in the context and enrich their work through a deeper experiential engagement with the problem to solve. The '*Galactic Defence*' simulation was that Parklands primary had been infiltrated by Dax, an evil robot master force. Dax had already possessed the senior staff and the classroom was the only safe place. Both classrooms were decorated to simulate a space laboratory. Employing teacher in role, I facilitated the workshops as a professor for '*Galactic Defence*', engaged the children as junior researchers and used writing in role for the children to bring themselves to the writing process. This involved developing group scenarios in the form of stories to present to the school's governing body regarding the potential risks of an evil robot infestation. Within this simulation, the workshops were structured around Alves and Limpo's (2015) writing process of planning, translation (composition – translating ideas into text) and transcription (including editing). This process included a '*what would happen if*' possibility thinking activity to generate ideas and shared reading, using a mentor text (Culham, 2014) or WAGOLL (What A Good One Looks Like) in the data, planning, composing, editing and revising in groups. This WAGOLL provided a model text for the children to see what they were aiming for.

During the writing workshops, observations were made around the children's creative thinking and, following them, focus group interviews with children and teachers were conducted. Once analysed, this evidence produced four key themes (larger boxes) and extrapolations at their side which are shown in Figure 0.2 below.

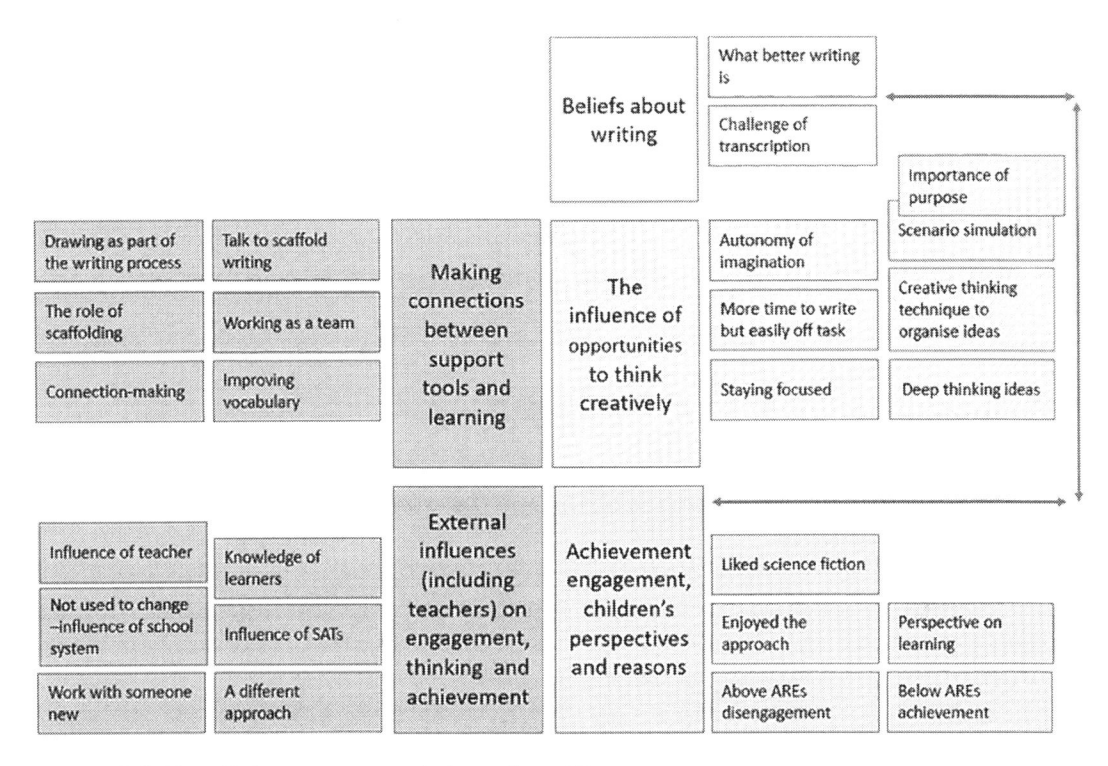

Figure 0.2 Year 6 theme map: workshops 1 and 2

While all of the evidence gathered was interesting, there were a couple of headlines that surprised me. The first was children struggling to make connections between the WAGOLL I had created and their own writing. Despite WAGOLLs being a regular feature of their usual English teaching, there appeared to be limited cognitive flexibility to magpie language and utilise it for their own purposes. The second headline was that children assessed at working above age-related expectations (AREs) seemed disengaged and writing produced did not cohere with their usual attainment, whereas the vast majority of children assessed at working below AREs were fully engaged and their written work was of a higher quality than usually produced. I don't wish to speculate here, but perhaps the 'external influences' in Figure 0.2 may be a factor. This evidence led to the first iteration of a *'thinking for writing'* framework. It emphasised the importance of making connections between the different elements of the writing process through writing discourse, within a thinking environment. This first framework is shown in Figure 0.3 below.

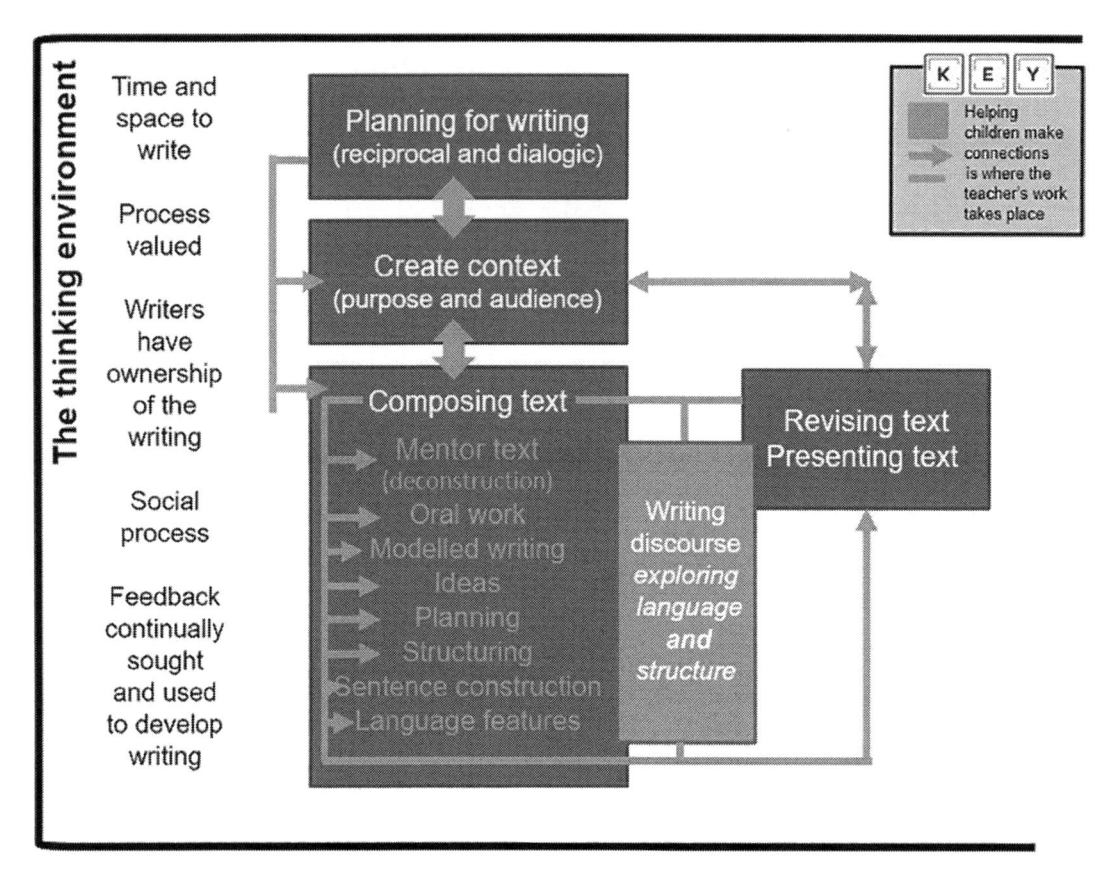

Figure 0.3 The first thinking for writing framework

Workshops 3 and 4: Year 2 – visualisation and creative connections

The design of workshops 3 and 4 was informed by Figure 0.3. This involved the setting and maintaining of a thinking climate through deployment of the factors that make up an effective thinking environment. It also involved making more explicit links for the children between elements of composing text, planning, context and presenting text. The theme of superheroes was chosen by both Year 2 class teachers as a school-wide '*superhero writers*' award had just begun to motivate children to improve their writing. The context of the Great Fire of London came out of a planning session with the classes a week prior to the workshops. This involved children working in pairs, creating mind maps focused on superheroes, and writing ideas. One of the pairs, drawing on their previous term's topic, remarked, '*I wonder what would happen if superheroes landed when the Great Fire of London started?*' This unlikely connection certainly demonstrated novel thinking (Sternberg, 2003) and proved to be the idea that motivated the workshop.

To provide a purpose for writing (Copping, 2018), it was agreed that a book would be created by each class with the title '*I wonder what would happen if superheroes landed when the*

Great Fire of London started?' Children would each create a 75-word story, so as to give less to write in the one-day workshop time available and more time to focus on editing and revising, part of the process that there was limited time for in workshops 1 and 2. These workshops were also designed to facilitate problem-solving (Meadows, 2006): could superheroes save London from the fire? The workshop began by facilitating curiosity (Robson, 2014) through the use of a large map of London (1666) with streets and landmarks laid out on the floor. This tool allowed the children to physically walk through London in 1666, see where the landmarks were and playfully visualise, as a way into composition. The workshops were again structured using Alves and Limpo's (2015) writing process of planning, composition (translating ideas into text) and transcription (including editing). This process included a film clip of London, featuring landmarks on the large map, engagement with the 1666 large map of London and discussing where they were in relation to the fire. Following this, ideas were developed in groups, and then planning the plot. The final stages of the processes allowed significant time to compose and revise text, as evidence from workshops 1 and 2 suggested children wanted more time to write. This links to developing creative thinking attributes of persistence (Robson, 2014) and self-regulation.

As in workshops 1 and 2, observations were made around the children's creative thinking and, following them, focus group interviews with children and teachers were conducted. Once analysed, this evidence produced five key themes (larger boxes) and extrapolations at their side which are shown in Figure 0.4 below.

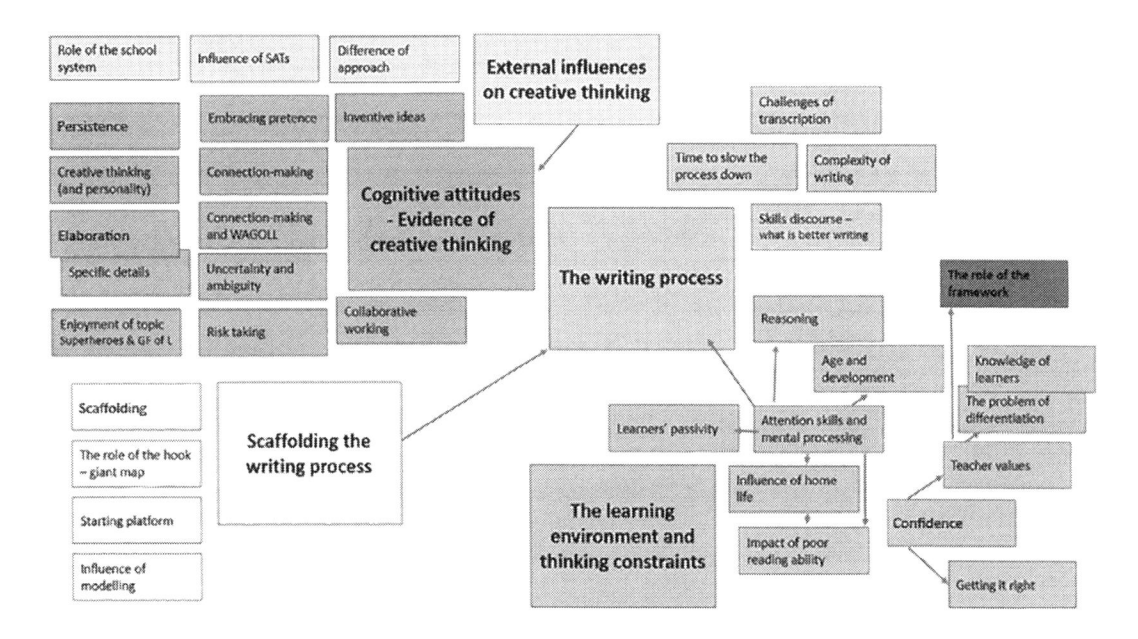

Figure 0.4 *Year 2 theme map: workshops 3 and 4*

It was evident through this pair of workshops that there were significant constraints on the children's capacity for creative thinking, mainly around cognitive load and information processing. This gave rise to a key development in my thinking for writing framework, the need for the teacher to get involved in the middle of the writing process, following some creative thinking training. This is demonstrated in the second iteration of the framework, shown in Figure 0.5 below.

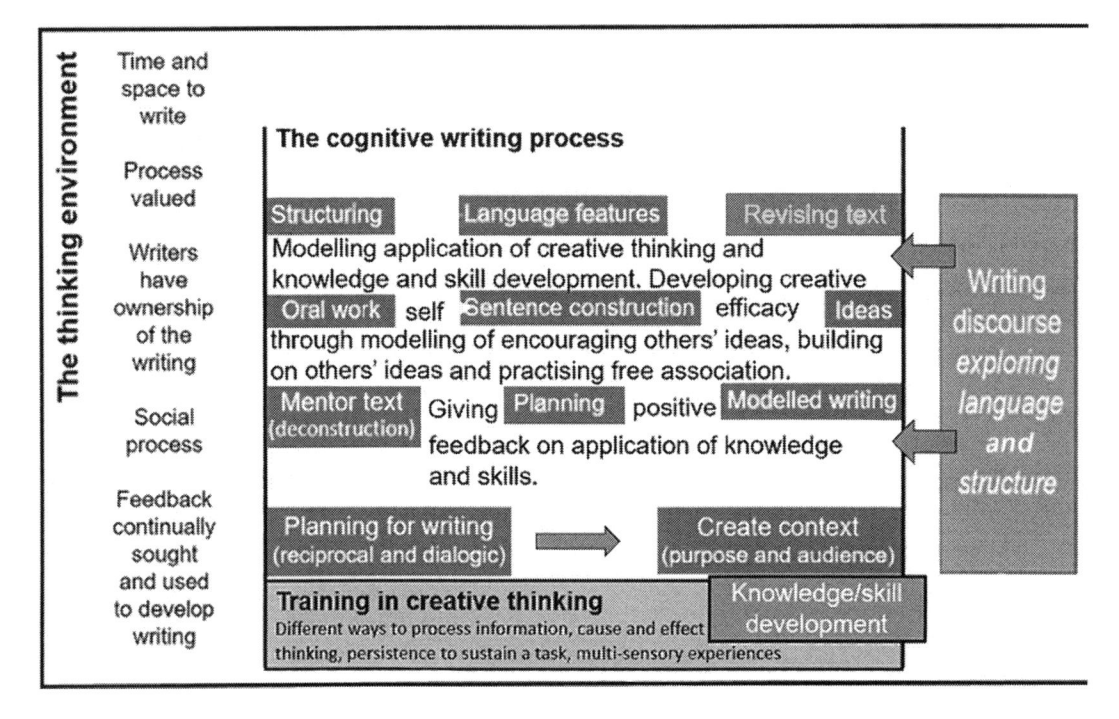

Figure 0.5 The second thinking for writing framework

Workshops 5 and 6: Year 4 – autonomous multi-sensory writing

The design of workshops 5 and 6 was informed by Figure 0.5. This involved, first, some creative thinking training. The training began a week prior to the workshop with some input on the purpose of mind-mapping and then idea generation for the workshops. Out of those ideas a multi-sensory experience of developing a musical play was decided upon both as a product and as a vehicle for developing creative thinking throughout the writing process. Also involved was making more explicit connections between the building blocks of the cognitive writing process.

The theme 'raindrops keep falling on my head' was chosen by both Year 4 teachers to tie in with their science topic on water and rainfall. 'Raindrops keep falling on my head' would also provide a vehicle for a problem-solving approach to writing (Meadows, 2006) through the use of creating playscripts that had to include certain ingredients:

- a musical element;
- a scientific fact about water;

Introduction • 11

- an imaginary land;
- a problem to solve; and
- a well-known character.

You can read more about this in Leo's case study in Chapter 4. The problem for the children to solve was how to incorporate all of these into a playscript which they could then perform. A week prior to the workshop, I had begun the ideation process with the children, including decision-making about what the workshops would entail. This, like workshops 3 and 4, involved creating mind maps but, despite modelling mind-mapping as a way to structure and extend ideas, many of the children's mind maps were essentially lists. To develop their understanding and training, I facilitated the synthesis of their ideas into a Year 4 mind map where they explored connections and idea development verbally and I depicted their collective thinking on paper. Figure 0.6 below is my depiction of their thinking.

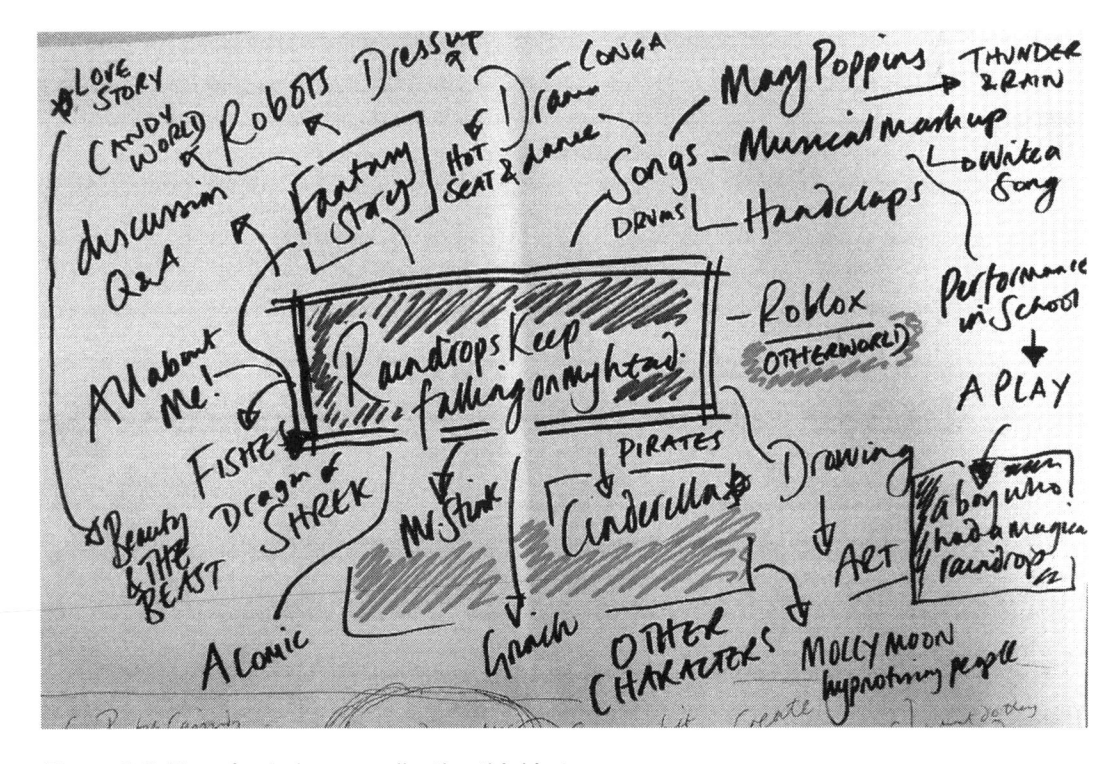

Figure 0.6 *Year 4 mind map: collective thinking*

This demonstrates their ability to see and make connections and develop ideas, but, perhaps not able to hold all of the information in their heads, to organise it on paper, as well as other demanding skills of writing: spelling, handwriting and letter formation.

Like the previous four, workshops 5 and 6 were structured using Alves and Limpo's (2015) writing process of planning, translation and transcription. The playscript was the form of writing chosen by the children, and this provided a slightly different focus for the transcriptional elements of the writing process; the finished product for these workshops was a performed play, not a piece of writing, so the transcriptional elements such as handwriting, spelling, punctuation and sentence structure all served a tangible purpose of communicating to the actors how they should perform their lines and create impact. This is different to the previous workshops where the product was a '*published*' piece of writing. The workshop process began with an explanation of the social process of thinking and writing and an introduction to the idea of each person in each writing group having a role, a co-operative learning strategy (Kagan et al, 1997). Each team member wore a lanyard with their role and an explanation of what that role meant; options to swap were given at points during the morning. The afternoon would be given over to preparing for their performances, refining the script and making decisions about musical instruments and costume. Uninterrupted time was given for this, allowing the development of persistence and self-regulation.

As in the previous workshops, observations were made around the children's creative thinking and, following them, focus group interviews with children and teachers were conducted. Once analysed, this evidence produced four interconnecting key themes (larger boxes) and extrapolations at their side which are shown in Figure 0.7 below.

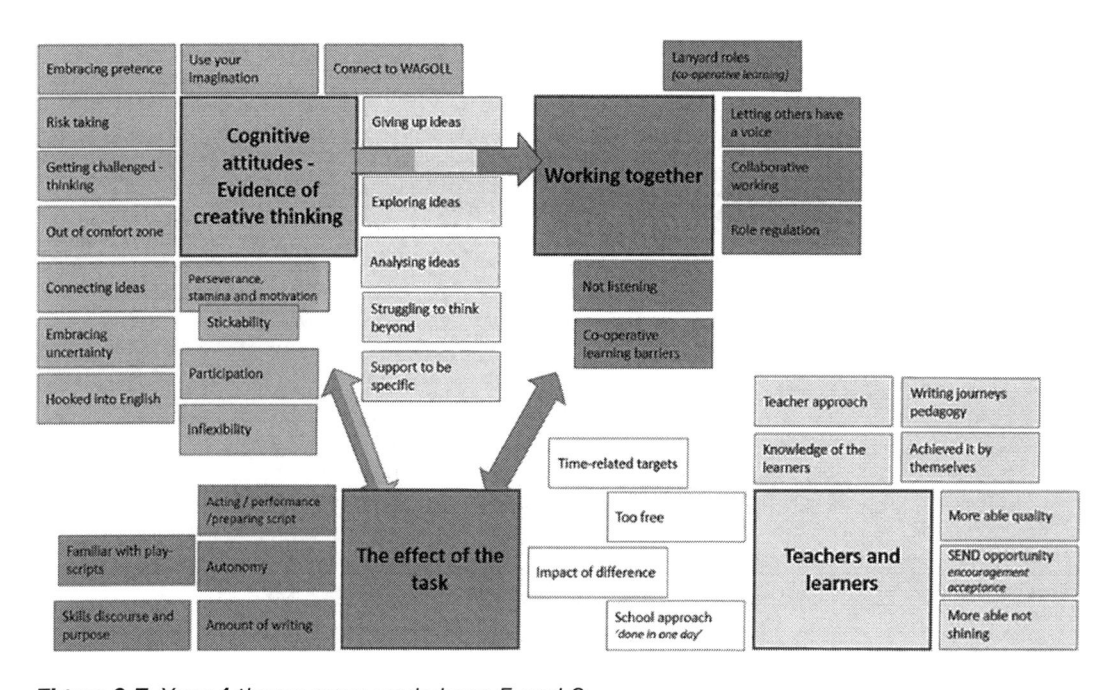

Figure 0.7 *Year 4 theme map: workshops 5 and 6*

The headline evidence here was the effect of the task on the children's creative thinking and their writing. In much of the writing, there was more evidence of risk-taking in use of language and using linguistic devices such as parentheses and rhetorical questions for intentional communication. Can the nature and design of the task have this much impact on thinking and writing? In this context, I have to say it did. It therefore led to what is the current iteration of my framework, presented in Figure 0.8 below.

Introduction • **13**

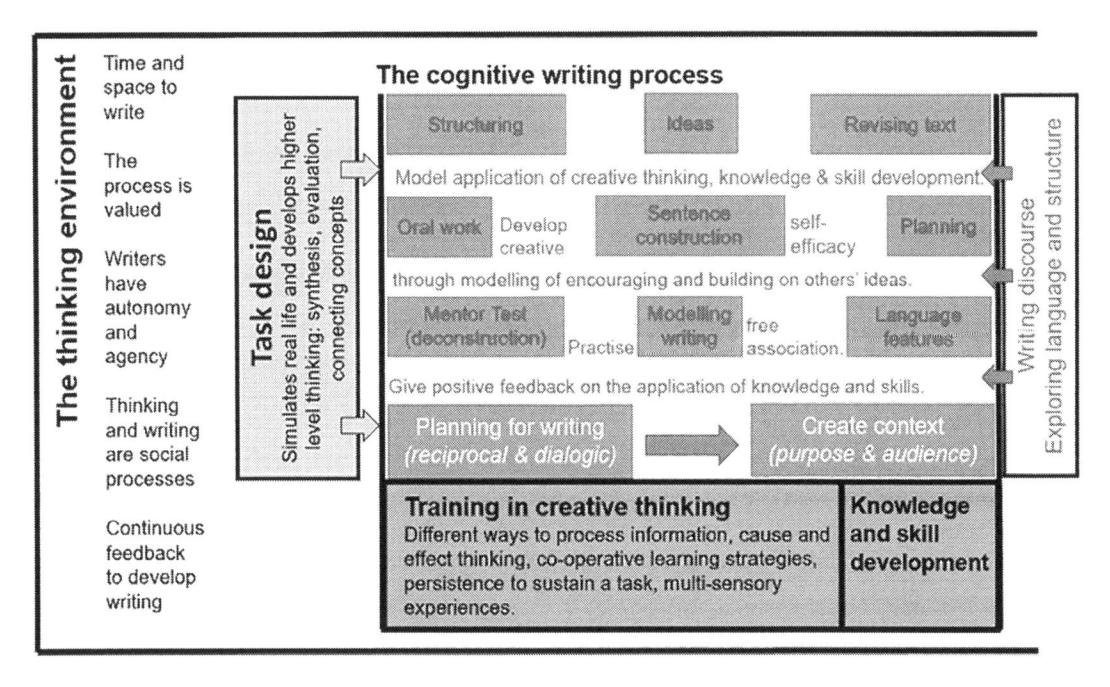

Figure 0.8 Current thinking for writing framework

Chapter summary

This introduction sets the context for the remainder of the book. Hopefully, it has provided an insight into my research adventure where I have sought to bring together the fields of creative thinking and children's writing and how one influences the other. Through giving you some insight into the learning I have gained along the way, the evidence gathered from the workshops carried out and the evolution of my thinking for writing framework, I hope to have built a foundation for you to get the most from the rest of this book.

1 The architect's brief: what is so hard about writing?

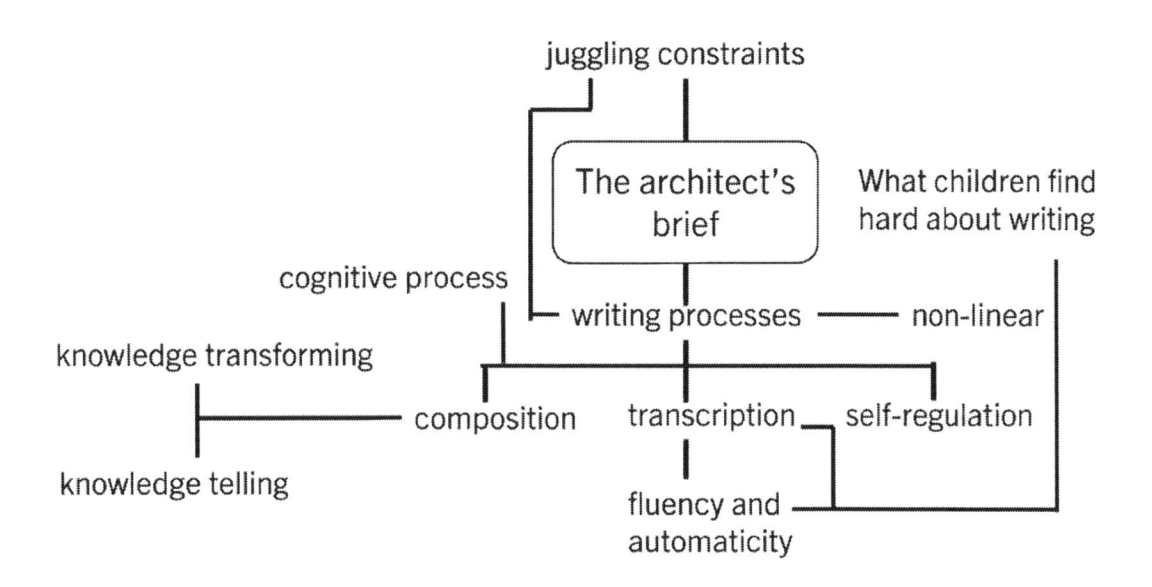

```
                    juggling constraints
                           │
                    ┌──────┴──────┐
                    │ The         │    What children find
                    │ architect's │    hard about writing
                    │ brief       │
        cognitive process         │
knowledge transforming  │ ── writing processes ─── non-linear
    ├──────────── composition   transcription ── self-regulation
knowledge telling                     │
                               fluency and
                               automaticity
```

Core Content Framework / Early Career Teacher Framework links

The Department for Education for England and Wales (DfE) provides a framework of minimum entitlement for trainee teachers which is then developed into your Early Career Teacher (ECT) years. This chapter links to the following:

- how pupils learn (Standard 2 – progress) – working memory, long-term memory, retrieval practice;
- subject and curriculum (Standard 3) – mastering foundational concepts, linking new ideas to existing ideas, mental models;
- classroom practice (Standard 4) – modelling, scaffolds, worked examples;
- assessment (Standard 6) – feedback to help regulate learning.

Introduction

I don't know if you are a fan of the type of television shows where people are looking to build their dream home, renovate a derelict building or reimagine their existing home. I will be honest and say I do get absorbed by them. I am always in awe of the architects who are tasked with bringing a range of ideas to a workable plan, looking at all the constraints and challenges of what is there in the landscape, then problem-solving to help realise their clients' dreams. If you have looked at the chapter headings in this book you will undoubtedly notice a building metaphor. I have applied this approach as I see the writing process as a series of building blocks. Thus, I have attempted to keep the metaphor running throughout the whole book. We start in Chapter 1, where a building often starts, with the architect's brief. In this context the brief was to develop a framework for teachers to use that brings together creative thinking and writing in a practical way. An architect also has to consider and address the varying constraints that may impact on the brief, so in this opening chapter the constraints and challenges that impact upon writing are explored. This chapter examines a range of research into what children say about writing and what they find hard about it. It considers areas that writers have to juggle – ideas, sentence structure, handwriting, letter formation and punctuation – as well as the challenge of communicating gesture and inflection through writing. I suggest that the cognitive challenge of juggling these many constraints is when writing can lead to cognitive overload. This in turn impacts on self-regulation, so important for sustaining and persisting in writing.

Keeping all the balls in the air

Hayes and Flower (1980) describe the process of writing as the juggling of simultaneous constraints. There is so much to think about when writing, as I have mentioned in the introduction to this chapter; so many balls to keep in the air at once. So, what are they?

Writing processes: composition, transcription and self-regulation

The various constraints mentioned in the introduction to this chapter – ideas, sentence structure, handwriting, letter formation and punctuation – can be categorised within three processes:

1. composition;
2. transcription; and
3. self-regulation.

These processes are not linear or even cyclical, they are simultaneous. But writing is not just a physical process; it is also a cognitive one. I also believe that writing is a problem-solving activity, which aligns to a key characteristic of creative thinking. This approach aligns with Bereiter and Scardamalia's (1993) models of composing as knowledge telling and knowledge transforming, knowledge transforming being more of a problem-solving process used by skilled writers. Struggling writers can be hobbled and often demotivated by the transcription elements of writing, as these are the processes they often struggle with.

The writing process is often seen as a series of actions or stages usually defined as planning, drafting, editing and revising (Seow, 2002, p 315). This process is also described as being difficult and requiring a variety of skills. Hiatt and Rooke state that:

> At the moment of writing children are struggling to bring together a clutch of different skills ... the act of writing is less about an artistic encounter and more about a practical and rather complicated process of construction.
>
> (2002, p 1)

In this statement, I suggest they are referring to skills needed within the stages of planning, drafting, editing and revising. Hiatt and Rooke suggest that the clutch of skills inexperienced writers need to bring together are *'the fine motor skills of handwriting ... alongside the skills of spelling, sentence construction, paragraphing and organisation of the whole text'* (2002, p 2). Alongside these I would add the skills of working with ideas, using imagination and applying knowledge of story. While all of this is happening, the internal dialogue of decision is taking place – word choice, punctuation, ideas, text structure and layout. What adjustments should be made? Hiatt and Rooke conclude their argument with a statement that adds what seems to me to be pressure on the junior writer: *'The quality of the child's composition depends upon the quality of this internal dialogue about what to use and how everything should be put together'* (2002, p 2). They seem to be suggesting that the quality of writing is dependent on the ability to connect and bring together different skills, which puts a lot of pressure on the writer.

Composition

This term is used regularly in the literature on writing (Kellogg, 1999; Harmey et al, 2019) to bring together the cognitive processes that support writing. Here you consider writing as not just a set of physical processes, but cognitive processes too. Hayes and Flower make the point that *'writing is best understood as a set of distinctive thinking processes which writers orchestrate or organise during the act of composing'* (1981, p 366). These cognitive processes are stated by Alves and Limpo (2015) as (1) planning processes – that support the generation of ideas; (2) translation processes – converting those ideas into written language; (3) transcription processes that utilise spelling, grammar and punctuation, handwriting or typing those written language ideas into written text; and then (4) revising processes that evaluate and adjust the stage 3 process to ensure the author's intended communication is achieved. Stages 1 and 2 above are often connected in literature under the umbrella term *'composition'* (Harmey et al, 2019), composition being the planning and translating of ideas into the written word.

Kellogg states that writing (he may be referring to the processes that encapsulate what I have termed composition) is the *'challenge of creating coherent ideas in the private realm of thought and mapping those ideas into the public world of linguistic symbols'* (1999, p 3). He is essentially saying that the act of composition is the act of making meaning, turning personal thought into public text; and he acknowledges the challenges that this presents. Understanding the composition process also makes it possible to see how that process can be influenced by creative thinking and how that can in turn influence pedagogy.

Communicating effectively using linguistic symbols means the communicator is denied what Gardner refers to as *'the potency of other symbol systems. Much knowledge is apprehended and communicated through gesture and other paralinguistic means'* (1991, p 56). In other words, written communication is denied the power of gesture, facial expression, pause, inflection and accent that, for example, oral communication enjoys. Written composition is therefore challenging: communicating meaning and intent with the aid of only words, structure and punctuation requires juggling a number of processes and also knowledge simultaneously, as I have referred to in the previous paragraph. Kellogg outlines some of these processes: *'retrieving information from memory, generating new ideas ... organising ... linguistic structures ... reading the evolving text ...'* (1999, p 10).

To suggest that composition is simply about turning private thought into text is probably not doing justice to the level at which skilful writers operate. Bereiter and Scardamalia (1987) suggest that there are two contrasting models of composition: knowledge telling and knowledge transforming. Knowledge telling, which I understand to be using cues from the brief of a given writing assignment to activate the writer's knowledge, retrieve that content and then write it. Knowledge transformation, however, is ascribed by Bereiter et al to more skilful writers as *'a variety of problem-solving operations involving ... identifying goals and constraints, searching, testing ... modifying knowledge in response to gaps, inconsistencies and the like'* (1988, p 261). While knowledge-telling is undoubtedly composition, it is little more than the *'arrangement of content reflecting what is salient in the mind of the writer'* (Bereiter et al, 1988, p 261). Yet Bereiter et al's viewpoint is that more skilful composing of text does more than just tell knowledge, it brings together existing knowledge, interprets it, connects it, tests it and pits it against other knowledge to create something transformative. It is a cognitive process of problem-solving.

Transcription

Transcriptional processes are the processes that cause struggling writers the most difficulty. MacArthur (1999, p 169) makes the point that children who struggle with writing find the mechanics – handwriting and spelling, grammar and punctuation – difficult. This is also posited by Graham and Harris (2009) in their meta-analysis of evidence-based writing practices. Transcription skills are, however, an important aspect of writing. In their discussion of the effects of grammar teaching on writing development, Andrews et al comment on why transcription skills are important. They state that *'different aspects of teaching grammar improve the quality and accuracy of ... writing in English'* (2006, p 39). MacArthur goes on to say that while these transcription processes (or mechanics) can often be seen as less important than communicating the message, they are of importance because *'errors distract readers from the message the writer is trying to convey'* (1999, p 170). In their work on self-regulation and transcription, Graham and Harris develop this idea of struggling with the mechanics of writing. They suggest that it is only struggling writers who *'may be hobbled by difficulties managing and co-ordinating the elements underlying the process of revising'*

(2000, p 6). They are referring here to the mechanics of transcription: checking spelling, punctuation and grammatical accuracy. Graham and Harris (2000) go on to make the point that because struggling and developing writers to an extent find the mechanics of transcription difficult, they will make fewer revisions than skilled writers and, as a result, it could be argued that their writing is not as well crafted or developed. They also put forward the argument that this lack of willingness to engage in revising (a transcription process) is down to a lack of self-regulation. Revising work requires the self-regulation disciplines of motivation, perseverance and persistence that contribute to '*mental subroutines for enhancing writing performance*' (Zimmerman and Risemberg, 1997, p 75).

CASE STUDY

Year 3: revising and editing text

Krishna, a student teacher, was on his final teaching placement before qualifying. He had been teaching a poetry unit using the poetic form of kennings. Although initially negative about poetry, his class had loved the fact that each line only had a two-word noun phrase, so there wasn't, as they put it, '*much to write*'. Krishna had found it a challenge to enthuse his class about writing throughout his placement and so thought that the opportunity to link this old Norse poetic form to his class history topic on Vikings would engage the class. Krishna had provided examples of kennings for the children to engage with and use the clues within the poems to work out who or what they were about. He had modelled the composing process and asked the children to add to his model, and he had then asked them to have a go in pairs. One of the key features of kenning poems is that the noun phrases start quite vague and provide stronger clues to guess the topic as the poem progresses, and Krishna wanted the pairs to edit and revise their work to understand this concept. Here is where the resistance began.

Figure 1.1 below shows the teaching and learning steps that Krishna planned and took. At first sight the approach is coherent, logical and makes sense. It is, however, linear.

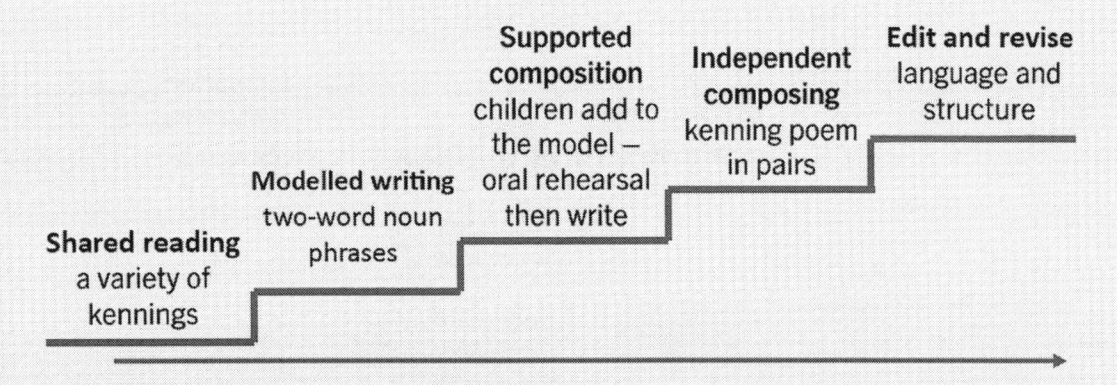

Figure 1.1 Krishna's teaching and learning steps

20 • *Thinking for Primary Writing*

Many of the pairs declared their kenning creations as already finished. Some confided that they didn't want to '*write it out again*', while others just felt their work was good enough and, despite recognising the need for improvement, they just didn't want to develop it. Krishna was yet again frustrated.

> ## *Reflective questions* ?
>
> » How do you think Krishna could have helped his class overcome their resistance of editing?
>
> » Was there any way Krishna could have modelled editing as part of the composition process? Editing and revising is often done at the end of the composing process, but if editing was an integral part of composing, would it feel like an extra burden?
>
> » What are some suggestions you might make to Krishna about approaches to composing or ways of recording their kennings that might make the class feel like editing was more purposeful? Could each noun phrase be on a strip of paper, thus easier to re-order? Would this help?

Part of the reflection process here is to think about how editing and revising can be included in the composing process rather than waiting until the end, when children have often run out of writing steam. Figure 1.2 below is a version of Krishna's same teaching and learning steps, but suggests that, instead of a linear process, the composition elements are more integrated. There are limitations to the diagram representation, but hopefully my meaning is clear.

Modelled writing
two-word noun phrases

Edit and revise
language and structure

Shared reading
a variety of kennings

composing

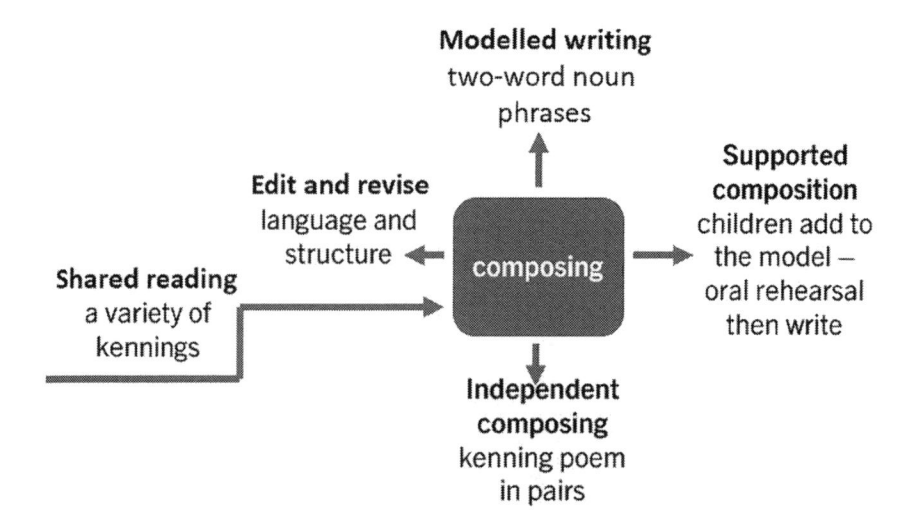

Supported composition
children add to the model – oral rehearsal then write

Independent composing
kenning poem in pairs

Figure 1.2 *Krishna's possible integrated composition process*

This suggests that all of these four stages are part of the composing process; editing and revising modelled as part of the composing process, and integral to it, may well support the development of self-regulation and hopefully minimise the cries of '*Yes, but I've finished*' in response to being asked to improve writing.

Self-regulation

A process too little discussed as part of writing is self-regulation. In Krishna's kennings example above, you can see the impact of that on his class's writing. There was a lack of willingness to persist in their writing, but I believe this can be developed. So, what is it?

Graham and Harris (2000) have cast writers into three categories: skilled, developing and struggling. One of the main differences between each category, they argue, is the writer's ability to self-regulate. Self-regulation is a necessity for skilled writing (Bereiter and Scardamalia, 1987; Zimmerman and Risemberg, 1997) and has long been considered a significant process towards writing alongside composition and transcription. Zimmerman and Risemberg state that '*Becoming an adept writer involves more than knowledge of vocabulary and grammar, it depends on high levels of personal regulation because writing activities are usually self-planned, self-initiated, and self-sustained*' (1997, p 73). They are arguing that writing is not just about physical and even cognitive processes, but also about motivation and the ability to motivate oneself, to initiate writing, plan it and then sustain the writing through the challenging processes of turning personal thought into public text. This is developed by Arrimada et al (2019) and Oddsdóttir et al (2021) in their work on teaching self-regulation strategies to young writers. Both studies found that teaching these explicit strategies led to more effective writing and affected more of the variables in writing. Harris et al (2011) identify a variety of self-regulation strategies that writers use to manage the complexities of the processes of composition and transcription. These include planning, gathering information, organising ideas, transforming knowledge for the writing purpose, revising, self-monitoring and self-evaluation. They go on to add that skilled writers are more self-regulated than struggling writers and that a writing pedagogy that combines teaching self-regulation with meaningful practice is the way to develop writing performance.

So, these are some of the constraints that a range of research and literature suggests need to be navigated as part of my architect's brief, but what do children say they find hard about writing?

What is difficult about writing? Children's voices

To explore this area, I have explored a meta-analysis by Ivanic (2004) evaluating writing discourse. I have compared this theoretical work to some empirical research by Lambirth (2016), exploring children's voices around writing, to see how they cohere together. Ivanic's (2004) work is more theoretical, providing an analytic tool to evaluate discourse from a range of sources such as documents, teaching and learning resources as well as interviews and focus groups. It is a '*meta-analysis of theory and research about writing and writing pedagogy*' (2004, p 220). As a meta-analysis it combines multiple studies and compares their findings, enhancing the reliability of the conclusions. Ivanic's (2004) framework has identified six discourses of writing:

1. skills discourse;
2. creativity discourse;
3. process discourse;
4. genre discourse;
5. social practices discourse; and
6. socio-political discourse.

Skills discourse appears most prevalent, as does creativity discourse, which appears later in discussion of and comparison to Lambirth's (2016) work. I have also utilised the work of Grainger et al (2003) to provide additional children's voice research to Ivanic's framework.

Ivanic defines a skills discourse as a *'belief that writing consists of applying knowledge of a set of linguistic patterns and rules for sound–symbol relationships and sentence construction'* (2004, p 226). This definition suggests that writing is about building sentences and applying patterns and rules. The implication may be that, within this view of writing, there is no room for the artistry of writing or cognitive problem-solving in writing. This discourse that writing is skills only and context free is also emphasised by Beard and Burrell (2010) in relation to the national curriculum (DfE, 2013) and an allusion to high-stakes testing. In their investigation of narrative writing by 9–11 year-olds, they emphasise the national curriculum expectations for this age group as being significantly skills-based: emphasising the more mechanistic elements of writing, including correct spelling, the correct use of full stops and other punctuation. This skills discourse is picked up by Grainger et al (2003) as their work suggests that it is the skills-based elements of writing that arguably makes for children's negative attitudes to writing. Grainger et al found that the pupils they spoke to in Years 3 and 4 expressed negative views about writing, their *'dislikes focused mostly on punctuation, spelling and aching hands'* (2003, p 7). They had also made judgements about their competence based on their perception of their punctuation and spelling skills. However, children in Foundation Stage and Key Stage 1 that Grainger et al (2003) spoke to expressed enjoyment of writing as it had a clear purpose and a real audience, for example making cards for special occasions and writing to fictional characters from books. These positive attitudes to writing were shared by children in Years 5 and 6 in Grainger et al's (2003) work. It seemed that enjoyment of writing was linked to freedom of task (2003, p 7) but also children enjoyed writing more when they felt they had mastered the more mechanical skills of writing. Grainger et al (2003, p 8) report that the influence prescribed curricula had on teaching was that *'early KS2 teaching became disproportionately focused on teaching transcriptional skills'*. This focus on the transcriptional skills of spelling, handwriting and punctuation could possibly account for Year 3/4 children in their research expressing negative attitudes towards English.

Lambirth's (2016) two-year project exploring children's discourses of writing focuses on two of Ivanic's (2004) discourses only as *'these were identified as recurring themes that emerged from the data: skills and creativity discourses'* (2016, p 217). Lambirth defines a skills discourse as one that *'concentrates on learners' attaining technical accuracy in their writing ... demonstrated by presentations of finished transcriptions of texts that adhere to the appropriate linguistic rules*' (2016, p 217). This develops Ivanic's definition through the use of language such as '*technical accuracy*' and suggests a learner focus on a finished, accurate piece of writing, arguably at the expense of learning through the process of content composition. Creativity discourse, as defined by Lambirth, '*highlights the quality of the content and style of a piece of writing*' (2016, p 217). These definitions take their basis from Ivanic's (2004) work but have been developed. Lambirth (2016) also draws upon Grainger et al's (2003) work exploring what children think about writing. Across these three studies, Lambirth (2016) posits that children were more ready to discuss aspects of writing they found most difficult, and as they became more confident with an aspect of writing they mentioned it less. This is an important piece of contextual information as it could suggest that if the children's views were primarily negative towards certain transcriptional aspects of writing, for example, this could mean perhaps that they were struggling with those aspects and this struggle was leading to the negative view. This coheres with MacArthur (1999) who puts forward the argument that it is these transcriptional elements of the writing process that writers struggle with. It is therefore perhaps of little surprise that the skills discourse is most prevalent in Lambirth's (2016) work. One of his conclusions was that children could use tools such as adjectives and adverbs effectively, use names of parts of speech and generally utilise these tools well, but do not necessarily understand how to best use these tools to make meaning effectively in their writing and improve quality.

In summary, then, the information above provides helpful insight into some of the writing challenges that need to be explored or even overcome as part of my architect's brief. The studies above agree that it is the transcriptional elements of writing that provide the most challenging constraints for children. For those of you reading this who are experienced teachers, this will not come as any surprise, as experience tells us that this is the case. However, for empirical, peer-reviewed, academic research to support our experience, greater weight is added to the argument.

The final part of this chapter '*draws up the plans*'. Can any solutions be found to the challenges of transcription? Ofsted's (2022) research review of primary English argues that building fluency and automaticity in the transcriptional elements of writing will then allow more cognitive space to focus on developing composition. The suggestion is compelling and makes sense. This research suggests that fluency and automaticity come through early practice, repetition and instruction in these elements. Again, this is a highly compelling argument. However, the context in which this is said is whole-school programme planning for progression in learning and does not take into account those who have not yet developed that fluency. Therefore, the plans I draw up have to take this into account.

Drawing up the plans, offering some possibilities

In terms of very young children, starting out on their writing journey, Cella (2022) provides a range of options to help develop transcriptional fluency. She provides some really helpful and practical suggestions, such as regular practice of a few letters at a time, using self-evaluation and providing a purpose. In this context, Cella (2022) suggests writing things like shopping lists, birthday cards or directions for a visitor coming to your house. The purposes provide a reason for writing accurately; simply, they have to be read, so meaning must be communicated clearly and the words accurately so meaning is not lost.

Providing a purpose is a helpful concept to apply to more experienced writers who perhaps have not yet developed that fluency in transcription and as yet lack the self-regulation to persist through to editing and developing their writing. Eleanor has just finished her Early Career Teacher Years and has now moved into the Year 6 class in her school. The case study below shows how Eleanor's innovative approach – to utilise her class's creative thinking skills and provide a purpose for their writing – also motivated them to be more self-regulated and as a result improved the transcriptional elements of their writing.

CASE STUDY

Year 6: writing for a purpose – class webpages

Eleanor's headteacher had suggested at a recent staff meeting that she wanted to increase their school's internet presence by overhauling the school's website. She had contacted several companies and had one booked to work with the staff on the design and technology elements. Eleanor took the opportunity to get her Year 6 class involved in leading this project. Monday morning arrived and the headteacher was waiting in the classroom when the children arrived. The head explained the website idea, the desire for class webpages and how she and Eleanor felt the class should lead the project. Needless to say, there was much excitement. Already, the real-life purpose had made an impact. Eleanor had spent the weekend planning the project – not in terms of lessons but in a flowchart of logical steps. Figure 1.3 shows Eleanor's planning flowchart.

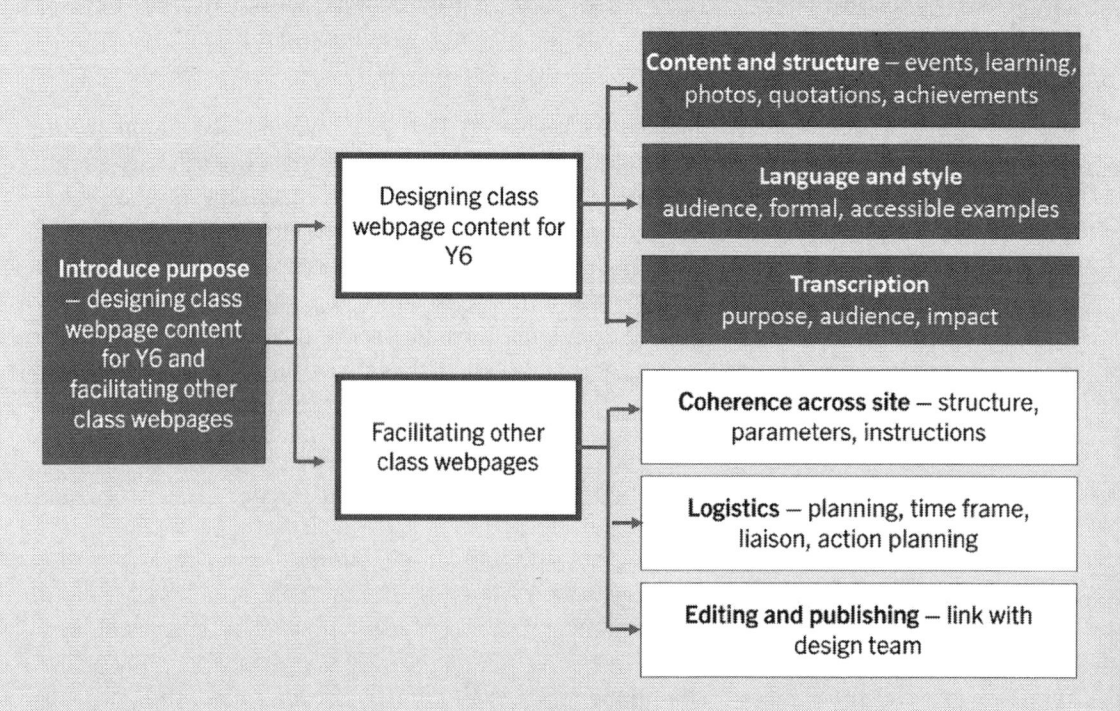

Figure 1.3 Eleanor's Year 6 class webpages planning flowchart

Eleanor put herself in role as project manager. The class divided themselves in half. One half took on the planning role of facilitating other class webpages and initially worked with Eleanor on developing an action plan. The other half focused on thinking about and mind mapping what they would want people to know and what they thought the headteacher would want the public to know about Year 6. The project progressed well; the children engaged with and seemed to relish the fact that this writing was going to be published. Throughout the composing process, the children, without prompting, made a point of focusing on accuracy of spelling, punctuation and grammar. Eleanor questioned a group on this and the reply was clear: it was going to be published and if it was badly written, the designers wouldn't let it be published and it would reflect badly on the school.

Reflective questions

» Eleanor was lucky in that she had seized upon an opportunity that this real-life purpose for writing brought. If this was not feasible in your context, how else could you provide a real-life purpose for writing?

» Eleanor's class naturally saw the connection between purpose, audience and accuracy of transcription. How will you help your class see this?

» Eleanor used a flowchart to help her break down a complicated project into several component parts so that she could make sure nothing was missed out. This is one of many approaches to planning in this book. How could you use this approach in your own planning?

Chapter summary

This chapter has explored some of the many constraints that writers have to juggle simultaneously when engaging in the writing process. I have used the metaphor of an architect's design brief to consider how the design of a framework to bring together creative thinking and children's writing needs to consider these constraints and the impact they can have on writing. The constraints have been categorised into three main processes:

1. composition, the act of developing text, bringing thoughts to life on the page or screen;
2. transcription, bringing those living thoughts into the accepted structures and features of text types and conventions of written language;
3. self-regulation, the motivation to persist and develop writing.

A key element of this chapter has been exploring, through literature, what elements of these processes children are likely to struggle with and, through case studies, some possible ways to think about how we can help our children keep those balls in the air.

Further reading

These three excellent and accessible readings alongside my focus questions will help develop your thinking from this chapter:

Cella, H (2022) Why Transcription is Important in Your Child's Writing and Reading Journey. [online] Available at: www.nwea.org/blog/2022/why-transcription-is-important-in-your-childs-writing-and-reading-journey/ (accessed 21 August 2023).

This excellent blog from NWEA (North West Evaluation Association) from the USA is really interesting. It focuses on the importance of transcription development from an early age, how this links to working memory and the simple view of writing.

Focus question

Cella subscribes to the view that automaticity in transcription needs to be developed through practice and this frees up working memory space for composition. How far do you agree? What does your experience and reading tell you?

Lambirth, A (2016) Exploring Children's Discourses of Writing. *English in Education*, 50(3): 215–32. [online] Available at: www.tandfonline.com/doi/abs/10.1111/eie.12111 (accessed 21 August 2023).

I have drawn upon this piece of research in the chapter to inform what children find difficult about writing. It is fascinating and really helped me understand some of the challenges children face when engaging in this challenging process.

Focus question

As you read this, how would you describe the discourse of writing in your class or classes you have been in? Is it different for teachers and children? Is a skills discourse prevalent?

Ofsted (2022) Research Review series: English. [online] Available at: www.gov.uk/government/publications/curriculum-research-review-series-english/curriculum-research-review-series-english (accessed 21 August 2023).

This research review provides headline data that takes you through suggested curriculum design, progression and assessment in English. It roots itself in the importance of foundational knowledge in spoken language, reading and writing.

Focus question

The review argues that '*when planning a curriculum, teachers and leaders should prioritise progression in knowledge of language and of its forms, usage, grammar and vocabulary*'. Which other areas, if any, do you feel should be prioritised in curriculum planning?

2 Choosing the tools: creative thinking skills to develop writing

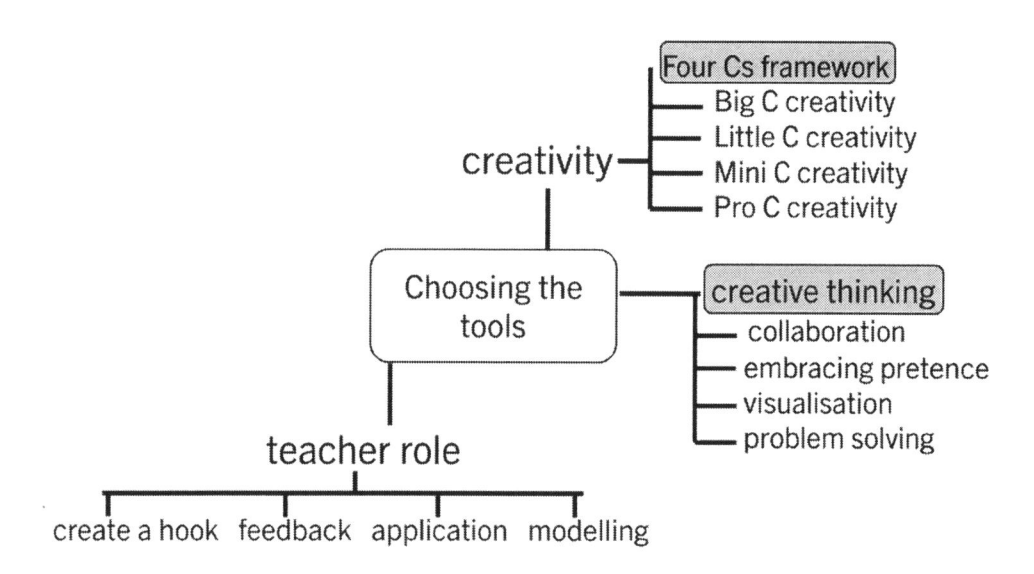

```
                              ┌─ Four Cs framework
                              ├─ Big C creativity
                              ├─ Little C creativity
              creativity ─────┤
                              ├─ Mini C creativity
                              └─ Pro C creativity
                   │
          ┌────────┴────────┐              ┌─ creative thinking
          │  Choosing the   │──────────────┤─ collaboration
          │     tools       │              ├─ embracing pretence
          └────────┬────────┘              ├─ visualisation
                   │                       └─ problem solving
              teacher role
    ┌──────────┬──────┴──────┬──────────┐
create a hook  feedback  application  modelling
```

Core Content Framework / Early Career Teacher Framework links

The Department for Education for England and Wales (DfE) provides a framework of minimum entitlement for trainee teachers which is then developed into your Early Career Teacher (ECT) years. This chapter links to the following:

- high expectations (Standard 1) – teachers influencing attitudes and values, high-quality teaching, long-term positive effect;
- how pupils learn (Standard 2 – progress) – working memory, long-term memory;
- subject and curriculum (Standard 3) – thinking critically, linking ideas;
- classroom practice (Standard 4) – metacognitive strategies;
- managing behaviour (Standard 7) – building resilience, intrinsic motivation.

Introduction

When our children were younger, summer holidays would be spent visiting their grandparents who lived in France. One of my favourite places to spend time was in my father-in-law's workshop. He was a carpenter/joiner by trade and his workshop was a big, converted barn. He had all the tools you would need, from a large table saw and table plane to a myriad of hand tools and hand-held power tools, all organised and ordered on shelves or on his huge tool board. Doing projects out there was great because the tools were all there, it was straightforward to choose the right tool, the best tool for the job.

This chapter heading follows the building metaphor throughout this book by exploring what some of the creative thinking tools are and which are the most effective creative thinking tools that I have found to support writing attainment. The chapter begins by introducing Kaufman and Beghetto's (2009) Four C Model of Creativity as the theoretical lens through which creative thinking is explored. This provides a context for looking at Little C or everyday creativity. In this chapter, creative thinking is defined as the cognitive process by which this everyday creativity such as problem-solving happens. From this underpinning, the creative thinking tools that my research found most impacted on writing attainment will be introduced, discussed and substantiated by literature. These include problem-solving, collaboration, visualisation, and embracing pretence.

Creativity and creative thinking

My interpretation of creativity is based on a wide variety of reading but has been informed largely by Robinson (1999) who states that creativity is a capacity possible in all areas of human activity. My first point regarding creativity is that I believe it is a capacity that all are capable of, not something you are born with or something only possessed by a few. Robinson (1999) also posits that creativity is possible in all areas of human activity. This is my second point. I believe that creativity is not confined to the arts or to people labelled as '*creative*', but as Beghetto and Kaufman (2010) suggest: creativity is accessible to all, possible for all in any subject, an integral part of classroom learning and teaching. Creative thinking I consider to be a complex, cognitive process involving exploration of a range of possibilities in problem-solving and setting, or possibility thinking (Craft et al, 2013). I also consider creative thinking to be the outworking of particular attitudes (Sternberg, 2003). These include choosing challenges, tolerating risk and enjoying ambiguity (Meadows, 2006). You may notice that I use the terms '*creativity*' and '*creative thinking*' together as I see creative thinking as being the cognitive process by which creativity is developed.

Having given my own perspective and starting point definition of the key terms '*creativity*' and '*creative thinking*', some of the complexities of these concepts are now explored more fully. In order to do this, I use Kaufman and Beghetto's (2009) conceptual framework, the Four C Model of Creativity, to structure my exploration.

The Four C Model of Creativity

Kaufman and Beghetto's (2009) model, developed from an earlier 2007 work, suggests four categories of creativity (four Cs). These are *'Big C creativity'*: *'clear-cut, eminent, creative contributions'* (2009, p 2), *'Pro C creativity'*: *'professional creators who have not reached eminent status'* (2009, p 4), *'Little C creativity'*: *'creative activity in everyday life and in everyday settings'* (2009, pp 2–3); and *'Mini C creativity'*: *'transformative learning'* or *'creativity within the learning process'* (2009, p 3). These are represented diagrammatically by Kaufman and Beghetto (2009, p 7) as a complete model (Figure 2.1 below) with end points and transitional periods, suggesting that everyone starts at Mini C and that there are pathways and the potential to reach Big C status.

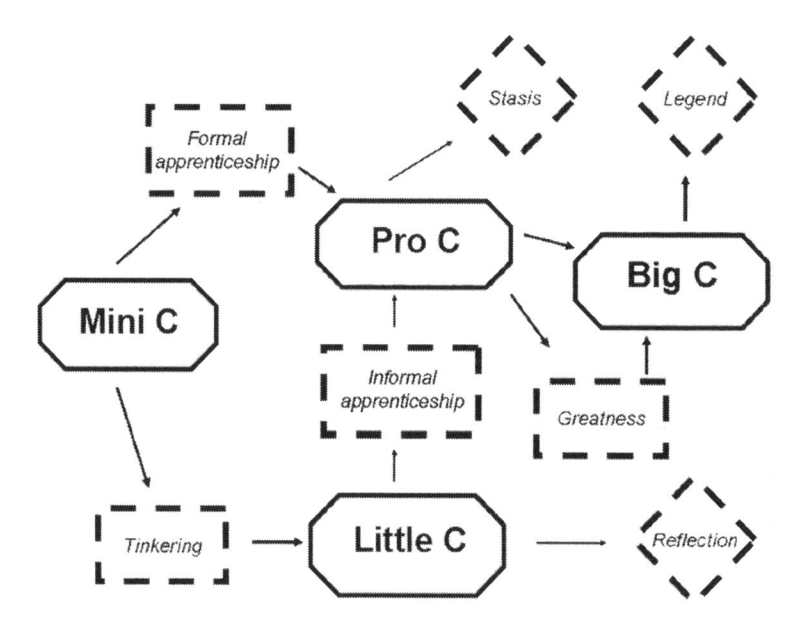

Figure 2.1 The complete Four C Model (Kaufman and Beghetto, 2009, p 7)

Big C creativity

This more traditional view of creativity, attributed to *'accomplished (often times eminent) creators'* (Beghetto and Kaufman, 2007, p 73), is, in their view, too narrow and does not take into consideration the role that creative thinking plays in the development of everyday new knowledge and problem-solving. Literature on this traditional view moves chronologically from focusing on creative individuals, to a focus on product or creative contributions. Amabile states that Big C creativity is centred around *'eminent creative individuals'* (2012, p 1) and Simonton states that creativity *'yields a product'* (2011, p 74). Connected together, these two elements are identified by Sternberg (1999) as creative contributions. Sternberg would therefore suggest that a Big C creative contribution can only come from an eminent individual and the two elements cannot really be separated. The word *'eminent'* is significant also as it is used more in the literature describing creative individuals than it is to describe contributions. The only work I have found using it to describe an *'eminent creative contribution'* as a feature of Big C creativity is Kaufman and Beghetto (2009). As examples of such eminence, they give winners of the Pulitzer Prize for literary fiction and people who have entries of over 100 words in length in *Encyclopaedia Britannica*. To summarise, a definition of Big C creativity put forward here is one which must include an eminent contribution as a product yielded from the creativity of an eminent individual.

The term Big C as a category of creativity is contested. Merrotsy (2013a) argues that there is little support in creativity literature that Big C creativity exists, let alone that it can be taught. His argument is that in order to try and make sense of creative thinking, writers, such as Kaufman and Beghetto (2009), have developed categories and models that are artificial and unhelpful. He makes the point that while the term Big C creativity is used prolifically, there is a failure in the literature to cite an original source for the term. Merrotsy (2013a) states that Plucker et al (2004), Csikszentmihalyi (1999) and Sternberg and Lubart (1995) all introduce the term but none of these sources lay claim to being the originator of it. In fact, they question whether there is really any difference between the thinking processes used by eminent creative individuals to produce creative contributions and the processes used in more everyday creative thinking.

Little C, Mini C and Pro C creativity

Having explored definitions of Big C creativity, this next section explores the remaining three Cs that make up Kaufman and Beghetto's (2009) model. However, it is worth saying at this point that I am not advocating a categorisation approach to creativity or creative thinking through this book or as part of the research on which this book is based. I believe the cognitive process of creative thinking transcends categorisation. My reason for using this model as a framework is that it is helpful to distinguish between the broad and wide-ranging definitions of creativity available and to position my research in a particular conception, helpfully defined as Little and Mini C through the Four C Model.

Little C creativity is defined by Kaufman and Beghetto as that which is *'more focused on everyday activities'* (2009, p 2). This aligns with the work of Plucker et al (2004), who emphasise the role creativity plays in diverse, everyday areas such as leadership, psychological functioning and conflict resolution. Creativity and creative thinking are processes that play an active role in everyday work, life and relationships (Cropley, 2006; Richards, 2007) rather than purely for eminent individuals making eminent contributions, as a Big C definition would suggest. In defining Little C creativity, it is also important to discuss variables required for this type of everyday creativity and creative thinking to occur. Amabile (1996) argues through her componental model of creativity that, for everyday Little C creativity to occur, domain-relevant skills, creativity-relevant skills and task motivation are needed. Using an example from primary English to illustrate this: domain-relevant skills would be an understanding of the genre, subject matter, content and language skills we might ask children to use; creativity skills could be demonstrating a willingness to take risks with language, being tolerant of the ambiguity of the task and that many responses to the task are possible (Robson, 2014). In order for creative thinking to occur, children would also need to be motivated by the tasks set.

The reason Kaufman and Beghetto (2009) give for the development of Mini C and Pro C creativity is that while the '*Big C, Little C*' distinction is helpful in distinguishing the eminent accomplishments that have big impact from the more incremental contributions made by everyday people, it does not take into account the more intrapersonal and developmental nature of creativity and creative thinking.

Beghetto and Kaufman state that Mini C highlights an important relationship between learning and creativity (2007). It includes the fact that knowledge is not merely transmitted but filtered and interpreted by the recipient in the light of their environment '*and through the lens of their existing conceptions, personal histories and past experiences*' (2007, p 73). This definition highlights the personal dimension of creativity and thinking, mentioned earlier, and also developmental elements, influenced by Cohen (1989). Mini C creativity is defined by Kaufman and Beghetto (2009) as the personal and meaningful interpretation of experiences, events and actions. This aligns to Craft's (2005) notion of responding flexibly and innovatively to the everyday events of life. It also links to Niu and Sternberg's (2006) concept of individual creativity. Central to Niu and Sternberg's concept is the idea of creativity and thinking as a dynamic process, where the product is less valuable. Mini C creativity is also based on the premise that everyone has the capability to think creatively, based on the conception that any individual can appropriate the necessary cultural tools and social interactions to create new learning. Mini C creativity also highlights the importance of learners' meaningful intrapersonal insights in response to subject matter and the way in which they can make connections between different elements of learning to create innovative ideas and thinking.

The fourth C is the concept of professional creativity and thinking (Pro C). This refers to individuals who are professionally creative in their chosen professions yet have not reached eminence, for example a chef who innovatively combines ingredients and methods but has not reached acclaim or fame for this creative thinking in both process and product. While Pro C creativity would seem to fit a process concept of creative thinking, it can also be aligned to a more objective, product-led concept. It coheres with an expertise acquisition approach (Ericsson et al, 2007) which suggests that ten years of preparation in a field of expertise is what is required to reach world-class expert status. This could suggest that everyone can therefore achieve this.

Creative thinking

Creative thinking as a process is central to my thinking for writing framework and the previous section provides theoretical underpinning for this. In this section, I articulate my definitions of this process, drawing on relevant literature.

The purpose of this book is to explore how the process of creative thinking can influence the pedagogy of primary-aged children's writing. In other words, how can this multi-faceted cognitive process improve the teaching of writing and therefore children's writing achievement?

Paul and Elder's (2019) work makes connections between the Big C focus of eminent thinkers and influential creative contributions to the processes they may go through in their thinking.

They, however, make a paradigmatic leap in so far as they suggest it is not just eminent thinkers who are capable of creative thinking, but anyone. They equate the term *'creative thinking'* with thinking that excels, and use the pronoun *'our'* to suggest this thinking is more inclusive than a traditional Big C definition might allow. They state:

> *Whenever our thinking excels, it excels because we succeed in designing or engendering, fashioning or originating, creating or producing results and outcomes appropriate to our ends in thinking. It has in a word, a creative dimension.*
>
> (2019, p 6)

Here, Paul and Elder (2019) explain what the brain does during creative thinking. By the term *'excels'* they are suggesting that the processes engaged during creative thinking are more advanced or of a higher quality, thinking that is purposeful. They do not suggest any caveats, or any particular classification of creativity, but they do list some helpful verbs to illustrate what the brain does during creative thinking:

- fashioning;
- originating;
- creating; and
- producing.

These verbs align with other definitions of creative thinking (Craft, 2003; Fink et al, 2007; Deejring, 2016). While Paul and Elder (2019) claim that everyone is capable of creative thinking, they go on to suggest that this type of thinking is not natural and needs training and development. They state that it is only with a *'fit mind'* (2019, p 7), a mind that is developed, honed and trained, that a person can *'engage successfully in designing, fashioning, formulating, originating or producing intellectual products'* (2019, p 7). Their definition aligns with Sternberg's (2003) suggestion that creative thinking is an attitude of mind and therefore something which all can develop. This idea, training creative thinking, forms part of my thinking for writing model.

Having provided a theoretical underpinning for creative thinking, the remainder of this chapter puts some specific creative thinking skills, or attitudes, under the spotlight. Using a case study to provide context, the roles that problem-solving, collaboration, visualisation and embracing pretence can play in developing writing are illuminated.

CASE STUDY

Year 2: superheroes at the Great Fire of London?

Part 1: planning, preparation and problem to solve

This piece of genius creative thinking (bringing together superheroes and seventeenth-century London) is first offered in the Introduction to this book as one of my writing workshops. Reframed as a case study here to illustrate the importance of some key creative thinking skills in developing writing, you will see how Richard, an experienced English subject leader, hooks his class into the world of London in 1666.

In the previous term Richard's Year 2 class had been studying the Great Fire of London and they had found it very engaging. Now into the spring term, Richard felt his class were ready to have some autonomy in their fiction writing and wanted to see if giving more ownership would help them develop. Richard approached the class with some thoughts but there was a certain leaning from the children that superheroes might be a favoured option. Richard set his class, in small groups, to create mind maps focused on superheroes writing ideas. One of the pairs, drawing on their previous term's topic, remarked, '*I wonder what would happen if superheroes landed when the Great Fire of London started?*' This unlikely connection certainly demonstrated novel thinking (Sternberg, 2003) and proved to be a piece of inspiration for the class. Two examples of the mind maps are pictured below in Figure 2.2.

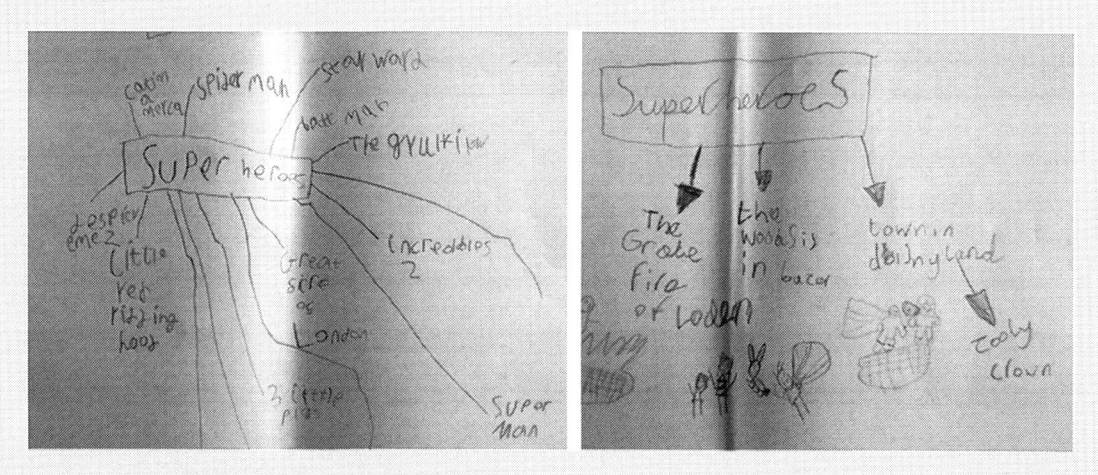

Figure 2.2 Superheroes writing mind maps

Richard's class wanted to write a book and be, as they called it, proper authors. It was decided that the title would essentially be the question asked by one of the children: '*I wonder what would happen if superheroes landed when the Great Fire of London started?*' Children would each create a 75-word story, so as to give fewer words to write, more opportunity to focus on quality of language and also set some clear parameters. This would also serve to eliminate one of the age-old questions children always want to know – '*How long does it have to be?*' These parameters also facilitated more time to focus on editing and revising, part of the key processes Richard knew the class needed to develop to become excellent writers. The problem to solve for Richard's Year 2 class was, quite simply, could superheroes save London from the fire?

> **Reflective question** (?)
>
> » What do you think of Richard's decision to provide a 75-word parameter to his class's stories? Is this an enabling constraint? Can you think of positive reasons for doing this?

A word on problem-solving

Problem-solving was the key creative thinking attitude driving Richard's superheroes and Great Fire of London writing unit of work. It also had the added bonus of engaging younger learners. Young children, Resnick (2007) argues, do think creatively. He posits the creative approach to learning in kindergarten helps learners develop the creative skills they need in the twenty-first century. Abbasi (2011) confirms this. Drawing on longitudinal research into divergent thinking that Robinson (RSA, 2010) discusses in his talk *'Changing Paradigms'*, she reports that in this work 98 per cent of kindergarten children scored at genius level in divergent thinking, yet this had dropped to 50 per cent by the time they were retested five years later. Literature does show that young children, then, are able to think creatively. Meadows (2006) takes this a step further, discussing the attitudes towards problem-solving that creative thinkers have. She suggests that creative thinkers enjoy the complexity of the process: familiarising oneself with the problem, gathering information, trying out every avenue towards a solution, letting the problem lie, the Eureka moment and then testing out the solutions. There is a recognition here that there is an enjoyment not only of the process and complex nature of challenging *'grey area'* problems, but also of the perseverance and tenacity to see it through.

CASE STUDY

Part 2: immersion and visualisation

Richard had committed fully to this writing unit of work. To hook the children into the Great Fire of London, Richard had made a 1666 news broadcast film of himself dressed in seventeenth-century attire, complete with wig, reading the *London News*, 1666. His starring role as news broadcaster probably wouldn't have won him an Oscar but he set the scene for the children, bringing some of their previous learning back into their working memory. The scene was set, the problem to solve laid out and the children were buzzing with excitement and questions, keen to share what they had remembered from the previous term's learning.

To help them understand where London was, Richard showed them a map and the class worked out how far away it was from them. He played them a film of London, showing some of the main sites, then showed them Google Maps and Google Earth so they could get a sense of London. Many of the children had been there, so they could contribute and make the connection between where they had been and the learning they were engaged in; again, this helped the children understand London. Finally, Richard revealed a huge floor map of London in 1666 that took up most of the classroom floor. Pictures of the key sites were labelled, as were the main roads, and children were starting to connect what they had seen in life and on film with the map. Figure 2.3 is a copy of the table version of the floor map.

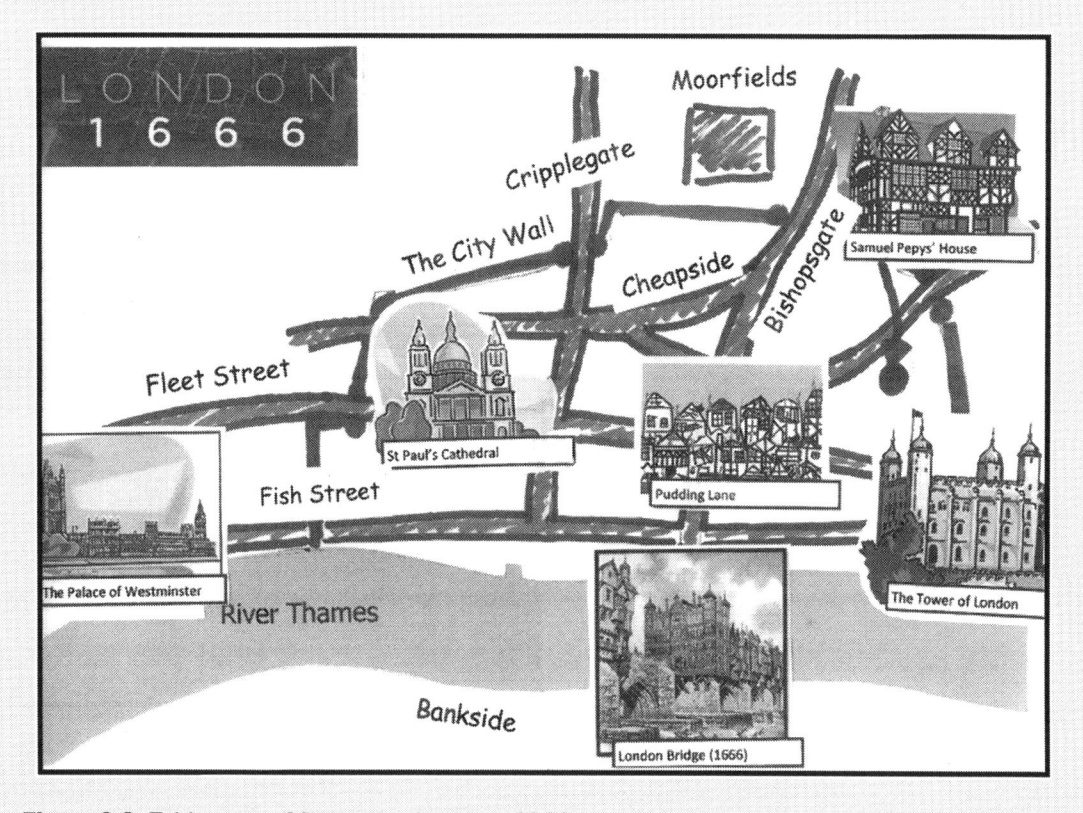

Figure 2.3 *Table copy of floor map, London, 1666*

Together, Richard and the children walked the streets of London, visualising the places, the views, the landmarks. They imagined the smells down Fish Street. They looked at where the fire started; they visualised the names and used the key language. They imagined themselves there and speculated where might be best for their superhero to land and how they might solve the problem. Content for their writing was already starting to form through their visualisation, sense of place and resulting collaborative discussion.

Reflective question ?

» Richard made a decision to invest time and energy in creating the floor map. What contribution do you think it made to the children's development as writers?

38 • *Thinking for Primary Writing*

A word on visualisation and collaboration

Building on his social constructionist beliefs about learning, Vygotsky (1978), cited by Foley, suggests that in order for learning to take place '*appropriate social interactional frameworks must be provided*' (1994, p 101). Richard's decision to create the giant floor map of London in 1666 could be described as this type of framework. It was a tool for children to engage with the Great Fire of London both historically and geographically, and to be able to imagine what being there might have been like. Pantaleo (2016) suggests that, to enable thinking and learning, a learner should be actively engaged with their environment, and this is also what the floor map sought to do. Following the lesson, the teaching assistant working with Richard commented on its success in achieving its aim:

> *I really liked how you set the classroom up at the beginning of the day. I think that was definitely a hook. It helped the reluctant writers give it a go … they were exploring the pictures of the buildings in London … they could see it and visualise.*

The visualisation also helped the children to embrace the pretence. Many of the class had no problem imagining superheroes in London 350 years ago. This was evident through Richard's observation and assessment of his class. One child had really immersed himself in the situation and told Richard why he was able to do such excellent writing.

> *Cos I'm playing a role, cos I was playing the role about each superhero.*

The story that this young writer (Tony) produced is found in Figure 2.4. below. His willingness to embrace the pretence to the point where he could imagine himself in the story is evident in his vivid description and coherence, developed from his ability to visualise himself in the situation.

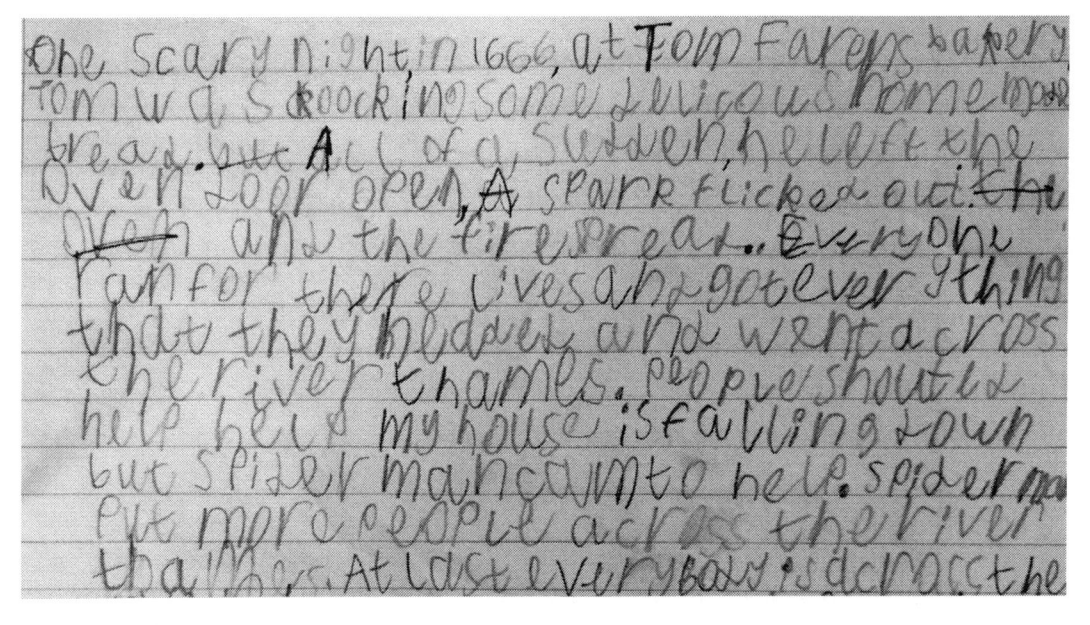

Figure 2.4 *Spiderman puts the Great Fire of London out (Tony, aged six)*

The collaborative thinking the children engaged in also impacted upon their writing significantly. Richard had created a pedagogical environment where learning and thinking together were synonymous. Craft et al's (2013) work on creating an environment for possibility thinking, an aspect of creative thinking, has peer collaboration as the context for possibility thinking to occur. Craft et al's (2013) work found that, across a range of tasks, children worked with ideas collaboratively, regardless of the product, and were able to share ideas effectively. Vass et al (2008) develop the idea of peer collaboration as a context for thinking by applying it to the cognitive process of creative writing. Vass et al's (2008) work explored some of the differences between collaborative writing and solitary writing, looking at some of the discourse taking place when writing collaboratively. Their findings suggested that collaborative discussion, even interruption, was a significant factor in more effective writing. Vass et al state, 'One child participant in our current study ... described this fuzzy, organic, non-linear type of collective thinking as ripple thinking'. When engaged in ripple thinking, '*ideas build on each other and get more and more rich and complex, expanding in all directions like ripples of water*' (2008, p 201). Vass et al (2008) argue a pedagogical environment that has collaboration at its heart develops ideas in a non-linear way, but these ideas expand, become richer and increase in complexity, as opposed to solitary thinking and writing.

CASE STUDY

Part 3: scaffolding the production of text

Figure 2.5 below shows the steps Richard took to scaffold the children's production of text including his role.

Teacher role

Shared reading
a quality short adventure story

Hook learners
Identify key language.
Identify structure

Modelled writing structure and application

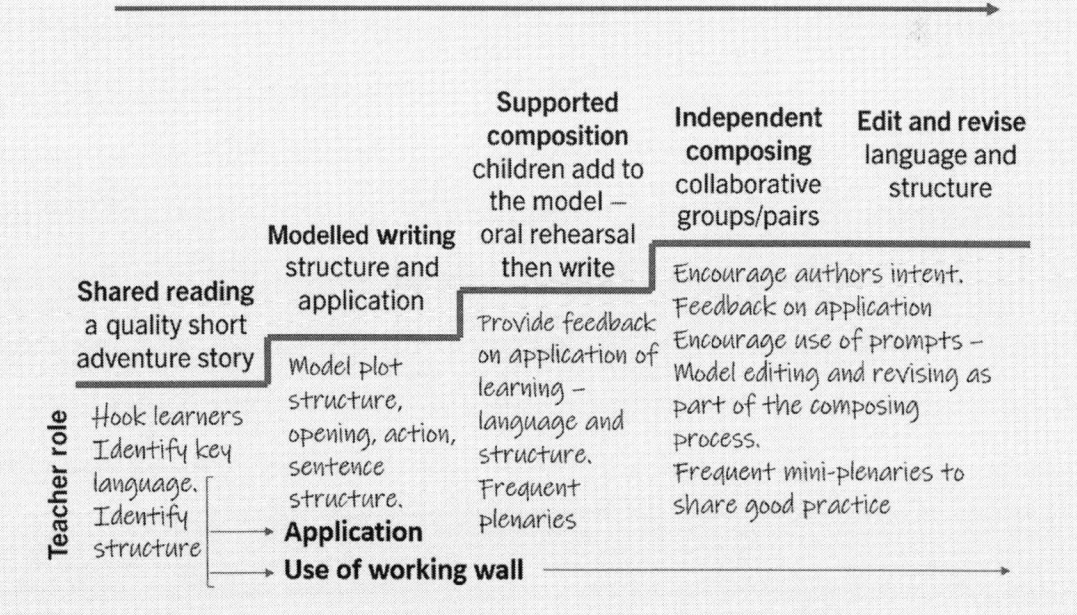

Model plot structure, opening, action, sentence structure.
Application
Use of working wall

Supported composition
children add to the model – oral rehearsal then write

Provide feedback on application of learning – language and structure.
Frequent plenaries

Independent composing
collaborative groups/pairs

Encourage authors intent.
Feedback on application
Encourage use of prompts –
Model editing and revising as part of the composing process.
Frequent mini-plenaries to share good practice

Edit and revise language and structure

Figure 2.5 Richard's steps to text production and his role in the process

You can see in Figure 2.5 many of the steps to writing you might expect to see in most English units of work. There is the important learning between reading and writing, seen right from the start. Richard modelled writing for the children: he unpicked the structure, some key story language and sentence structures, and plot structure, and showed how to get all of that into 75 words. His role in the process here was crucial. Richard's approach started from his knowledge that children find applying learning from one context to another very difficult. With this in mind, he knew that his modelled writing, editing and shared text would only be helpful if the children could apply his teaching to their learning. Therefore, Richard needed to focus his work on '*meddling in the middle*' (McWilliam, 2009) of their writing. You can see in Figure 2.5 above that Richard's emphasis is on frequent feedback, frequent engagement with learners and learning, using collaboration to help him with that and a lot of encouragement to use the models and scaffolds, including the maps, to help them. Figure 2.6 below is another example of one of the stories from Richard's class. This one is from Nero, a boy whom Richard had previously identified as working well below age-related expectations; now he has to rethink Nero's attainment. It had been typed up. Please note Nero's application of Richard's modelling – use of a rhetorical question, short sentences to build up suspense and internal rhyme with '*crashing*', '*smashed*' and '*trashed*'.

> It is 1666 in London. A dark, crashing, loud hulk smashed into the bakery demolishing it. The whole city was on fire. Batman appeared out of nowhere and used his laser beam eyes but it didn't work. How can we stop this? Suddenly Superman appeared using his cape to fly but there was no way to put it out. Then people were like "OMG! Why are they running away?" It is because Hulk is crashing and everything was destroyed and London was trashed.

Figure 2.6 Fire out, but London destroyed. Whoops! By Nero

When he finally had enough confidence to read it to the class, with support from Richard, everyone cheered and applauded, and Richard confessed that he did shed a tear.

> **Reflective question** ?
>
> » Richard expended a lot of effort in helping the children to apply his modelling and scaffolds in this element of the unit of work. What impact do you think this had on the quality of the writing?

Chapter summary

This chapter has explored some of the key creative thinking tools, skills or attitudes that positively influence children's writing attainment and engagement with the process. Beginning with creativity more generally, I have used Kaufman and Beghetto's (2009) Four C Model of Creativity as the theoretical framework to conceptualise and define it. Following this more general discussion of the concept, I have defined creative thinking as the cognitive process by which creativity happens, with a focus on everyday creativity. Keeping alive the building metaphor, I have then suggested several skills or attitudes of creative thinking that my research has shown specifically influence writing. These are:

- problem-solving;
- visualisation;
- collaboration;
- embracing pretence.

Richard's Year 2 class writing 75-word stories exploring what might have happened if a superhero had landed when the Great Fire of London started provided the pedagogical context to explore practically how these skills and attitudes can influence writing in terms of both process and product.

Further reading

These three excellent and accessible readings alongside my focus questions will help develop your thinking from this chapter:

Merrotsy, P (2013) A Note on Big-C and Little-c Creativity. *Creativity Research Journal*, 25(4): 474–6. [online] Available at: www.tandfonline.com/doi/full/10.1080/10400419.2013.843921 (accessed 22 August 2023).

This excellent discussion from Paul Merrotsy challenges some of the categories of creativity that exist, including those discussed in this chapter. If you are interested in developing your thinking, this is a really good place to start.

Focus question

What do you think of the terms Big C and Little C creativity? Are they helpful to you in your understanding of the concepts?

Craft, A, Cremin, T, Burnard, P, Dragovic, T and Chappell, K (2013) Possibility Thinking: Culminative Studies of an Evidence-Based Concept Driving Creativity? *Education 3–13*, 41(5): 538–56. [online] Available at: www.tandfonline.com/doi/full/10.1080/03004279.2012.656671 (accessed 22 August 2023).

An interesting element of creative thinking alluded to in this chapter but not explored fully is possibility thinking. This piece of empirical work by some eminent researchers is highly practical and really helpful in understanding this concept.

Focus question

The authors make some interesting observations about the use of possibility thinking in children aged 9–11 (Years 5 and 6). They suggest that it is used less in these age groups than earlier in school and cite performativity and curriculum overload as contributing factors. What do you think?

Copping, A (2018) Exploring Connections Between Creative Thinking and Higher Attaining Writing. *Education 3–13*, 46(3): 307–16. [online] Available at: www.tandfonline.com/doi/full/10.1080/03004279.2016.1250801 (accessed 22 August 2023).

This piece of research explores the influence of problem-solving on the writing process, through a Victorian murder mystery. Drama techniques are discussed and explored in terms of their impact on writing.

Focus question

How far do the findings of this piece of research resonate with the thinking in this chapter? What are some of the similarities and differences in the conclusions?

3 Laying the foundations

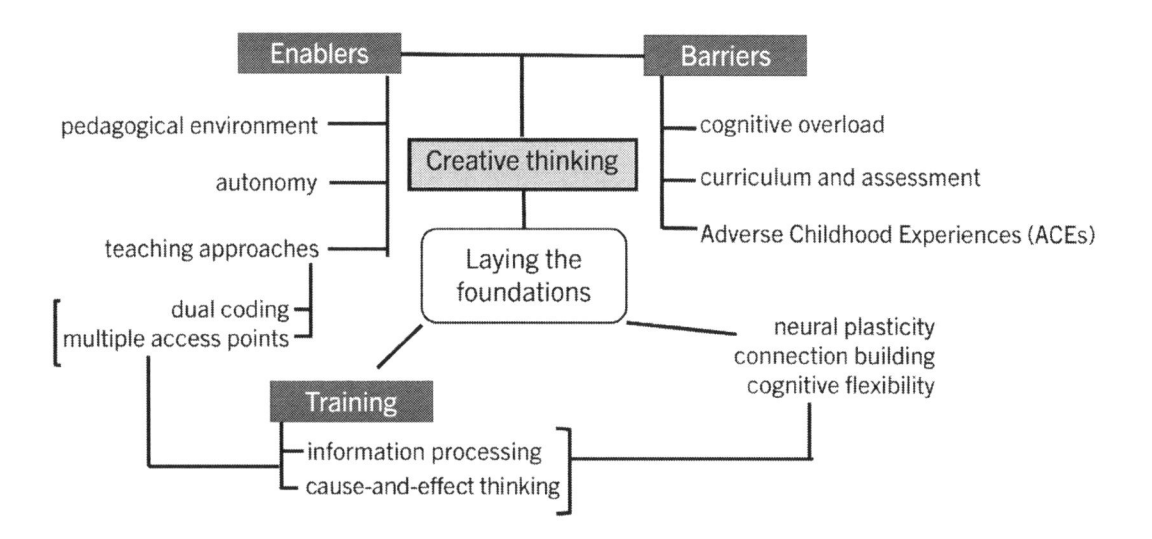

Enablers
- pedagogical environment
- autonomy
- teaching approaches
- dual coding
- multiple access points

Creative thinking

Barriers
- cognitive overload
- curriculum and assessment
- Adverse Childhood Experiences (ACEs)

Laying the foundations
- neural plasticity
- connection building
- cognitive flexibility

Training
- information processing
- cause-and-effect thinking

Core Content Framework / Early Career Teacher Framework links

The Department for Education for England and Wales (DfE) provides a framework of minimum entitlement for trainee teachers which is then developed into your Early Career Teacher (ECT) years. This chapter links to the following:

- high expectations (Standard 1) – expectations, teachers influence and affect outcomes;
- how pupils learn (standard 2) – working memory, long-term memory, worked examples;
- classroom practice (standard 4) – questioning, metacognitive strategies, modelling, talk;
- adaptive teaching (standard 5) – flexible grouping, understanding barriers to learning;

→

- assessment (standard 6) – effective assessment provides understanding of pupil need;
- managing behaviour (standard 7) – influence pupils' resilience and ability to succeed.

Introduction

I am getting a new shed. When my family recently moved to our current house, a compromise I had to make was giving up my garage; so currently my tools, work bench, the family's bikes, general stuff that I do sometimes need is all stacked in a partially rotten shed left by the previous houseowners. However, before I can get my new shed, there is some work to do. The ground where it would stand is not level, it is not fully solid and therefore work is needed to make it ready and for foundations to be laid. You see, before my big, new, heavy shed arrives, there have to be strong foundations made or the shed will sink into the ground, or it won't be level and everything would slide. Laying strong and level foundations are fundamental for a safe and secure shed.

The same is true of creative thinking. If you want creative thinking to influence writing, or even be helpful for learning at all, then strong foundations for cognition must be laid. Having introduced creativity and creative thinking skills in Chapter 2, this chapter explores the importance of training and developing those skills so as to provide a firm foundation for writing. It starts with the premise that all children are capable of thinking creatively, but also explores some of the barriers to that. These include cognitive overload, lifestyle challenges, curriculum and teaching approaches. This chapter suggests that children do not automatically think creatively but need some training, and it suggests activities and approaches in everyday teaching that will support children to do that through questioning, coaching and reframing activity.

Everyone is capable of creative thinking

Sternberg (2003) suggests, as previously stated, that creative thinking is an attitude of mind and therefore something which all can develop. This is supported by Paul and Elder (2019) who claim that everyone is capable of creative thinking; but they go on to suggest that this type of thinking is not natural and needs training and development. They state that it is only with a '*fit mind*' (2019, p 7), a mind that is developed, honed and trained, that a person can '*engage successfully in designing, fashioning, formulating, originating or producing intellectual products*' (2019, p 7). However, it is important to consider here that this perspective has only been recognised really in the twenty-first century. Merrotsy (2013a) notes that, in the 1990s, researchers and writers were recognising only '*Big C*' types of creative thinking – thinking and innovation had led to eminence in their fields. But there were a couple of notable exceptions – Weisberg and Runco. Weisberg (1993) focuses on the innovative power of '*ordinary*' thinking, the everyday skills of problem-solving, idea creation and question posing. He suggests these creative thinking skills are as valid to be labelled creative as the more eminent '*Big C*' thinking. This is echoed by Runco (1996), who emphasises personal creative thinking (rare at the end of the twentieth century), everyday experiences of adults and children as creative, giving rise to possibility thinking – acting effectively, as Craft (2005) states, with flexibility, intelligence and novelty in the everyday tasks of life. So creative thinking has moved from the domain of the eminent genius, making a significant global contribution, often connected to a specific subject-relate domain such as art, music, science or maths to the everyday tasks of life.

Barriers to creative thinking

If you are to align with Paul and Elder's (2019) perspective from the previous section, you would be expecting me to write that the first barrier to creative thinking is a lack of training in thinking excellence. You would probably be right. But what I want to focus on in this section are barriers that often the child (creative thinker) can do little about, but also barriers that teachers can do quite a lot about. You may not be able to fully remove them, but you can certainly make those barriers lower, easier to jump over.

CASE STUDY

Adverse childhood experiences (ACEs) and cognitive overload

Sunita is coming to the end of her first ECT (Early Career Teacher) year. Her school employed her following a successful final teaching placement during her PGCE year. Sunita was delighted as she had found her placement very rewarding. Many of the children in her school have chaotic lives, and are growing up in poverty, and there is a high level of deprivation in the area. Sunita loved the challenge, the children and the tight-knit staff team. This term, she had begun a non-fiction topic with her Year 3 class. In the previous term the class had been really engaged with a science topic of habitats and animals adapting to their environment. The class had worked with the local conservation group to make the most of the wildlife in the woods next to the school and made bug hotels to place there. Sunita wanted to draw upon this knowledge and experience to provide content for the information texts they would be writing. The learning activities and writing process that Sunita had planned are shown below in Figure 3.1. The planning format is designed to show what Sunita would do and what the children would do, so you can see her role in the process clearly.

→

	Learning episodes 1–4 →			
Sunita activity	Facilitate learner visit. Support learners in mind mapping, assist in bug identification and Take photographs to support writing content.	Create wall display – use photos from visit. Select sections from mind maps. Explain purpose – Information text for Year 2 – 'Wildlife in the Woods'. Support information selection.	Shared reading – wildlife information text. Modelled writing using sections developed in previous episode. Focus on text structure, text style and language features. Model how to use her text as a model.	Provide feedback on how the children are using her model. Assess use of information text language, model how to use photographs to help with content. Frequent use of mini plenaries to guide the learners.
Learner activity	Learners revisit woods. Explore bug hotels. Who is staying? Identify wildlife, discuss climate and colours. Create a multi-sensory mind map of their experiences.	Share memories of the visit. Work together to pick out important information to share with Year 2. Work collaboratively to develop sections for the information text based on photos.	Children have a copy of a double page of the text and read along – underline key information. Work together to identify structure. Use Sunita's model to start working together to add their own details from their visit.	Draft, edit and revise text in pairs. Work with another pair to evaluate.

Figure 3.1 Sunita's information text learning episodes

Following the second learning episode, Sunita began to get frustrated as many children were not able to connect the different elements together. As you will see from the plan, Sunita was working hard to support her learners draft and produce quality writing. She had provided a huge variety of models and scaffolds, but the children were just not using them. For some reason they were not able to make the connections that Sunita had planned.

> ### *Reflective questions* ⓘ
>
> » Look at some of the learning and teaching decisions Sunita made in Figure 3.1. Which do you think should have helped the children make connections between the learning episodes?
>
> » What reasons can you suggest for the children not being able to make the learning connections that Sunita had put in place?
>
> » Do you think there is any more Sunita could have done?

Critical commentary on the case study

Sunita's experience, shared in the case study above, is not uncommon. As Sunita reflected mid-way through the unit, she noted that there was a significant lack of memory, recall and application in the way the children worked, and this may well have inhibited their connection-making ability. Dietrich (2004) ascribes cognitive abilities of working memory and sustained attention to the brain's prefrontal cortex, associated with creative thinking. There is evidence here therefore that, for some reason, possibly adverse childhood experiences (Dahlitz, 2017), the brain architecture of some of the children was not sufficiently developed to think creatively.

Earlier in this chapter, I have cited the work of Paul and Elder, who state that creative thinking, of which making connections is a part, does not just come naturally, and that a *'fit mind'* (2019, p 7) is needed to do this. This I have linked to Sternberg's (2003) view that creative thinking is attitudinal, again introduced earlier in this chapter. It is possible that these children did not seem able to make connections because their minds have not been trained and motivated to do so.

Sunita's reflections gave rise to the realisation that perhaps she was asking too much of the children. They were not inside her head while she was planning and therefore were not able to recognise those connections or see Sunita's intention. Her conclusion was that perhaps this type of creative thinking does need embedding and perhaps more time and opportunity to develop. Kaufman and Beghetto (2009), whose Four C Model of Creativity I have discussed extensively in Chapter 2, do suggest that creative thinking is developmental in nature.

This theory of embedding creative thinking through training and development of creative thinking with regard to making connections also applies to other creative thinking elements. Elements such as risk-taking, persistence, elaboration of ideas and embracing uncertainty and ambiguity can often cause difficulty for children without mindset training, support or understanding. For example, Sunita found that her class also struggled with the creative thinking skill of tolerance of risk (Robson, 2014). Sunita found that when responding to her model towards the end of learning episode 3, the children seemed to just focus on the language they knew; there was no out of the box thinking, no desire to try something out. While it was good that they were starting to use her model, Sunita had expected some of those identified as working at greater depth to incorporate some of their own thinking.

Curriculum

The second barrier to creative thinking under consideration here is curriculum. I mean curriculum here in its broadest sense, not necessarily particular schemes, although the marketisation of education is not necessarily an enabler of creative thinking for teachers or children. In this section, how the curriculum is assessed will also be considered.

It could be argued that the national curriculum (DfE, 2013) requirements do not stipulate or favour a particular pedagogy. The content of the curriculum is purely statements of what should be taught, not how. However, it is perhaps the way the content is assessed that drives prevailing pedagogic approaches (Skidmore, 2006; Alexander, 2008; Donnelly, 2015). It could also be argued that it is not just the way the content is assessed but what those measures are used for. One way that assessments are used is as a measure of outcomes to make schools accountable (Acquah, 2013). Hutchings, in his research into the impact of measures to hold schools accountable, found that the high-stakes testing in English *'results in an improvement in test scores because teachers focus their teaching on the test; however, higher test scores do not necessarily represent an increase in pupils' level of understanding and knowledge'* (2015, p 2).

This finding demonstrates how high-stakes assessments drive pedagogy but also could suggest that a higher score on a test does not necessarily correlate with a higher level of understanding or thinking, implying that the high-stakes test is not perhaps fit for purpose. Marshall (2017) makes the point that high-stakes testing is not a recent phenomenon. Since 1989, governments have used exams to rate a school's success, creating a marketised sector through the use of league tables. Assessment, a product, therefore has had an impact on pedagogy as Hutchings (2015) purports: a focus on a product, a test. A product approach to teaching writing is defined by Nordin and Mohammed (2017) as writing imitating a pattern with a focus on a product. They go on to describe a product approach as focused on structure, language and often an imitation of input from a teacher. This approach is arguably formulaic, focused on the mechanics of writing. This approach is evidenced through the grammar test, introduced for Year 6 children from 2016 (Marshall, 2017) and focuses on children's knowledge of word classes rather than how to use grammar effectively to communicate in writing. However, Badger and White (2000) argue that children can learn linguistic knowledge of texts partly through imitation, and that a product approach, through imitation of native texts, helps children to not repeat errors. Pincas (1982), cited in Badger and White (2000), focused on the appropriate use of vocabulary, syntax and cohesive devices that a native text helps children imitate and develop their learning.

The product-based approach to writing pedagogy, it could be argued, is currently prevalent, not because of the content laid out in Department for Education national curriculum (DfE, 2013) requirements for teaching writing but because of how that content is assessed: decontextualised tests in grammar and spelling (Marshall, 2017) and the fact that these tests are an accountability measure used to judge a school's effectiveness.

With a product-based approach, the process of writing can often get lost. The process of writing is where the learning takes place, the messiness of playing with language, thinking, problem-solving, trying things out, daring to take risks with language to create bold communication. This is not measured, cannot be standardised, and often doesn't adhere to Teacher Assessment Frameworks. It therefore takes a courageous teacher to bring it to the fore.

Teaching approaches

In the final barrier to creative thinking considered in this chapter, rather than explore teaching approaches that provide barriers, I want to turn it on its head and explore some teaching approaches that enable creative thinking.

Creating an effective pedagogical environment

The reason I have chosen to explore learning environments that enable effective writing and creative thinking together is because the literature I have considered suggests significant crossover between them. Where Parr and Limbrick (2010) have used the term '*cognitive environment*' to describe the interaction between learner, teacher and learning materials, Davies et al (2012, p 85) use the term '*pedagogical environment*'. Davies et al (2012), in their systematic literature review of creative learning environments in education, define this in terms of activity, task authenticity and ethos. The term '*pedagogical environment*' is therefore a more effective one than '*cognitive*' as it alludes more to teachers' values and beliefs through design, whereas the term '*cognitive environment*' seems, potentially, to leave a designed ethos out.

What, then, does this look like? It is important to say here that several teaching approaches that enable creative thinking are part of an effective pedagogical environment.

First, an effective pedagogical environment is social and collaborative. Pantaleo (2016) argues that an effective pedagogical environment that enables writing is rooted in a socio-cultural approach. Drawing on the work of Vygotsky (1978), Pantaleo defines a socio-cultural theoretical approach to teaching and learning in schools as one that '*recognises how human thought originates in and is shaped by the social world of the classroom*' (2016, p 84). Pantaleo (2016) here posits that learners' thoughts do not arise from nowhere but are formed, developed and influenced by the social environment in which learning takes place. Smagorinsky develops this idea further by suggesting '*we learn not only words, but ways of thinking, through our engagement with people around us*' (2013, p 197). This sense of engagement with people comes back to the idea of pedagogy as dynamic and interactive. Smagorinsky (2013) is therefore suggesting that thinking and learning come about not just from the influence of the learning environment but active engagement with it. It could therefore be surmised from these arguments that an effective pedagogical environment that enables writing and thinking is one where learners engage with other learners.

A pedagogical environment which enables effective creative thinking and writing should therefore have a strong social element (Berninger et al, 2002; Craft et al, 2013). A pedagogy which encourages social engagement and learners engaging with other learners can enable creative thinking. The Durham Commission's second report into creativity (Durham University and Arts Council England, 2021) also emphasises social engagement through collaborative learning as significant for creative thinking. Writing is a cognitive activity, not merely a physical one; if a social environment aids thinking and cognition, then a pedagogy encouraging social engagement should, arguably, enable more effective writing.

CASE STUDY

Creating an effective environment to enable thinking

Mario, an experienced Year 1 teacher, was working with his class to compose text by sequencing sentences. Mario was using Jez Alborough's (2014) text *Where's My Teddy?* as his starting point. The previous week, Mario had introduced his class to his own teddy, Bingley the Bear. To hook the children in, Mario had created short film clips of Bingley in different places in his home, and after registration each morning the children had to watch

→

the clip, guess where he was and try and answer the question 'Where's Bingley Bear?' Each day they added to Bingley's adventure journey by putting their answers on a big Bingley Bear adventure journey timeline. This would add some chronological structure to their own version of Where's My Teddy? Having read Alborough's book together, they knew that Eddy in the story had gone to search for his teddy in the woods and found a bit of a surprise. What surprise could Bingley find?

Mario wanted his children to enjoy the process of composing text and he knew that working together might help them. Using some of the text from the timeline, he gave small groups sentences which they had to put into a sequence. But he wanted them to consider lots of other possibilities: what else could happen to Bingley? Immediately there was a buzz in the room. The children began talking, sharing, laughing, even challenging each other's ideas, such as Bingley couldn't be in space, because he was in Mr Sozzi's (Mario's) house. Mario found he enjoyed listening in, questioning to reveal a deeper understanding and supporting the children to shape their versions of Bingley's journey. The collaborative environment, with permission to take risks with ideas within the parameters of Mario's house, produced some really interesting and creative suggestions. Each sentence was written on a separate piece of paper, so in their groups the children could order them, orally rehearse them, decide if they liked them and make amendments, a sophisticated process for five-year-olds. One example from a group is typed out in Figure 3.2 (spellings corrected). The original was six sentences, six pieces of paper with a range of creative ideas to develop Bingley's adventure.

Where's Bingley Bear?

Bingley is eating his dinner

Bingley is cleaning himself in the washing machine

Bingley is hiding under stairs so he doesn't have to go to bed

Bingley is being quiet

Bingley is going up the stairs with Mr Sozzi

Bingley is tired, what a day!

Figure 3.2 Where is Bingley Bear?

Notice the complex sentence with the conjunction 'so'. Mario was surprised that giving a level of autonomy and freedom to play with language could have led to this use of a sentence type. Mario hadn't yet thought the class ready to look at joining clauses using 'and', but perhaps he now needs to revise his expectations?

Figure 3.3 is a representation of the impact of the environment on thinking and writing. It is an adapted section from my thinking for writing framework and illustrates Mario's work.

teacher facilitates

The thinking environment
- Time and space to write
- Process valued
- Writers have ownership of the writing
- Social process
- Feedback continually sought and used to develop writing

enables

writing process and creative thinking

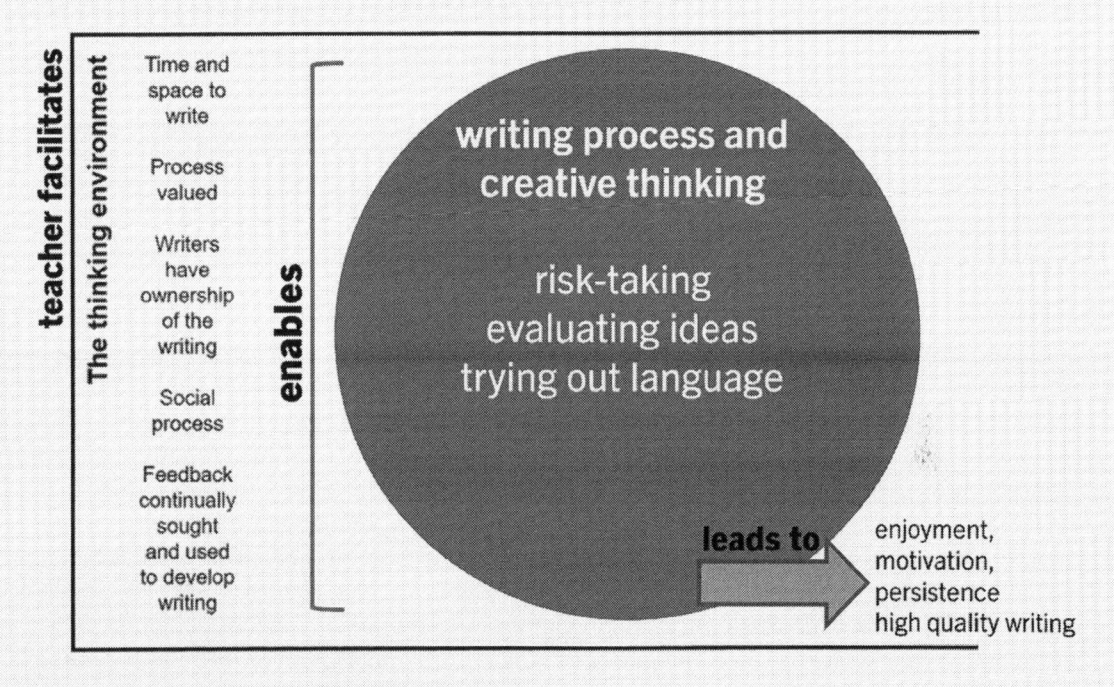

risk-taking
evaluating ideas
trying out language

leads to → enjoyment, motivation, persistence, high quality writing

Figure 3.3 The impact of the environment on creative thinking and writing

---

Reflective questions ⑦

» In what ways do you think Mario enabled his learners to think creatively?

» Mario developed some of the content and structure for the children's writing during the week prior to the writing itself. What impact do you think this had on the children's thinking and writing?

» Mario's role in creating an effective pedagogical environment was crucial. He, as the teacher, sets the classroom ethos. What will you take away from Mario's approach illustrated in Figure 3.3?

Enabling autonomy in writing

An enabling pedagogical environment for creative thinking also has autonomy and freedom at its heart. This is alluded to in the previous section and illustrated in Figure 3.3. Craft et al (2013) speak of a playful environment as one that fosters creative thinking. Cremin and Chappell (2021), in their systematic review of literature, also identify playfulness as a key feature of creative pedagogy. This involves questioning as a driving process leaving children freedom to explore, play, try out and develop self-determination, while the teacher stands back from the child's engagement with the task. Craft et al (2013) go on to discuss the importance of an environment that facilitates imagination and risk-taking in responding to the questions and problems set. This gives children much more ownership of the tasks set and how to go about them. This theme of autonomy is developed by Falconer et al's (2018) exploration of creativity in primary school children. They go on to suggest that for an enabling environment for creative thinking to occur teachers need to allow children to demonstrate initiative and involve them in the decision-making process around learning tasks. Falconer et al (2018) go on to state that this pedagogical environment should be positive, open, democratic and free. This provides an argument for a pedagogy that is interactive, where pupils have significant input into their learning and freedom of opportunity and choice.

An enabling pedagogical environment should also promote learner agency. The reason for exploring this separately to autonomy is because the term suggests something more than 'autonomy and freedom'. The reason is based around learner identity as agents of their own learning. Lantolf and Pavlenko define learner agency thus: '*Learners are viewed as agents who actively engage in constructing the terms and conditions of their own learning*' (2001, p 145). Autonomy implies personal choice within set parameters, whereas agency, as defined above, implies being involved in setting those parameters. Gadd and Parr (2016) discuss effective literacy teachers whose pedagogy involves learners in constructing tasks. One of the teachers involved in their research recognised the importance of their class '*writing on self-selected topics*' (2016, p 98). They identified that the challenge was maintaining motivation while students were identifying their own learning goals and meeting prescribed learning outcomes. Craft et al (2013) suggest that a teacher placing high value on learner agency is a key enabler for creative thinking, alongside standing back and allowing time and space.

Through case study and critical commentary, this chapter has so far explored some of the potential barriers to creative thinking in the classroom alongside some of the enablers. Following the building metaphor, this could be digging out the ground in preparation for the foundations. The remainder of this chapter lays the foundations for children's creative thinking, exploring some ways to train children's brains to think in this way. It could be argued from some of the case study material you have read that, given the right pedagogical environment, creative thinking just happens naturally. I think providing the environment really helps, almost like by digging out the ground ready for the foundations you are providing a strong and receptive piece of ground, but it is not the full picture; some training, as Paul and Elder (2019) suggest, is needed to develop a fit mind and cognitive flexibility.

Training for creative thinking

Placed to illustrate a foundation for the cognitive writing process, Table 3.1, taken from the training in thinking section of my thinking for writing framework, makes some suggestions as to what the focus of that training might be.

Table 3.1 Foundation extract from my thinking for writing framework

| **Training in creative thinking**

Different ways to process information, cause-and-effect thinking, co-operative learning strategies, persistence to sustain a task, multi-sensory experiences | **Knowledge and skill development** |

Different ways to process information

Cantor et al (2019), in the context of how children learn and develop, discuss the importance of neural plasticity and malleability so that the brain can adapt as it responds to changing contexts and experiences. They make the point that the development of this neural flexibility is not linear but very diverse, and that for the whole child to develop in terms of the full capacity of their learning, there needs to be an interconnection between cognition and other processes that influence learning, such as emotion. If this insight is placed alongside the more conventional ways learners process information: visual, verbal (oral) and kinaesthetic (Rigsbee and Keith, 2023), there are some implications for you. The implications are about interconnectedness of processing, or, as I often term it, creating multiple access points to learning. Therefore, in order to train children in this, teaching must enable learners to process information in different ways. Some practical examples are below.

- Use dual coding (combining words and visuals) in your teaching. Not only does this reduce the learner's cognitive load, it also develops neural flexibility by enabling the brain to process information visually.

- Model and encourage the use of action, gesture, manipulatives, role-play, human Likert scales, practical activity. These approaches will often motivate children, and also help them to process information kinaesthetically.

- Allow talk, call and response games, vocabulary tennis, discussion, collaboration, co-operative learning strategies. By talking together, children process the information given and can test it out with their peers. They may even create new knowledge.

The key here is ensuring that within the learning and teaching there are opportunities to process information and demonstrate learning in different ways. This develops neural plasticity and flexibility in thinking, but also deepens learning and has the added impact of being more motivating for the learners.

Cause-and-effect thinking

Cause-and-effect thinking helps children have reasons and be able to make inferences about why things are happening around them (Bailey-Galreith, 2015). Invariably this is natural in young children; it is both wonderful and frustrating in equal measure when your child is constantly asking '*why?*' But this is a genuine desire to understand the world, to make sense of why things happen. It is a fundamental part of neural flexibility because it facilitates the making of connections and building of new neural pathways, an essential part of creative thinking (Meadows, 2006). This type of thinking leads to the application of the answer to the why question to other contexts. For example, *'Why did my rabbit die?' 'Because it got sick.' 'So does that mean when I get sick, I might die?'* The child here is trying to apply this meaning to other context and develop new neural pathways of understanding. We can train this through the following:

- asking why questions of a character in a text with follow-up application;
- asking why a particular spelling rule might not work, and applying it;
- playing some cause-and-effect matching statement games. Give additional credit for those links that require more creative explanation. For example, see Figure 3.4.

Figure 3.4 Cause-and-effect matching game

Chapter summary

This chapter has explored the idea that everyone is capable of creative thinking. It is not a set of skills only for those who might be described as genius status or who have made some considerable contribution to knowledge and society. Creative thinking is ostensibly about the navigation and solving of problems that daily life throws at you. This chapter has also considered some of the barriers that can impede creative thinking, particularly those around adverse childhood experiences and cognitive overload, the latter of which teachers can do something to influence. Following this some teaching approaches have been explored that are rooted in the creation of effective environments for thinking, supported by cognitive training in different ways to process information and cause-and-effect thinking. In this chapter, the ground has been prepared and the foundations laid through the re-wiring of neural pathways and the establishing of greater connections.

Further reading

These three excellent and accessible readings, alongside my reflective questions, will help develop your thinking from this chapter.

> Cantor, P, Osher, D, Berg, J, Steyer, L and Rose, T (2019) Malleability, Plasticity, and Individuality: How Children Learn and Develop in Context. *Applied Developmental Science*, 23(4): 307–37. [online] Available at: www.tandfonline.com/doi/epdf/10.1080/10888691. 2017.1398649?needAccess=true&role=button (accessed 22 August 2023).
>
> *In this excellent article, the authors delve into the neuroscience of how children learn and what the brain does when thinking. The authors highlight the importance of flexibility and plasticity in thinking for effective development.*
>
> ## Focus question
>
> On page 4 of the article, the authors state that '*Instructional and curricular design can optimise learning*'. What do you think this could look like and what are the connections between how you design your curriculum and instruction and how your learners process information?

> Bailey-Galreith, A (2015) 'Explain yourself': A Powerful Strategy for Teaching Children Cause and Effect. [online] Available at: www.learningandthebrain.com/blog/cause-and-effect/ (accessed 22 August 2023).
>
> *This engaging and practical article focuses on cause-and-effect thinking. It also focuses on children processing information and understanding this process more by self-explaining, suggesting that concepts are understood more effectively than, for example, by reading.*
>
> ## Focus question
>
> Why do you think self-explaining a concept or explaining it to someone else is more effective for learning? What does this have to do with information processing?

Rigsbee, P and Keith, L (2023) Learning Styles and Information Processing. [online] Available at: https://edp304.wordpress.ncsu.edu/processing-with-technology/ (accessed 22 August 2023).

This article, perhaps a bit controversially, as it is contested, draws your attention to learning styles and information processing, making the point that a large part of creative thinking is about being able to process information in different ways.

Focus question

What do you think about the concept of visual, auditory and kinaesthetic learning styles? Should this be a contested term, as the ITT Core Content Framework states?

4 The building blocks

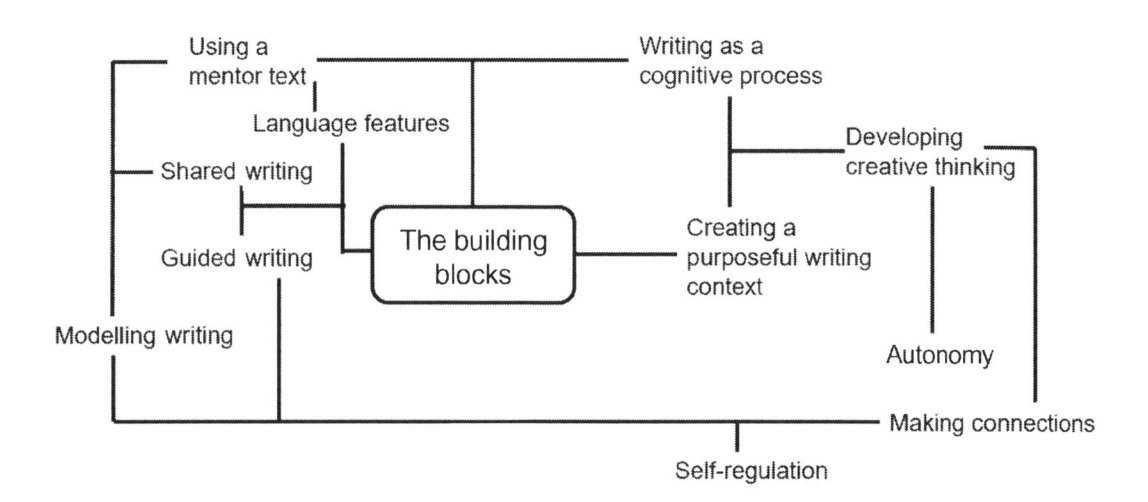

```
Using a mentor text          Writing as a cognitive process
    Language features           Developing creative thinking
Shared writing
                    ┌─────────────┐    Creating a purposeful
Guided writing ─────┤The building ├──── writing context
                    │   blocks    │
                    └─────────────┘
Modelling writing                       Autonomy
                                        Making connections
                    Self-regulation
```

Core Content Framework / Early Career Teacher Framework links

The Department for Education for England and Wales (DfE) provides a framework of minimum entitlement for trainee teachers which is then developed into your Early Career Teacher (ECT) years. This chapter links to the following:

- high expectations (Standard 1) – setting clear expectations and a positive environment;
- how pupils learn (Standard 2 – Progress) – working memory, breaking complex material into smaller steps, purposeful practice, retrieval, the use of worked examples;
- subject and curriculum (Standard 3) – linking ideas to existing knowledge, secure knowledge of the subject area being taught, modelling;
- classroom practice (Standard 4) – modelling, scaffolds, worked examples, introducing new material in steps, questioning, talk for learning, the role of practice;
- adaptive teaching (Standard 5) – flexible grouping.

Introduction

There are, within the English language, a great many exquisite and fanciful collective nouns. Some you may have heard of: a murder of crows, an army of caterpillars and a shiver of sharks. But have you heard of a rhumba of rattlesnakes? I wonder what the collective noun for the different components of an English lesson might be? You may have already noticed the '*building*' metaphor used in the structure of this book and, if so, you will hopefully also have noted my attempted collective noun phrase for these components – '*building blocks*' of the writing process.

This chapter builds on the foundations laid in Chapter 3, with the assumption that creative thinking is the underpinning foundation for this chapter. Building on this, I discuss some of the important building blocks of the writing process that will be familiar to all teachers. These include shared work, the role of a mentor text, teaching grammar and punctuation, developing ideas, and editing and revising. These blocks, identified in my thinking for writing framework in the Introduction to this book, are shown in Figure 4.1.

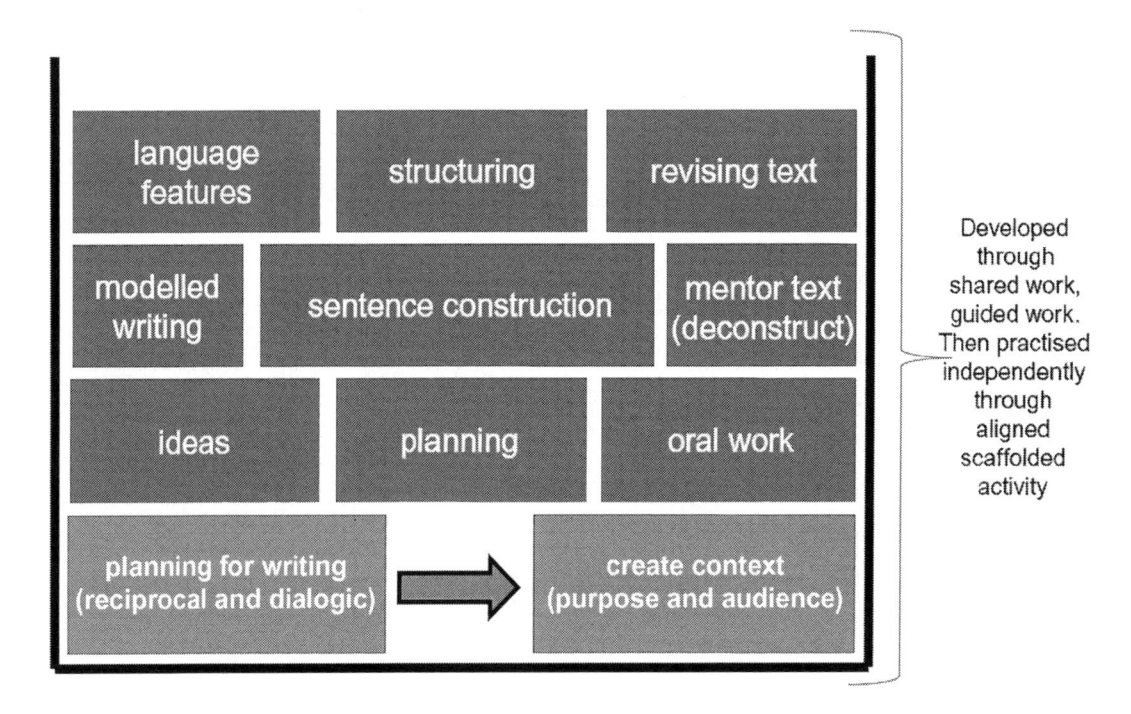

Figure 4.1 Building blocks of a cognitive writing process

This chapter explores each building block alongside teaching approaches and activities. It also demonstrates how to utilise each approach effectively to maximise writing attainment and at the same time develop learners as writers who can make effective authorial decisions.

Planning and creating a context for writing

First, let me clarify what I mean by creating a context for writing. Here I am not building on Chapter 3's exploration of the classroom environment as a context; instead, I am discussing the importance of the writing contexts teachers create for their learners. Church (2010) links the writing context with the nature of the writing task teachers set. Her work on engagement theory and facilitating higher-level thinking suggests that an activity and context that build thought, synthesis and evaluation different to traditional routine school activities can help build connections, a desirable creative thinking behaviour.

A word on real-world writing contexts

Research evidence for the impact of a real purpose and audience on motivation and progress is extensive (Copping, 2016; Rothwell, 2016; Wong and Moorhouse, 2018; Block and Strachan, 2019). Both Rothwell (2016) and Wong and Moorhouse (2018) use blogging to provide this for their learners. Wong and Moorhouse's work also includes writing peer feedback as an authentic task, learners drawing upon writing instruction from previous learning to evaluate their peers' blog posts. What a creative way to employ retrieval practice and pull previous learning back into the working memory.

The fundamental role of the task in developing creative thinking is developed further in Chapter 7; however, in the context of creating authentic writing contexts, the role of the task is integral. Therefore, it is also discussed here.

Reciprocity, dialogue and autonomy

An important factor in developing authentic contexts that foster writing development and creative thinking is listening to your learners and giving them a voice. Cremin (2006) describes this act as developing an enabling pedagogical environment, which Waitman and Plucker (2009) agree must include facilitating the autonomy to explore ideas. Why is this important? Well, it's mainly about learner enjoyment and engagement. According to research by Grainger et al (2003), learners enjoyed the freedom of writing at home, where they could control the direction of their stories. This was also, according to Grainger et al (2003), more motivating for learners as they had more choice and control over how their writing developed. This follows the work of Myhill (2001), who found that young writers preferred writing tasks that allowed them freedom of expression. The same theme of autonomy and freedom is also found in Lambirth's (2016) work on exploring discourses of writing. The teachers he engaged with responded to their learners' writing preferences offering more choice, freedom and independence. Autonomy is also one of Cremin and Chappell's (2021) features of creative pedagogy found through their systematic review of creative pedagogies literature. Providing a pedagogical environment that partners with learners in a reciprocal way and therefore offers autonomy and choice is also a theme developed by Gadd and Parr (2016). They argued that the exceptional teachers within their study on task orientation in writing involved their learners in the construction of learning tasks, thus giving more autonomy and freedom in their work. An enabling context for writing, therefore, seems to be one that recognises individual difference, provides more autonomy and is therefore more effective.

With this in mind, read the case study below where Leo, an Early Career Teacher, is working with his Year 4 class on some science-inspired writing.

CASE STUDY

Year 4: science-inspired writing

In his second ECT year, Leo had a science focus for term one. His topic was the water cycle and he wanted to try and help his class bring forward some of their learning into other curriculum areas. He challenged them to think of some ideas. One of the learners ventured the song *'Raindrops Keep Falling on my Head'* as a starting point and lots of varied ideas developed. Leo put together the mind map below (Figure 4.2).

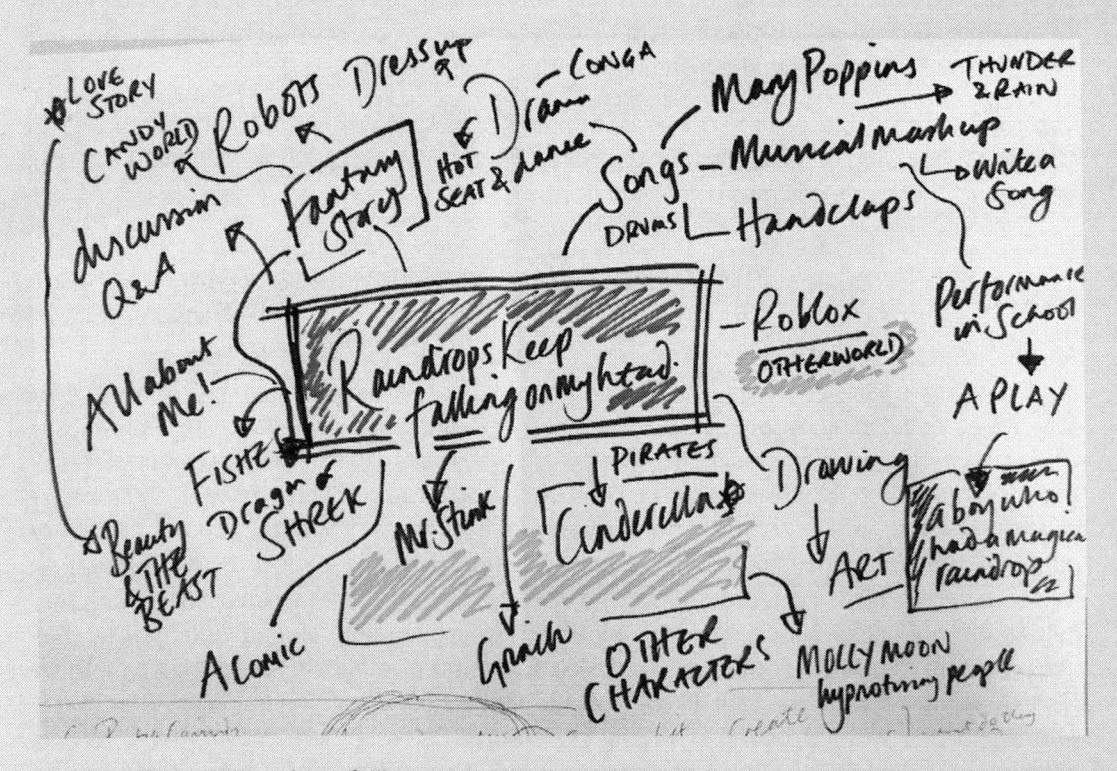

Figure 4.2 *'Raindrops keep falling on my head' mind map*

Leo's class agreed together that they would write playscripts that they would like to perform to other classes to teach them about the water cycle. In order to refine their thinking, Leo gave them some parameters. Their play must have a fictional world, a musical element, a scientific concept from their learning and at least two opposing characters. The stipulation was that everyone must be involved. Leo supported those who needed help with organisation and decision-making. Following idea development, Leo modelled playscript structure and the use of stage directions for the class. Learners were working in interest groups and the dialogue about these worlds they had created enhanced their vocabulary. Leo was surprised at their creativity of language and use of punctuation to communicate. For some learners their oral and written language, sentence structure and understanding of how authors communicate meaning was far in advance of other work Leo had seen from his class. Figure 4.3 is an example from a group where many of the learners were assessed as working below age-related expectations (AREs).

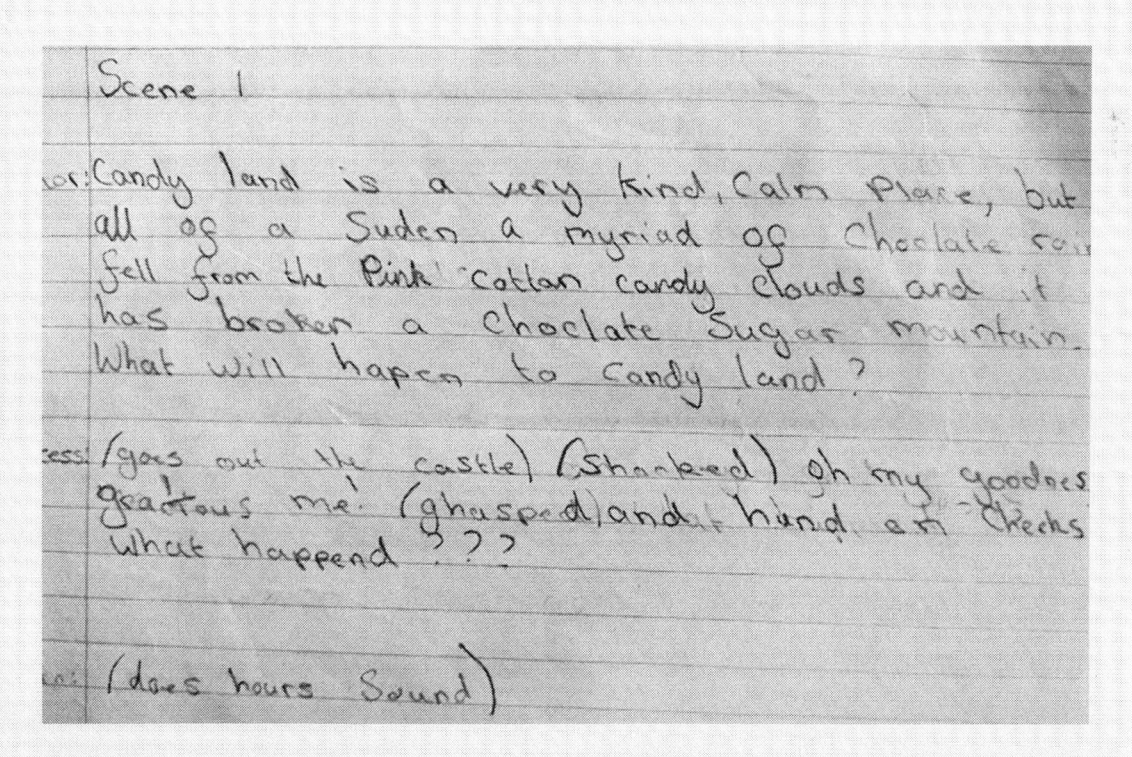

Figure 4.3 Playscript extract

Leo was impressed with the group's understanding of stage directions, vocabulary – '*myriad*' – and the use of a rhetorical questions.

Despite Leo's heavy involvement in management issues – mediating in debate about character actions and the assigning of roles – on reflection, he was pleased with this unit of work. His eyes had been opened to the elevated levels of thinking demonstrated by many of his learners, their writing capabilities not seen before and their creative engagement with the task that they had created.

> **Reflective questions** ?
>
> » How do you think the autonomy of task choice and co-creation of the writing context has influenced Leo's class's writing?
>
> » How does Leo's teaching help develop creative thinking behaviours such as making connections, problem-solving and collaboration?
>
> » What are some of the indicators of effective writing that have been demonstrated?

The case study above illustrates two building blocks of the writing process – planning and creating a learning context. This is what you as busy teachers will be doing several times a day without even thinking about it. The pressures upon you to deliver the curriculum in preparation for high-stakes assessment does not naturally create space for autonomy and co-creation of learning contexts. However, taking the kind of learning risks that Leo did could produce some positive impact in terms of both process and product.

Teaching to enable learners to forge connections

The DfE's Core Content Framework for Initial Teacher Training (2016, p 14) states that *'Pupils are likely to struggle to transfer what has been learnt in one discipline to a new or unfamiliar context'*. I have found this to be true in my own research into creative thinking and children's writing. Through this research I noticed that many learners struggled to connect learning from shared work through to guided and independent work. Making connections is part of what Beghetto and Kaufman (2007) term 'Mini C' creativity. This is defined as everyday creativity, such as solving common problems, and therefore seeks to make connections between different elements of learning to create innovative ideas and thinking. It is this type of thinking that writers use to create text, to juggle the many constraints of sentence structure, ideas, handwriting, punctuation, tense agreement and voice simultaneously. So how do we teach this type of thinking? Well, first we acknowledge that writing is not just a physical process but a cognitive one. Writing is a problem-solving activity. It is expression and communication.

Using a mentor text

A highly appropriate tool that teachers use in shared work is a mentor text, sometimes called a WAGOLL (What A Good One Looks Like). A mentor text is defined by Culham as any text that can be *'read with a writer's eye'* (2014, p 31). In other words, it is a model rooted in the idea that reading can be used to teach writing. Writers would therefore examine and analyse a piece of text, engage with its features and *'magpie'* or steal any that might develop their own writing. Graham and Perin (2007), in their work on improving writing, state that mentor texts should be studied and learners should analyse text structure and language, and emulate the important elements in their own writing.

Herein lies the problem: the application to their own writing. The job of the teacher in using a mentor text is to work with the learners to apply the language and structures and appropriate them into their own writing context, then help learners mould mentor text language into what they want to communicate. So here are a few practical tips for you when using a mentor text.

- Actively involve learners through focused tasks as you are reading the text with them; do not wait until afterwards for activity. It can often be too much for the working memory to cope with to remember the teaching and then do the activity. Do them together. This might be text marking, highlighting, anything that gets the learners using the text in the moment.

- During the above process, get regular feedback from the learners, read work out. Let them be in no doubt what success looks like. Having other learners' examples alongside the mentor text can build confidence and cement success criteria.

- Give feedback to learners on how they are applying the language and structures to their own work. This helps build creative self-efficacy and leads to perseverance, part of self-regulation, which is important for effective writers.

A word on self-regulation

Self-regulation is a necessity for skilled writing (Bereiter and Scardamalia, 1987; Zimmerman and Risemberg, 1997). It has long been considered a significant element of writing alongside composition and transcription. Zimmerman and Risemberg state that '*Becoming an adept writer involves more than knowledge of vocabulary and grammar, it depends on high levels of personal regulation because writing activities are usually self-planned, self-initiated, and self-sustained*' (1997, p 73). They are arguing that writing is also about motivation, an ability to motivate oneself, to initiate writing, plan it and then sustain it through the challenging processes of turning personal thought into public text. This is developed by Arrimada et al (2019) and Oddsdóttir et al (2021) in their work on teaching self-regulation strategies to young writers. Both studies found that teaching these explicit strategies led to more effective writing. Harris et al (2011) state that skilled writers are more self-regulated than struggling writers, and that a writing pedagogy that combines teaching self-regulation with meaningful practice is the way to develop writing performance.

Activity ?

The next time you are using a mentor text in your English lesson, provide your learners with a cognitive activity that engages with the text, linked to your learning objective. Get them active while you are reading the text with them. Reflect on their learning. If you want them to magpie language or structures from the mentor text, give them feedback on their application, read out successful work and explain why it is effective. Reflect on how this motivates the learners to persevere in their writing. Also ask yourself, are you overloading the learners by asking them to write too much? Can they meet your objective in writing, for example, in a 75-word story?

Modelling writing and the cognitive process

Using a mentor text as part of shared work can be an effective way of helping learners improve their writing and develop their own cognitive skills within the writing process. Another important teaching tool, often used in conjunction with a mentor text, is teacher modelling. Within this section we will explore effective ways to model writing with a focus on sentence construction, but also how to model the cognitive process alongside the physical process and the impact that can have on writing. This will be explored through a case study with some reflective questions.

CASE STUDY

Year 6: Galactic Defence

Maariya, an experienced Year 6 teacher and English subject leader, was developing plot lines in fiction with her class. She had chosen science fiction as a genre as she felt this would best motivate them. Maariya had placed biohazard and no entry posters on her classroom door and windows and used hazard tape to seal her classroom off. In role as a professor from fictional cyber security department '*Galactic Defence*', Maariya let her class in and set the context. A malignant alien force known as '*Dax*' had infiltrated the school, seeking to take it over. The only safe place was their classroom. Maariya, in role, made her class Galactic Defence researchers, gave them lanyards and badges and set them the morning's task. The task was to develop plot lines for possibility stories should the school's governing body not take action, and give Galactic Defence control to expel Dax and thus save the school. The class were hooked.

Maariya's learning objectives for writing were taken from the National Curriculum for England and Wales (DfE, 2013), upper Key Stage 2. They were:

> *plan their writing by: identifying the audience for and purpose of the writing.*

> *draft and write by: selecting appropriate grammar and vocabulary, understanding how such choices can change and enhance meaning.*

Maariya provided some clear parameters for the writing task. It would be a 100-word flash fiction story focusing on plot – what could happen. She asked the learners what they would need to consider in writing for the governing body of the school. Responses reflected the seriousness of the simulation, focused on clarity of expression and the gravity of the possible outcomes should Dax take over. Responses also recognised the importance of transcriptional elements – spelling, handwriting and accuracy – as the stories would probably be discussed at a governors' meeting.

Maariya asked her Galactic Defence researchers to collaborate together in pairs and record their initial ideas for the plots for their stories. What could be the possible devastating outcomes for their school, should Dax take over?

Maariya made the decision to develop her own mentor text, focusing purely on plot, with her researchers to help embed the thinking that she would also model. She selected some of their plot ideas and put them together on an hour-by-hour timeline. She articulated her authorial choices, demonstrating logical progression of actions. While modelling this, she gave the same blank timelines to her learners to follow her thinking and develop their own timelines. She gave feedback to them on their application of her thinking to their work. Maariya's timeline of ideas in preparation for her modelled writing is Figure 4.4.

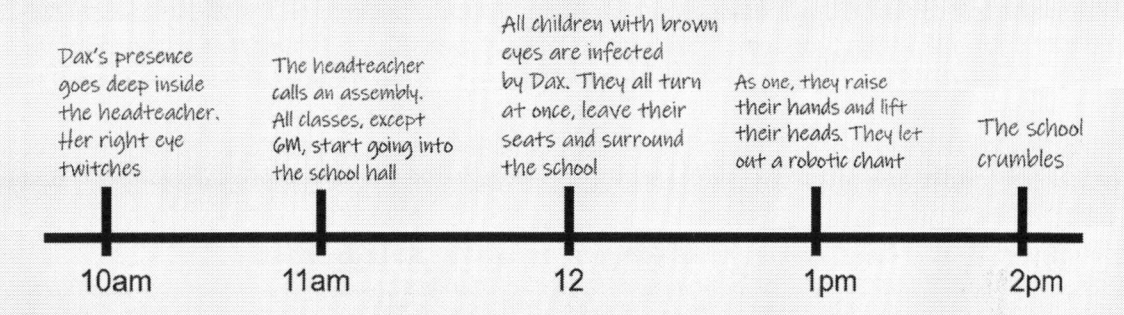

10am	11am	12	1pm	2pm
Dax's presence goes deep inside the headteacher. Her right eye twitches	The headteacher calls an assembly. All classes, except 6M, start going into the school hall	All children with brown eyes are infected by Dax. They all turn at once, leave their seats and surround the school	As one, they raise their hands and lift their heads. They let out a robotic chant	The school crumbles

Figure 4.4 *Maariya's Galactic Defence and Dax possible plot timeline*

Through her modelled writing, Maariya wanted to also focus on Year 6 word and sentence level objectives from the national curriculum (DfE, 2013). These included *'The difference between vocabulary typical of informal speech and vocabulary appropriate for formal speech and writing'*, and also using a variety of sentences, including short sentences to build suspense. With only 100 words, word choice was crucial, and Maariya needed to model this.

As Maariya modelled the 10am plot line in formal language, and she asked the pairs to do the same, with her. She wanted her articulation of thinking to signal to her researchers how they should be thinking. As Maariya wrote, she explained her word choices, revisited her sentences, structure and language and checked for formality. After these first few sentences, Maariya picked out examples from the work of her researchers and praised their application of her thinking; she sought articulation of thinking from her researchers and in the moment addressed any misconceptions.

> ### Reflective questions ?
>
> » How could the writing context Maariya had created through the '*Galactic Defence*' simulation impact on her learners' thinking, writing and self-regulation?
>
> » Why do you think Maariya made the decision to provide a 100-word parameter? What impact might that have on thinking, writing and self-regulation?
>
> » In this case study, Maariya's modelling of thinking and writing decisions was as important as her modelling of physical writing. What do you think was the impact on her learners' thinking, writing and self-regulation?

The explicit teaching of grammar

In the case study above, Maariya modelled relevant grammatical conventions in the context of her writing. Ofsted's Research Review of English (2022) highlights the importance of explicitly teaching the foundational knowledge of grammar and punctuation. The review states *'Explicitly teaching pupils the knowledge and skills they need to succeed within particular subject areas is beneficial'* (2016, p 13). Andrews et al (2006) posit that teaching grammar improves the quality and accuracy of writing, while Graham et al's (2012) work includes the importance of explicit strategy instruction in transcriptional skills and grammar teaching alongside learner self-regulation and how text structure works. This is also developed by Higgins (2015, p 14) who is clear that the explicit teaching of strategies is important for success; these include, as we see through Maariya's teaching, writing for a purpose, writing for a real audience and also explicitly teaching writing as a process.

Language features, structure and revising text

As illustrated by the *'Galactic Defence'* case study, modelling the writing process is an excellent teaching tool. Its uses are not confined to those described in the case study; modelling is an English teaching multi-tool and can certainly be used to teach genre-specific language features, text structure and how to revise text effectively. However, in this section, I will explore the teaching tool of guided writing and how it can be utilised effectively to develop learners' understanding of genre-specific language features and revising text. To do this we will explore a guided intervention in the writing process co-constructed by PGCE primary trainee Luke and his mentor Lisa.

What is guided writing?

Guided writing is a teaching tool, whereby the teacher facilitates a short (approximately 20 minute) focused and targeted piece of learning for a small group of learners, usually five or six. I believe it to be most effective as an intervention in writing development for a group of learners with similar writing needs at the point of need in the process. It might involve you as a teacher modelling, it will definitely involve learners writing and it will certainly involve learners thinking. The aim of guided writing is to lead your learners into writing independence. Does it work? Medfouni et al (2021) suggest that the use of this technique improves writing performance and Khatri (2014) found this tool effective in teaching composition. Both articles cite the instrumental role of the teacher. In an earlier text I have written (Copping, 2016), I suggest that the role of the teacher in guided writing is not to transmit information but to support enquiry, investigate language and think like authors, making intentional choices about language and structures. Supporting learners to find their written voice, giving permission to use the language they want, and to communicate what they want to communicate guided by your focus on the learning objective is crucial to their motivation and independence.

CASE STUDY

Year 2: writing a missing chapter

Lisa's Year 2 class had been exploring the text *Bill's New Frock* by Anne Fine. By the end of their two-week unit of work, Lisa wanted her learners to have written a new chapter for the book, focusing on an incident or event that is mentioned in the text but isn't explicit. Having spent the first week reading the text, Lisa and her PGCE primary trainee Luke are now ready to support some writing. Together, they have planned with the class, mapped out some plot lines, and developed a working wall with ideas, characters and extracts from the chapters either side of the one they will write. Lisa is now modelling writing including the use of dialogue. Lisa's objectives are taken from the national curriculum (DfE, 2013) and include the use of co-ordination and sub-ordination in sentence construction and also expanded noun phrases. Lisa has modelled these for the learners, articulated her thinking and put examples up on the working wall. Lisa and Luke have planned together two guided sessions – Lisa will teach the first session on Monday focusing on using genre-specific language (adventure stories) which Luke will observe, and Luke will work with a group on Friday on editing and revising text.

Figure 4.5 is Lisa's plan for her guided session. She is using an adapted format based on McGill's five-minute lesson plan (McGill, 2023).

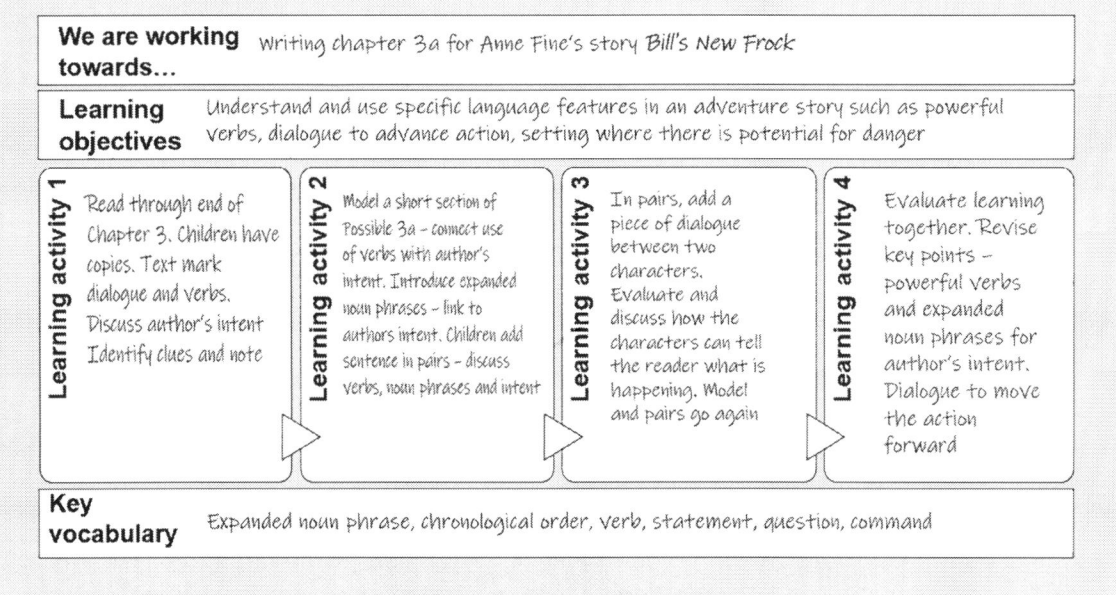

We are working towards...	Writing chapter 3a for Anne Fine's story *Bill's New Frock*
Learning objectives	Understand and use specific language features in an adventure story such as powerful verbs, dialogue to advance action, setting where there is potential for danger

Learning activity 1	Learning activity 2	Learning activity 3	Learning activity 4
Read through end of Chapter 3. Children have copies. Text mark dialogue and verbs. Discuss author's intent. Identify clues and note	Model a short section of Possible 3a – connect use of verbs with author's intent. Introduce expanded noun phrases – link to author's intent. Children add sentence in pairs – discuss verbs, noun phrases and intent	In pairs, add a piece of dialogue between two characters. Evaluate and discuss how the characters can tell the reader what is happening. Model and pairs go again	Evaluate learning together. Revise key points – powerful verbs and expanded noun phrases for author's intent. Dialogue to move the action forward

Key vocabulary	Expanded noun phrase, chronological order, verb, statement, question, command

Figure 4.5 Lisa's Year 2 guided writing plan for Bill's New Frock

First, notice Lisa's subject knowledge. Lisa's knowledge of specific language features and their function in text linked to author's intent enabled her to move her learners on in their writing. She also advanced their thinking through her insistence on discussion and articulation of thinking modelled by herself. The evaluation at the end, led by the learners, allowed Lisa to assess progress and understanding.

This was an excellent model for Luke, Lisa's PGCE primary trainee. They deconstructed the session together afterwards and supported Luke in planning his guided writing focusing on editing. Figure 4.6 shows the progression of his planned learning episodes.

Learning activity 1: Revise language features and author's intent. Model using content of working wall to help with editing. Revise purpose of editing

Learning activity 2: Model editing process. Focus on articulating reasons for editing, language choice, remain focused on author's intent

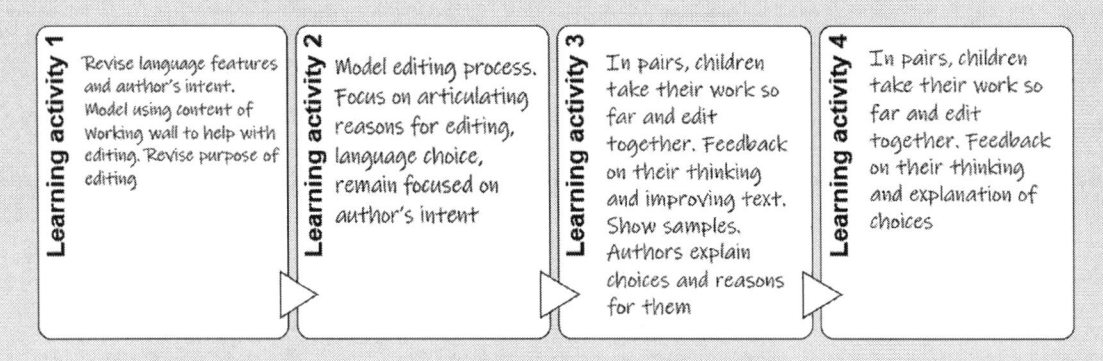

Learning activity 3: In pairs, children take their work so far and edit together. Feedback on their thinking and improving text. Show samples. Authors explain choices and reasons for them

Learning activity 4: In pairs, children take their work so far and edit together. Feedback on their thinking and explanation of choices

Figure 4.6 Luke's learning episodes – guided work – edit and revise

> ### Reflective questions ?
>
> » Notice Lisa's understanding of the importance of writing as a cognitive process through use of a working wall. (This weblink will give you a great insight into working walls for English – https://literacywithmissp.com/2018/08/07/harnessing-the-power-of-working-walls.) What impact might that have on thinking, writing and self-regulation?
>
> » How do you think the focus on thinking and articulation of language choices will support the learners into becoming independent writers?

Chapter summary

This chapter has started to explore some of the building blocks of the writing process. While exploring the practical and physical approaches associated with these blocks we have also focused significantly on the cognitive elements. Writing is a cognitive process and for us as teachers to first recognise that, then to articulate and model it and finally to support learners to apply it, is very powerful. This approach helps learners make connections through the different elements of your teaching through the writing process. We have also considered the importance of setting a meaningful and relevant real-life context for writing. A key element of this chapter has been to use the teaching tools of shared, modelled and guided writing to explore the building blocks in the context of creative classroom pedagogy. During shared learning and teaching, learners should be fully active. If learners are engaging in related activity alongside your teaching, this will help alleviate cognitive load and ease the processing of information. We have also explored the effective use of mentor texts and modelling writing. Again, the focus here has been developing learners' creative self-efficacy and self-regulation through developing thinking and supporting their decision-making as authors.

Further reading

These three excellent and accessible readings alongside my reflective questions will help develop your thinking from this chapter:

Culham, R (2014) *The Writing Thief: Using Mentor Texts to Teach the Craft of Writing.* Newark, NJ: Stenhouse Publishers, International Literacy Association.

This text will really help develop your thinking around using mentor texts. Ruth Culham has a passion for great writing. She is an avid collector of mentor texts, describing her approach as looking through the eyes of a writing thief.

Focus question

While reading, consider Ruth Culham's 4 Ws of writing – writing process, writing traits, writing workshops and writing modes. How do these help develop learners as writers?

Bushnell, A, Smith, R and Waugh, D (2018) *Modelling Exciting Writing.* London: Sage.

This is a practical text which is packed full of excellent evidence-informed practice. It takes a context-based approach to teaching writing and focuses on the power of modelling.

Focus question

While reading, consider the authors' focus on articulating the writing process during modelling. How does their advice connect to this chapter?

Hermansson, C and Lindgren, E (2019) Writing as a Cognitive Process. [online] Available at: www.cambridge.org/elt/blog/2019/12/19/writing-cognitive-process/ (accessed 22 August 2023).

This excellent blog from the University of Cambridge emphasises the complexities of writing and the challenges for young writers alongside practical ideas for using mentor texts. It is intended for teachers of learners who are learning English as an additional language, but the advice and discussion is relevant for all.

Focus question

How does the authors' focus on purposeful practice help with their automation of writing? How does this align to the idea of writing as a cognitive process?

5 The importance of cement: connecting the blocks

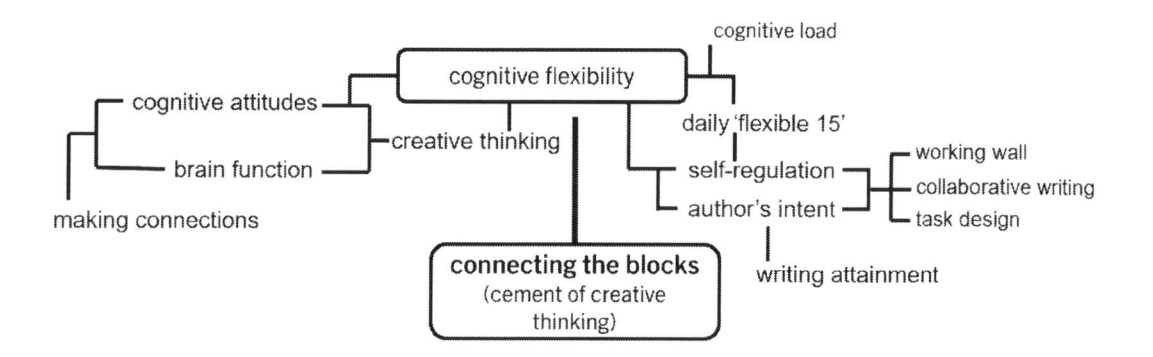

```
                              cognitive load
                                  |
          cognitive flexibility
  cognitive attitudes ─┘    │    └ daily 'flexible 15'
                      ├─ creative thinking                      ┌─ working wall
       brain function ─┘    │    ┌ self-regulation ─┬─ collaborative writing
making connections          │    └ author's intent ─┴─ task design
                      connecting the blocks          |
                      (cement of creative      writing attainment
                            thinking)
```

Core Content Framework / Early Career Teacher Framework links

The Department for Education for England and Wales (DfE) provides a framework of minimum entitlement for trainee teachers which is then developed into your Early Career Teacher (ECT) years. This chapter links to the following:

- high expectations (Standard 1) – setting goals that challenge and stretch pupils;
- how pupils learn (Standard 2 – Progress) – working memory, active processing, retrieving information from memory;
- subject and curriculum (Standard 3) – learning new ideas by linking to existing knowledge, transferring knowledge from one discipline to another;
- classroom practice (Standard 4) – modelling, metacognitive strategies, high-quality talk, practice;
- assessment (Standard 6) – good assessment avoids misleading factors, identifies misconceptions. High-quality feedback encourages further effort and helps pupils regulate their own learning.

Introduction

If I built a house or wall with just blocks, it may not stand up for very long. I would have to rely on the way the blocks are balanced for them to remain standing. For those blocks to stand firm as a structure they need to be connected together using cement. Cement connects the blocks to form a cohesive and strong structure, particularly when built upon a strong foundation, which is laid in Chapter 3.

Having discussed building blocks of the writing process in Chapter 4, this chapter suggests that of equal importance are the connections made between each block. It begins with the premise that children do not necessarily make connections between each of the building blocks, and their learning and writing development can be impaired as a result. The chapter explores the creative thinking skill of making connections and some of the benefits this can bring to children's attainment in writing, drawing upon Dunsmuir et al's (2015) Writing Assessment Measure, which is rooted in the Department for Education's Teacher Assessment Frameworks for writing.

Why do learners need '*cement*'?

In my experience as a teacher, lecturer and researcher, children do struggle to make connections between different elements of the learning process. Part of the challenge, I think, is that the children in your class are not inside your head as you are planning. Whether you are using a scheme or published resources or planning from scratch, you will be designing the learning process, creating connections in your head between your shared reading and writing, your modelling and their writing, and to you it all makes sense. But to the children it may not. To your learners, the incredible connected design that you have created for their learning may well just be a series of unrelated tasks to be completed and hopefully get right. In other words, they are blocks that are not joined together. In order to get the most from the learning and make it make sense, your learners need to be able to connect those blocks with the cement of creative thinking.

Creative thinking: definitions and characteristics

So, what is meant by creative thinking? This section explores and discusses some wide-ranging definitions from social, psychological and neuroscience perspectives, before landing on making connections and cognitive flexibility. Figure 5.1 below is a knowledge organiser which will help you connect the key definitions.

The importance of cement • 73

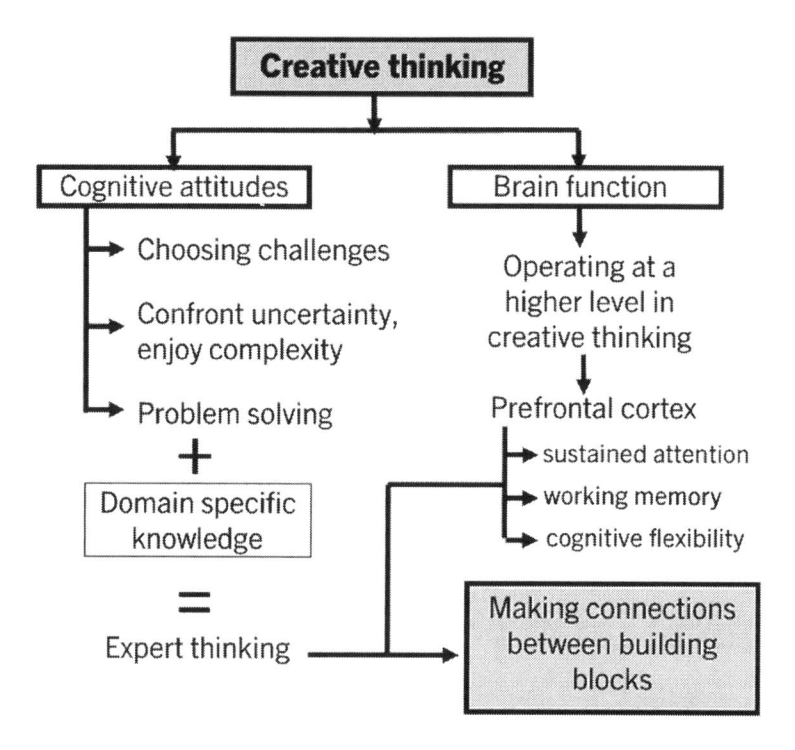

Figure 5.1 *Creative thinking knowledge organiser*

Creative thinking as an attitude is developed by Meadows. In her discussion of how cognition is acquired and developed in childhood, she suggests three important *'cognitive attitudes'* that creative thinkers display (2006, pp 194–5). The first is *'choosing challenges'*. By this she means embracing a challenging task or situation and coming to it with an attitude that is all about personal development and learning. The second is *'confronting uncertainty and enjoying complexity'*. Aligning with McWilliam and Haukka's (2008) dispositions of flexibility and adaptability, Meadows suggests that creative thinkers enjoy operating within the grey areas of a task or problem, rather than the more certain black and white. The third is to do with problem-setting and solving. This is a key feature of creative thinking across a range of literature over a significant time period, for example Guilford (1967), Ward (2007), Craft et al (2013) and Deejring (2016).

Meadows (2006) and Sternberg (2003) also suggest that not only are these attitudes important for creative thinking, but they are also important for domain-specific knowledge. Meadows states that the creative thinker has an *'exhaustive knowledge of his or her field, a sizeable basic repertoire of strategies and skills and information'* (2006, p 195). Both make the argument that in order to think around a particular topic or domain creatively, an attitude is not enough; knowledge of that topic or domain is of fundamental importance. Sternberg emphasises creative thinking as an attitude; he claims, *'creative people are creative in the large part because they have decided to be creative'* (2003, p 333) and he also acknowledges that having a greater domain-specific knowledge facilitates a greater degree of creativity (2003, p 334). This aligns with Sweller, who in his work on cognitive load during problem-solving, makes the point that *'domain specific knowledge in the form of schemas is the primary factor distinguishing experts from novices in problem solving skill'* (1988, p 257). Here Sweller is referring to skills such as working flexibly, being adaptable, embracing challenge – the attitudes that Meadows (2006) shared – and domain-specific knowledge, the concepts, understanding and knowledge of the field or area in which the problem sits.

Having explored some of the key characteristics of creative thinking from a sociological and psychological perspective, I now examine this from a neuroscience viewpoint. Understanding brain function is helpful in further understanding the creative thinking process. If, as Dietrich states, we understand that the *'neural circuits that process specific information to yield non-creative combinations of information are the same neural circuits that generate creative combination of information'* (2004, p 1011), then the assumption that all have the capacity to be creative has some proof through scientific study of brain function. While Dietrich states that the neural circuits in normal and creative thinking are the same, drawing on the work of Cabeza and Nyberg (2000) and Damasio (2001), he does equate creative thinking with higher brain function (2004, p 1011). According to Dietrich (2004), it is not clear in any of the work listed above if this is the same as an increase in brain cells sending messages to each other, but the implication that creative thinking involves the human brain operating at a higher level than in other thinking is crucial to understanding why the capacity or ability to think in this way is desirable for learners. Dietrich (2004, p 1011) states that the prefrontal cortex part of the brain contains many of the cognitive abilities ascribed to creative thinking. These are working memory, sustained attention, cognitive flexibility and judgement of propriety. Cognitive flexibility, linked to Guilford's (1967) divergent thinking and Craft's (1999) possibility thinking, discussed in the previous section, is stressed as the epitome of creative thinking. This is *'what helps humans pursue complex tasks, such as multitasking and finding novel, adaptable solutions to changing demands'* (Ionescu, 2011, p 190). The prefrontal cortex is therefore crucial in problem-solving activity, bringing to bear *'the full arsenal of higher cognitive functions to the problem'* (Dietrich, 2004, p 1015). These are defined as sustained attention or persistence, retrieving relevant information, buffering it, ordering it and making connections with other relevant information.

Making connections, or following the metaphor, applying cement to the learning blocks, is seen as a higher cognitive function, requiring cognitive flexibility. If children are to gain the most from your teaching, then there is the need to support them to develop this important skill. In Chapter 6, I explore in more detail specific practical approaches of applying metaphorical cement, but to help apply the principle of cognitive flexibility to your teaching, read the case study below. Elise, a recently qualified teacher (RQT) is looking to develop cognitive flexibility in her Year 5 class using what she terms a daily *'flexible 15'*.

CASE STUDY

Year 5: developing cognitive flexibility – the daily flexible 15

Elise had been working with her new class for a week. As she reflected on her class's progress, their ways of working, social dynamic and lack of independence, Elise knew she had to act. She wanted the children in her class to experience more success in learning, develop more sustained writing and be able to make connections between the building blocks of their learning. She had noticed many children in her class were good at following a method to get an answer but found understanding processes and applying principles difficult. She decided to try out cognitive flexibility exercises every day for three weeks to see if any difference was made. She chose to use 15 minutes after lunch each day, a '*flexible 15*' to develop her class's thinking. Figure 5.2 is an annotated version of Elise's '*flexible 15*' weekly visual timetable.

Flexible 15. Our daily challenge

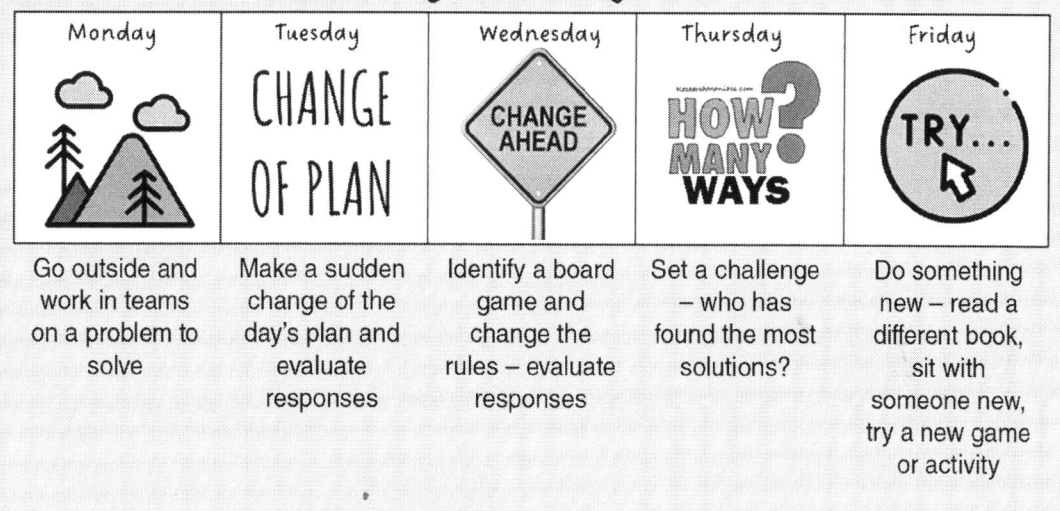

Monday	Tuesday	Wednesday	Thursday	Friday
Go outside and work in teams on a problem to solve	Make a sudden change of the day's plan and evaluate responses	Identify a board game and change the rules – evaluate responses	Set a challenge – who has found the most solutions?	Do something new – read a different book, sit with someone new, try a new game or activity

Figure 5.2 Annotated visual timetable for 15 minutes of cognitive flexibility a day

Each of the activities involved developing cognitive flexibility. Monday's outside activity required collaboration and trying out a number of possible solutions. Tuesday's sudden change of plan required children to be able to adapt to changing environments. Wednesday's making up new rules for a game meant that children had to think outside of what they already knew. Thursday's challenge involved understanding there may be several solutions to a problem and Friday's involved opening their mind to new experiences. If you look back to Figure 5.1 you will see that these activities also develop the cognitive attitudes that Meadows (2006) discusses, and in so doing engage the prefrontal cortex part of the brain, crucial for making connections in learning.

→

By the end of the third week, Elise noticed changes in the way many of her class engaged with each other and with their learning. More children were willing to have a go at an activity and enjoyed taking on a learning challenge; some had even developed an acceptance that getting it wrong meant they were learning. More children were able to apply language and sentence structures from shared and modelled writing and some could adapt the modelled writing to suit their own author's intentions. Elise was staggered at how successful her cognitive flexibility activities had been; she had not made any changes to her teaching approaches, instead she had developed her children's cognitive flexibility through short, focused tasks and experiences. In so doing, Elise had provided tools to lay the creative thinking cement onto the building blocks of learning and start to connect them up.

Reflective questions ?

» How do you think Elise's activities were underpinned by the literature on creative thinking I have shared in this chapter so far?

» What do you think is the significance of regular and repeated short, focused cognitive flexibility activity daily?

» Were you surprised at the impact Elise's cognitive flexibility activities made on the children's engagement with their learning?

» Reflect on why Elise chose to introduce some cognitive flexibility exercises to her class. Think about your own class and the struggles they have with learning. Cognitive flexibility is a vital skill to have in many areas of learning. For example, to grasp hold of the different graphemes for some phonemes, eg 'a' 'a-e' 'ai' ay', cognitive flexibility is essential.

» Consider how you will build the cognitive flexibility of your learners – you could use some of Elise's activities and try a flexible 15 every day to build learner resilience and persistence.

» Reflect on the impact of what you do and how it helps your learners make connections between the building blocks of the writing process, or any learning, for that matter.

The remainder of this chapter discusses three important impacts that making connections through cognitive flexibility can have on children's writing. These are self-regulation, author's intent and attainment against standardised writing criteria. In fact, I would suggest that the first two of these also lead to the third, as Figure 5.3 demonstrates.

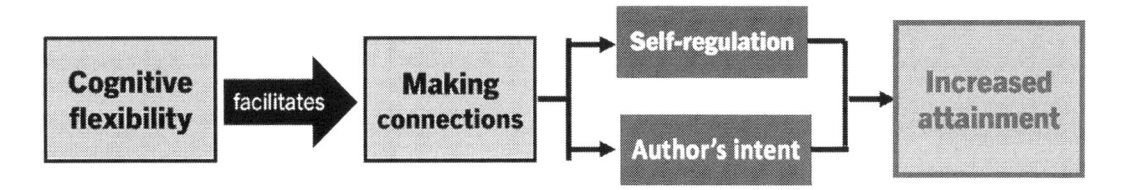

Figure 5.3 Impact of cognitive flexibility on attainment

As much as I would like it to be, I know the process is not as simple as Figure 5.3 might suggest. You will know your class, your learners and reasons why this may not be straightforward for them. Ji and Wang (2018), for example, discuss the effects of adverse childhood experiences (ACEs) on cognition, learning and cognitive flexibility. You will also be aware of the seminal work of Maslow (1943) on human motivation. His hierarchy of needs makes the point that learning cannot really take place effectively unless basic needs such as food, shelter, love and a sense of belonging are in place. Earlier in this chapter I have referred to Sweller's (1988) work on cognitive load theory and how having simply too much going on in your brain can cause it to overload. Overload can be attributed to in-school factors such as too many instructions and the speed of curriculum delivery, but also external factors such as the home environment. While there are a number of influences on cognitive processing (Ford and Stein, 2016), McManus and Poehlmann (2012) suggest that social deprivation can impact cognitive processing negatively. What Figure 5.3 is aiming to demonstrate and what I am exploring here is that developing cognitive flexibility in learners can have a positive impact on attainment, notwithstanding the many factors that can impact negatively on cognition.

Self-regulation

Self-regulation as part of the writing process has been previously discussed in Chapter 4, but here I explore it as a product of making connections in learning through creative thinking. Graham and Harris (1997) state that self-regulation is necessary to become an expert writer. They draw upon Zimmerman and Risemberg's (1997) cognitive model of self-regulation and writing, who argue that because writing is often self-sustaining and sometimes self-initiated, self-regulation is crucial. How, then, does one achieve self-regulation? What exactly are the key indicators? You will, I am sure, have found reluctant editors amongst the children in your classes, as I did throughout my teaching career. Children who, when invited to develop their sentence structure, strengthen the verb, add more detail, improve the description, reply '*but I've finished*'. Editing and revising takes self-regulation, the willingness to sustain writing, to persist and persevere. Self-regulation is also a key part of the composing process. It is needed so that writers can pay more attention to focusing on the choice of topic, the needs of the audience to whom they are writing, and the text type conventions. Writing, as Hayes and Flower (1980), cited in Myhill (2009, p 47), state, is *'the act of juggling simultaneous constraints'*. It is not a linear procedure, but a set of complex processes and so self-regulation is vital to manage them. Self-regulation requires cognitive flexibility to create brain space for these constraints and the mechanical processes of putting pen to paper or fingers to keys. To see the potential impact that self-regulation can have on writing attainment, let's return to the case study of Elise and her Year 5 class. You will remember that Elise had done some intensive daily cognitive flexibility development for a three-week period. Following this, through her topic of the impact of the Second World War on Britain from the history national curriculum, a significant turning point in British history, Elise had introduced her class to Michelle Magorian's 1981 text *Goodnight Mr Tom*. The case study below explores the writing the class did in terms of process and attainment.

CASE STUDY

Year 5: self-regulation and writing attainment

The writing task Elise had set for her class was a challenging one as it demanded they apply the cognitive flexibility skills they had been practising over the previous few weeks. Her plan for her daily learning and teaching over the week uses the same adapted format from Chapter 4.

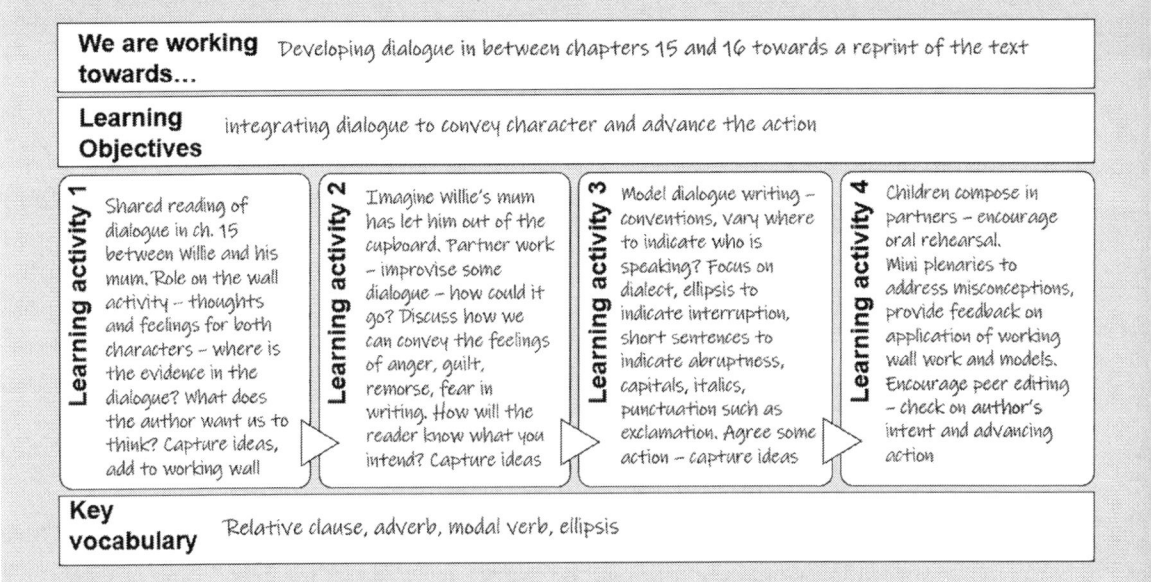

We are working towards…	Developing dialogue in between chapters 15 and 16 towards a reprint of the text
Learning Objectives	integrating dialogue to convey character and advance the action

Learning activity 1	Learning activity 2	Learning activity 3	Learning activity 4
Shared reading of dialogue in ch. 15 between Willie and his mum. Role on the wall activity – thoughts and feelings for both characters – where is the evidence in the dialogue? What does the author want us to think? Capture ideas, add to working wall	Imagine Willie's mum has let him out of the cupboard. Partner work – improvise some dialogue – how could it go? Discuss how we can convey the feelings of anger, guilt, remorse, fear in writing. How will the reader know what you intend? Capture ideas	Model dialogue writing – conventions, vary where to indicate who is speaking? Focus on dialect, ellipsis to indicate interruption, short sentences to indicate abruptness, capitals, italics, punctuation such as exclamation. Agree some action – capture ideas	Children compose in partners – encourage oral rehearsal. Mini plenaries to address misconceptions, provide feedback on application of working wall work and models. Encourage peer editing – check on author's intent and advancing action

Key vocabulary	Relative clause, adverb, modal verb, ellipsis

Figure 5.4 Elise's learning episodes over a week: Year 5 Goodnight Mr Tom

Elise's plan and thinking around connection-making has some key features that build on her cognitive flexibility development. The first is activity during shared reading. Her class will have large cut-outs of Willie Beech and his mum from the story; as the dialogue is being read, they record on the cut-outs (role on the wall) what the dialogue is communicating about thoughts and feelings. These cut-outs are added to the second cognitive flexibility tool, the working wall. Working walls have been used by teachers for many years; they recognise the importance of writing as a process and making best use of all the excellent development work that leads to a final written piece. Working walls are also a great way to alleviate cognitive overload; they act almost as another part of the long-term memory, storing all of the process information from previous learning ready to bring back into the working memory when needed. At the end of each of the first three learning activities Elise's plan reads *'capture ideas'*. She will develop her working wall with her class's ideas over the learning episodes as part of the cognitive process of composing.

There are two final elements of Elise's plan to note.

1. First, the task. The task is writing dialogue; it has a clear form and a clear purpose, instantly lessening cognitive load. Quality of language to convey thoughts and feelings and to advance the action is desired over quantity. Again, cognitive load is lessened, giving more space to flexibly use language.

2. Second, children are writing in pairs and using oral rehearsal first so risk is lessened. Note the use of mini plenaries to assess learning, address misconceptions early and intervene if needed.

During learning and teaching Elise reflected on the design of this unit of work. She wanted to see if her cognitive flexibility training had any impact on the writing. What surprised Elise most was the seeming closing of the attainment gap between those previously assessed at working below age-related expectations (AREs) and those working above. Elise chose to use an adaptation of Dunsmuir et al's (2015) Writing Assessment Measure, shown in Table 5.1. Each element of writing has four criterion statements; they are in order of high to low attainment from the top down.

Table 5.1 Adaptation of Dunsmuir et al's (2015) Writing Assessment Measure

Element of writing	Criteria
HANDWRITING	Writing is consistent and fluent
	Writing is clear, neat and legible
	Handwriting may vary in shape and size
	Handwriting is difficult to read
SPELLING	Correct spelling of complex and irregular words
	Polysyllabic words are usually spelt phonetically
	Spells the majority of high-frequency words correctly
	Monosyllabic words spelt correctly

Table 5.1 (Cont.)

Element of writing	Criteria
PUNCTUATION	Range of punctuation used for structure and effect
	Secure use of full stops and capital letters
	Largely accurate use of capital letters and full stops
	Shows an awareness of full stops used in writing
SENTENCE STRUCTURE AND GRAMMAR	Complex sentences and clauses manipulated for effect
	Extending sentences using some subordination
	Conjunctions used to create compound sentences
	Simple sentences used
VOCABULARY	Well chosen, vivid and powerful vocabulary used
	Varied use of adjectives, verbs and specific nouns
	Selects interesting and varied verbs
	Uses simple vocabulary appropriate to content
ORGANISATION AND OVERALL STRUCTURE	Paragraphs well organised based on themes, cohesive
	Identifiable structure using cohesive ties
	Themes are expanded upon and logic is apparent
	Communicates meaning but flits from idea to idea
IDEAS	Creative and interesting and engages reader
	Imaginative with varied and descriptive detail
	Ideas developed and elaborated upon by adding detail
	Short sections of repetitive and limited text

Elise noticed that while the writing from her learners working below AREs did not score highly in handwriting and spelling, their improvement in ideas, sentence structure, vocabulary and punctuation for effect was vast. Many of those working below AREs achieved as highly as those working above AREs in terms of ideas and vocabulary. Figure 5.5 is an example of a piece of writing from a pair working together in Elise's class, both previously identified as writing below AREs. It has been typed but the spelling, punctuation, grammar, vocabulary and ideas are as written.

> "Aaaarrgghhh!" The light was too bright and the pain in his ankel was too bad.
> "Stop your cryin, you always was soft" scoldded Mrs Beech as she unloked the cupboard.
> "Why did ya do it? Why did ya 'it me?"
> "You need to learn, that's what"
> "But mum..."
> "Don't you but mum me, boy or it'll be bad for ya"
> "But I didn't do nuffin"
> "There you go, lyin' again. I see you still aven't learnt" She reached for the belt.
> Willie tried to back further into the corner but he had reached the end.
> "Why is there a knok at the door? If you've told enyone you're ere I'll..."

Figure 5.5 Extract from Year 5 dialogue writing: Goodnight Mr Tom

These learners used oral rehearsal and wanted to show that Willie was scared and that his mum believed that the discipline she had meted out had been necessary, but also, she didn't want to be found by anyone else to be hitting her son. Note the use of dialectic speech, ellipsis and adverbial phrases. This example highlights two important points.

1. First, that having more cognitive flexibility alongside a clearly defined task where cognitive overload is alleviated may well have been contributing factors in this writing.

2. Second, children find transcriptional elements of writing (handwriting, spelling, punctuation) difficult (Graham and Harris, 2009; Lambirth, 2016). This can often be the difference between learners identified as working above and below AREs; however, using an assessment measure such as that in Table 5.1 can help gain an understanding of attainment in the more cognitive elements of composition.

Reflective questions ?

» What role do you think cognitive flexibility played in higher levels of writing attainment?

» What, in your opinion, were the key elements of Elise's plan that impacted most on writing?

» What will you take away from this case study and apply to your own practice?

Author's intent

If you look back at Figure 5.4, Elise's plan, you may well notice the idea of author's intent is embedded into the writing process. Learning activity 2 facilitates the learners' problem-solving how to convey intent and meaning through language, punctuation and grammar. I suggest that understanding how grammar works and how to use grammatical conventions helps writers make choices in their writing to convey meaning (Copping, 2016). In order for children to have the capacity to make these choices they have to see themselves as writers with something to say that is important. I also suggest that the cognitive processes involved here are eminently creative (Copping, 2016), and therefore require cognitive flexibility. Gardner (2014) argues that many teachers lack confidence in teaching writing and in themselves as writers, and so fall back on teaching purely discrete skills (Bailey, 2002) and traditional conventions of writing. There is a danger that this approach, while a necessary foundation, is not sufficient. Children need to know they can take risks with language, play with it and have fun with it to communicate effectively with the target audience. Gardner's (2014) work highlights the importance of teachers positioning themselves as writers. This helps to understand the challenges that children face when writing, and the risk involved in making those private thoughts public text (Kellogg, 1999), but also the high reward of creating a linguistic masterpiece.

Chapter summary

This chapter has begun to explore the concept of working between the building blocks of the writing process. Using cement as a metaphor for creative thinking, this chapter has explored the importance of connecting these building blocks together to make a strong and stable learning structure. Building on the broader discussion in Chapters 2 and 3, definitions of creative thinking from social, psychological and neuroscience perspectives are brought to the fore, providing a foundation for this chapter's key concept, making connections. The concept of cognitive flexibility is introduced as a process of creative thinking that supports the making of connections between stages of learning. We have considered the importance of this for learning and, through case study, activities that can help develop learners' cognitive flexibility. The case study has then been developed into exploring the potential impacts of these *'flexible 15s'* on writing. Using a four-stage learning plan, the case study also demonstrated ways in which the teacher can work between the building blocks of the writing process using teaching techniques such as working walls, collaborative writing, modelling and feedback on how learners are applying the models. Finally, this chapter has developed the case study, focusing on the self-regulation and author's intent aspects of the learning and teaching to impact upon writing attainment. There has also been reflection on the challenging and complex processes of writing that may present cognitive overload for some learners. This chapter has considered, again through the case study, how some of this overload can be alleviated, again through the design of activity and use of teaching tools such as working walls.

Further reading

The following three excellent and accessible readings, alongside the reflective questions, will help develop your thinking from this chapter.

> Gardner, P (2014) Becoming a Teacher of Writing: Primary Student Teachers Reviewing Their Relationship with Writing. *English in Education*, 48(2): 128–48. [online] Available at: https://doi.org/10.1111/eie.12039.
>
> *This interesting and informative study considers how teachers of writing need to be writers themselves, so they understand the processes and challenges from a writer's perspective. Study participants discussed the positive impact on their teaching and the importance of a safe psychological environment for writing.*
>
> ## Focus question
>
> Consider whether you position yourself as a writer. If so, how does this impact on your teaching of writing? If not, do you think positioning yourself as a writer is important for developing your writing pedagogy?

> Sahakian, B, Langley, C and Leong, V (2021) IQ Tests Can't Measure It, but 'Cognitive Flexibility' is Key to Learning and Creativity. [online] Available at: www.languagesciences.cam.ac.uk/news/iq-tests-cant-measure-it-cognitive-flexibility-key-learning-and-creativity (accessed 22 August 2023).
>
> *This article from the University of Cambridge Language Sciences Research Centre gives a helpful insight into the importance of cognitive flexibility for learning in a general sense. It makes the point that cognitive flexibility can be trained.*
>
> ## Focus question
>
> As you read the article, consider how it applies to the learners in your class. Are there any you think of who display cognitive rigidity? How is that impacting upon their learning and attainment?

Education Endowment Foundation (2014) IPEELL: Using Self-Regulation to Improve Writing. [online] Available at: https://educationendowmentfoundation.org.uk/projects-and-evaluation/projects/ipeell-using-self-regulation-to-improve-writing (accessed 22 August 2023).

This interesting project by the EEF explored the importance of self-regulation in the writing process. The project had an impact on a variety of learners, including the writing attainment of children who were described as low attainers.

Focus question

The project used memorable experiences to help children take ownership of their writing. In what ways can you develop self-regulation in your learners through the use of memorable experiences that help children own their writing?

6 Working within the gaps

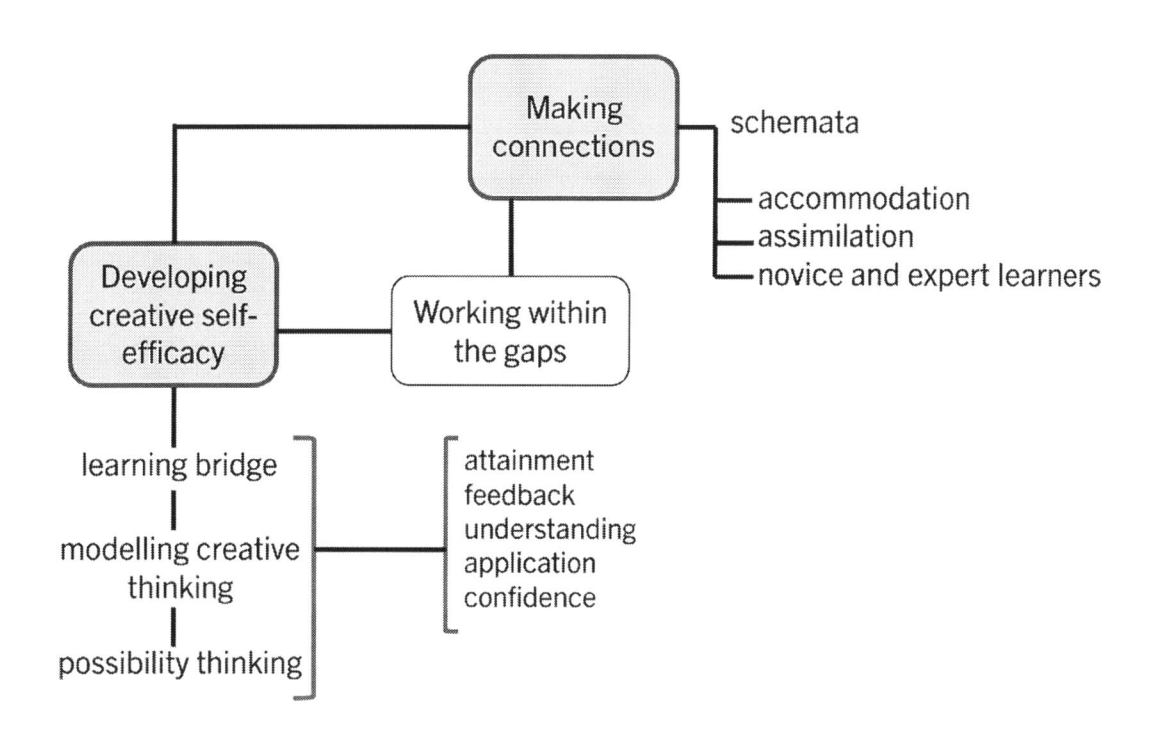

```
                    ┌─ schemata
       Making connections ─┼─ accommodation
              │            ├─ assimilation
              │            └─ novice and expert learners
              │
Developing ──┴── Working within
creative self-    the gaps
efficacy
    │                ┌ attainment
learning bridge      │ feedback
    │                ┤ understanding
modelling creative   │ application
   thinking          └ confidence
    │
possibility thinking
```

Core Content Framework / Early Career Teacher Framework links

The Department for Education for England and Wales (DfE) provides a framework of minimum entitlement for trainee teachers which is then developed into your Early Career Teacher (ECT) years. This chapter links to the following:

- high expectations (Standard 1) – teachers as role models and teacher expectations;
- how pupils learn (Standard 2 – Progress) – integrating new ideas with existing knowledge;
- subject and curriculum (Standard 3) – transferring learning to another context;

→

- classroom practice (Standard 4) – modelling process, guides and scaffolds;
- adaptive teaching (Standard 5) – adapting teaching in a responsive way;
- assessment (Standard 6) – high-quality verbal feedback, encourage effort and improvement.

Introduction

Many years ago, I worked on a building site as a builder's labourer. As the youngest and least experienced person on site, many of the duties I had to perform were not deemed to be the most desirable. For example, I made the tea, swept up the mess, emptied bins, carried materials, fetched anything I was asked to get and was often sent to the shop for snacks. However, for a couple of weeks I was asked to fill in for the bricklayers' labourer who was unwell. That meant mixing the cement for them and making sure they always had enough to turn the stacks of bricks into strong, stable, uniform walls. This, I discovered, was not as easy as it looked, and was also very hard work, even with a cement mixer. The consistency had to be right, the mix of cement, sand and lime had to be right; if not, then it wouldn't do the job. The cement and its quality were essential for the wall to be strong and the bricks to hold together.

In a lot of the books on primary English that I have read and contributed to, it is often the building blocks of primary English pedagogy that get the most coverage. The chapters focus on shared and guided reading and writing, for example, teaching spelling, grammar and punctuation and effective teacher instruction. However, very little focuses on the cement that connects these building blocks. I suggest that just like in the building trade, the cement does the work to hold the wall together; there is significant work that needs to happen in the gaps between the building blocks of primary English pedagogy to impact positively on understanding and attainment.

This chapter, therefore, presents some very practical ways in which teachers can '*work within the gaps*' of the building blocks and cement them together. It explores the development of children's creative self-efficacy by taking a coaching approach to teaching writing, supplementing the more common instructional approach. It focuses on modelling the application of creative thinking, modelling and encouraging the using and developing of others' ideas, building confidence, practising free association and giving feedback to learners on their use of these processes. This chapter also demonstrates how these practices can support higher attainment in writing, with reference to the Department for Education Teacher Assessment Frameworks for writing.

Working within the gaps: a rationale

In the Introduction to this book, I have outlined some of my own research upon which it is based. Within workshops 1 and 2, with Year 6, framed as Maariya's case study in Chapter 4, it became apparent that the tried and tested building blocks of working with a mentor text and modelling writing from it were just not working. Prior to my workshops, the classes had used mentor texts (Culham, 2014) weekly. The children were used to, with support, examining and analysing text, engaging with its features and using any that might develop their own writing. In these two workshops, a mentor text was used to help develop descriptive writing. This is referred to as 'What A Good One Looks Like', with the acronym WAGOLL. A large copy of the text was read with the class, displayed, highlighted and discussed together, then analysed for key features to magpie. Despite the regular use of this tool in the class, in my reflective diary, while working with class 6H, I observed:

> *There was very little ability to pick out language.*
> *The children seemed to really flounder with the WAGOLL, just because it was in a different format to what they are used to.*
>
> (My reflective diary, p 3)

These reflections were corroborated by observations of 6H during the workshop,

> *Children didn't connect what I was doing with the WAGOLL to how they could use it and magpie ideas, they didn't know what to do with it and seemed to see it as a separate activity to the writing.*
>
> (6H observation extract)

In an interview with the class teacher, this observation was followed up. The reason suggested for the children's lack of application of the mentor text was that I had used it differently to how they are used to and had not given them copies. However, during the focus group interview with 6H, children could clearly articulate how a mentor text should be used, and one participant's perspective was that she had used it to develop the opening of her story.

> *When we all did the openers first … I put about where they were coming from … 'the moon and every day they get closer', from the Iron Man.*
>
> (Child B, 6H focus group)

However, when analysing her writing, there was no evidence of this line in her work, demonstrating a lack of connection between the purpose of the mentor text and her writing.

A similar lack of connection was apparent when working with class 6D. While some children in 6D worked effectively with the mentor text, an extract from observation noted,

> *I made more of reminding them to use the WAGOLL but still many didn't have it in front of them.*
>
> (6D observation extract)

The class teacher of 6D, however, rated the use of the mentor text highly, recognised my use of it as being helpful to the children and understood that the purpose of the mentor text was to emulate elements of it. She stopped short of articulating how the children's writing had developed from it, and again there was limited evidence in the children's writing of the mentor text's use.

Graham and Perin, in their work on improving writing, state that mentor texts should be studied and children should be encouraged to '*analyse these examples and to emulate the critical elements … embodied in the models in their own writing*' (2007, p 20). Evidence from my findings suggests that while a mentor text is a recognised support tool to aid writing, the challenge is helping learners make the connection between a mentor text and their own composition. There is, however, a paradox within this issue of a mentor text. It was seen by some of the children as a useful support tool,

> ... having all the support, WAGOLLs, success criteria and big masses of paper to write all the things ... could have edited it and built it up to make it much better.
> (Child D, 6D focus group)

So, what was the problem? Looking back to the start of this chapter, the ITT Core Content Framework gives us a clue. In the section on subject and curriculum (Standard 3), there is some core understanding that '*Pupils are likely to struggle to transfer what has been learnt in one discipline to a new or unfamiliar context*' (2021, p 14). The problem is centred around how children learn. Kirschner and Hendrick (2020) cite the work of Piaget (1952), who explains two important processes in a child's learning: assimilation, '*new knowledge inserted into existing knowledge schemata*' (2020, p 9) and accommodation, '*existing knowledge schemata adapted to new knowledge*' (2020, p 9). Kirschner and Hendrick (2020) also remind educators that novice learners (in this context, children) are not miniature versions of expert learners. So, what can be expected of an expert learner – to problem-solve, apply concepts, evaluate and judge what might be the most effective language and linguistic techniques to steal from a mentor text – cannot be expected of a novice. The novice learner does not have the relevant schemata (or mental model) of what effective writing should look like in every context to make those choices.

So, what can be done? It is my belief that working within the gaps is partly about developing children's schemata. The remainder of this chapter provides some practical ways to develop mental models of effective writing and help novice learners assimilate new knowledge into what they already know and enlarge their existing knowledge to accommodate it.

Practical approaches to working within the gaps

Developing children's creative self-efficacy

Tierney and Farmer (2002), cited by Steele et al (2018), state that creative self-efficacy can '*provide the confidence needed to take risks and adopt perspectives and actions that may defy social norms*' (2018, p 22). Evidence from my research suggests that the children lacked this confidence and therefore arguably creative self-efficacy. Bandura (1997) notes that creative self-efficacy comes from knowledge and application. This is the knowledge of rules and strategies related to the task in hand, or domain-specific knowledge (Sweller, 1988) and the self-assurance to apply them. Mathisen and Bronnick (2009), citing Schunk and Rice (1987), argue that self-efficacy also comes from positive feedback. This feedback, they argue, in order to develop self-efficacy, should confirm that children are applying strategies well rather than practice in the strategies.

Working within the gaps • 89

This aligns with findings from the workshops discussed in the earlier part of this chapter, where I concluded that, instead of more effort helping children to understand what the building blocks of the writing process are, more effort needs to go into teaching in the gaps, making connections and helping learners apply learning. Schunk and Rice's (1987) work adds feedback between the gaps and helps build creative self-efficacy, which in turn improves creative performance. The importance of developing creative self-efficacy is also emphasised more recently in the Organisation for Economic Co-operation and Development's (OECD, 2019) PISA Creative Thinking Framework. In their study on motivation for writing, Limpo et al (2020) also convey the importance of developing self-efficacy. Their findings suggest that self-efficacy had a big impact on the story length and quality written by their third-grade research participants.

CASE STUDY

Year 4: poetry – creating images

Simeon, in his first ECT year, had planned a unit of work on creating images in poetry, building on his class's previous learning around figurative language. Simeon's intention was for his class to apply their knowledge of simile, metaphor and personification to build pictures in their readers' minds. He had chosen '*A Birthday*' by Christina Rossetti as his mentor text. The poem is full of similes and has a distinctive rhythm and clear rhyme scheme, which Simeon felt his class would respond to. Figure 6.1 is a representation of the building blocks Simeon had put together for this unit of work.

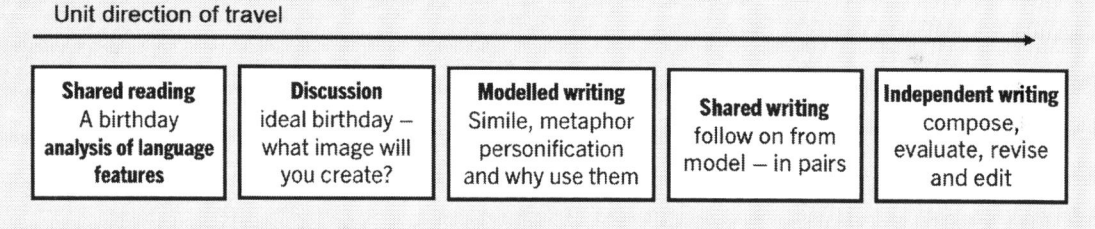

Unit direction of travel →

Shared reading	Discussion	Modelled writing	Shared writing	Independent writing
A birthday analysis of language features	ideal birthday – what image will you create?	Simile, metaphor personification and why use them	follow on from model – in pairs	compose, evaluate, revise and edit

Figure 6.1 The building blocks of Simeon's poetry unit

Despite having already explored the poetic tools of simile, metaphor and personification, it became clear to Simeon that the children were unable to make informed authorial decisions. Despite having provided a mentor text, unpicked it and modelled the features himself, the fact that they were novice learners and novice poets meant they did not have established mental models (schema) of effective poetry to assimilate this new knowledge. Simeon also felt that the learners' lack of confidence and willingness to have a go was a huge barrier. Following his modelled writing and discussion, Simeon decided to provide a learning bridge between this and the next stage, shared and supported composition. Figure 6.2 illustrates the revised outline plan, showing his planning between the gaps of the blocks to help build self-efficacy in his learners.

→

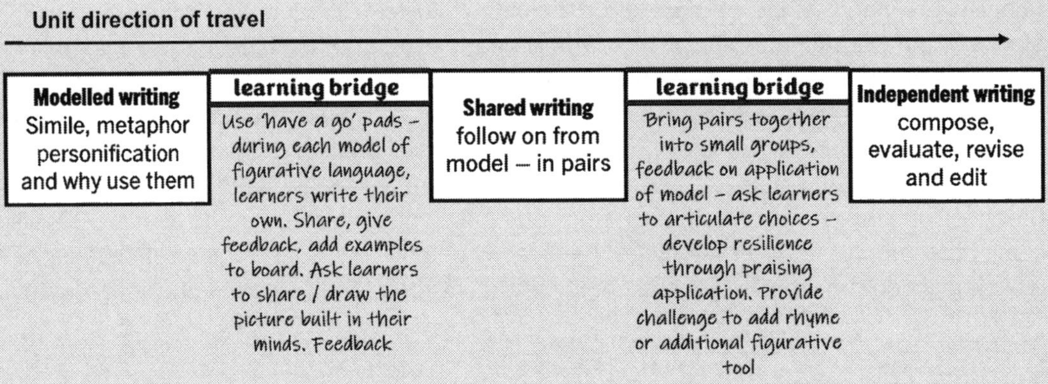

Unit direction of travel →

Modelled writing	learning bridge	Shared writing	learning bridge	Independent writing
Simile, metaphor personification and why use them	Use 'have a go' pads – during each model of figurative language, learners write their own. Share, give feedback, add examples to board. Ask learners to share / draw the picture built in their minds. Feedback	follow on from model – in pairs	Bring pairs together into small groups, feedback on application of model – ask learners to articulate choices – develop resilience through praising application. Provide challenge to add rhyme or additional figurative tool	compose, evaluate, revise and edit

Figure 6.2 Simeon's revised plan to include working in the gaps – the 'learning bridge'

Kirschner and Hendrick (2020) suggest that the novice learner needs to be given a more structured approach to using key principles, in this case the use of figurative language. Simeon, in his revised version, provided that scaffolding through his work between the planned building blocks. There are some key approaches Simeon used which developed his learners' self-efficacy, and this led to greater writing attainment. These are:

- learners using the new concept while it is being modelled. This helps reduce the load on the working memory;

- providing frequent process feedback. This can be on the application of the mentor text, other learners' ideas and modelled writing;

- collect and use learners' work. This helps develop persistence through confidence building and a range of examples for learners to use – again reducing cognitive load;

- asking learners to articulate their writing choices and receive feedback. This develops understanding of how the concept works, builds schema, develops confidence and persistence and provides a foundation for more effective writing.

Reflective questions ⓘ

» What do you think might be the impact on Simeon's class of building creative self-efficacy?

» What do you think of Simeon's plans for working within the gaps of the building blocks of his unit of work? Would they be approaches you could apply to your teaching context?

» What strategies have you used to help your learners assimilate new knowledge into existing schemata or enlarge their schemata to accommodate new knowledge?

Modelling the application of creative thinking

This practical strategy for working within the gaps has been alluded to in the previous section. It is also a helpful tool for developing learners' creative self-efficacy. Gist (1989) suggests that in order to help develop learners' mental models, teachers should model not just the physical tasks set for learners, but also the thinking processes needed to be successful. Gist (1989) uses the term cognitive modelling to describe this process. He studied cognitive modelling and its effects on creative self-efficacy, noting that the most effective cognitive modelling for building creative self-efficacy includes modelling not criticising others' ideas, building on others' ideas and free association. A good example of this, taught and modelled, in my experience, on primary English modules on initial teacher training programmes, is talking aloud your thinking when modelling writing. The teacher models effective writing while also modelling the cognitive processes behind the text creation. They may talk out word choices, strategies for revising text, where to put punctuation, tense cohesion, inclusion of key language features and text formality. This cognitive modelling can help the learners see what they should be thinking while writing. This is a helpful strategy, but the challenge is for learners to apply it.

Fahrurrozi et al (2019) suggest that creative learning is needed to engage effectively in writing. Their work, although in an Indonesian education system context, is transferable. Their research focused on the use of experiential learning to model creative thinking skills that then transferred into the writing of their participants. In Chapter 2 of this book, I have suggested that the approach to creative thinking underpinning this book is that of everyday experience. Modelling creative thinking through everyday life choices can therefore apply to creative thinking in the writing process. One component of creative thinking helpful to model here is possibility thinking (Craft, 2005). This is defined by Craft as '*acting with flexibility, intelligence and novelty in the everyday tasks of life*' (2005, p 19). In the introduction to the book, I have outlined the political context within which this book and the research behind it takes place. Here I have suggested, supported by literature, that high-stakes assessment has led to a narrowing of the curriculum and, with adherence to decontextualised mark schemes and criteria, the need to find the correct answer or language to use in writing. This is the opposite of possibility thinking. The National Literacy Trust's annual report into children and writing (2022) found that only 40 per cent of the children they surveyed enjoyed writing; one of the key enablers to writing engagement was found to be writing for creativity. Perhaps modelling possibility thinking can help with engagement, which will develop confidence and attainment.

Kim (2011) states that creative thinking declines through school. Using the Torrance Tests of Creative Thinking as a measure (although using a test to measure creative thinking is contestable), she notes a huge decline in creative thinking between kindergarten (Reception) and third grade. This suggests that young children have a natural ability to think creatively, and perhaps schooling is not the place for it to develop, maybe for some of the reasons I have stated. To look at this modelling the application of creative thinking practically, let's return to Simeon and his work on creating pictures through poetry from earlier in this chapter. In this part of the case study, Simeon's class are finding the lack of a right answer or a right way to write their poems a real struggle for their brains to cope with.

CASE STUDY

Year 4: poetry – creating images – possibility thinking

Simeon's work between the gaps had been largely successful. The children seemed to be sharing their ideas with one another. Simeon's hard work to speak to each group, discuss their work with them, respond to misconceptions and give them permission to communicate their thinking had paid off. However, another challenge had arisen. One of his class, Bethany, identified as working above aged-related expectations (AREs), wanted to get the poetry right. As he went round the class, discussing with the children, Simeon found that this concern was shared by most of his other above ARE learners. Thinking on his feet, he posed them a question – *'Could you come and help me reorganise the bookshelf please?'* The group of eight children followed Simeon over to the class library. Simeon then asked them, *'How should we do it?'* A variety of answers came back, by author, genre, fiction and non-fiction, colour, height. Simeon was modelling possibility thinking to them, everyday problem-solving. This came easily to the children, whereas it had not with the writing. To help, Simeon created another learner bridge, illustrated in Figure 6.3.

Unit direction of travel →

Independent writing

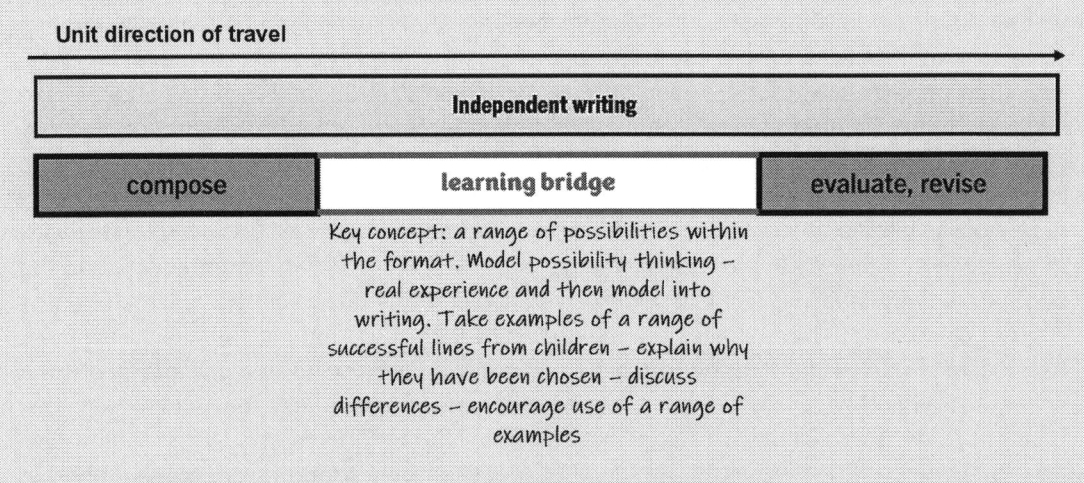

| compose | learning bridge | evaluate, revise |

Key concept: a range of possibilities within the format. Model possibility thinking – real experience and then model into writing. Take examples of a range of successful lines from children – explain why they have been chosen – discuss differences – encourage use of a range of examples

Figure 6.3 Simeon's scaffolding to model and apply possibility thinking

Simeon recognised that the independent writing part of his initial plan needed to be broken down, not because the learners couldn't use the figurative language they had been taught, but because their creative self-efficacy needed some more development. Through working within the gaps and engaging with his learners, Simeon was able to adapt his plan to meet his learners' needs. They needed to know that they had permission to use the figurative language autonomously, and Simeon had to model that for them.

> ***Reflective question*** ❓
>
> » In what ways have children you have worked with found embracing a range of possibilities in their learning difficult?

How working within the gaps supports higher attainment in writing

During the earlier part of this chapter I have drawn upon evidence from the first two writing workshops undertaken as part of the research on which this book is based. In this section, I return to evidence from these workshops to discuss the impact of working within the gaps on attainment. By way of context, in response to an Ofsted report, the school where my research took place had developed their approach to English pedagogy. In order to facilitate levels of consistency required across the whole school, the senior leadership alongside the English subject leader brought in and later developed a whole-school systematic, skill-based pedagogy approach scheme for staff to utilise. This whole-school system standardised the approach to writing pedagogy across the school. It is based on educational trainer and author Pie Corbett's talk for writing approach and used his language of cold task and hot task (Corbett, 2020). Each week followed a structure of introducing a genre, children then having a go at writing in that genre (a cold task), deconstructing a text, then reconstructing it through scaffolded support, leading to an individual written piece (hot task). Therefore, as I began my writing workshops, this system had been embedded for a full academic year and children and teachers were used to it. Ofsted had later returned, reporting on the success of the new English approach in raising performance and attainment. They noted that teachers had now developed pupils' writing skills carefully, and as a result writing had improved across all groups of pupils. Against the measure that Ofsted use to evaluate effectiveness, which includes attainment test results and data, this approach was clearly bearing fruit in terms of attainment for these children in this context.

However, the following questions are to be considered around the pedagogical approach that this school implemented.

- What impact does the approach have on children's understanding?
- Is attainment against externally imposed assessment criteria having to be prioritised at the expense of children's development of creative thinking skills?
- Are there some learners whose attainment is adversely affected by this approach?

What was the impact on understanding?

Despite the fact that the school's systematic approach to teaching writing involved mentor text deconstruction, evidence suggested that children could not apply their previous knowledge of using a mentor text to the different context of the workshops. It was evident that the learners knew what the building blocks of the writing process were – for example, mentor text, composing and editing text, drawing a comic strip, modelling writing, and teamwork, and how to use them discretely; what evidence shows they struggled to do was make connections between them to develop writing. The lack of connection-making ability perhaps illustrates a lack of creative self-efficacy to apply the knowledge they had.

Prioritising attainment over creative thinking skills?

This question suggests that attainment and creative thinking have to be mutually exclusive. However, I do not think they are. Earlier in the chapter, I cited the work of Fahrurrozi et al (2019), who provide evidence regarding creative thinking through experiential learning on writing attainment. In Chapter 2 of this text, I have suggested a look at an earlier piece of work I have done which explores connections between creative thinking and higher attaining writing. What I think this product-based approach to writing pedagogy does is give teachers more control in measuring attainment. I would argue that this is necessitated by standardised testing as high-stakes measures of school effectiveness. These measures, in my experience, have often driven the introduction of structured systems for teaching writing that, while doing their job, increasing test scores, have influenced teachers creating pedagogical environments that have not supported learners to develop their cognitive processing and connection-making or engage with writing as a process.

Were any learners adversely affected?

Evidence from my workshops did show that those working above AREs struggled with the creative thinking elements. For those children identified as working above AREs, involving others proved to be more of a challenge and the teamwork element of the workshops was a barrier for many of them to achieve what was normally expected. Evidence suggests that, for these children, many of whom had a high level of attainment using the school's individual approach to writing, giving up control was difficult. Hallam et al (2004) suggest that children working above AREs may get frustrated with group work, particularly when they are working with children who are not achieving as highly as they are. Hallam et al (2004) go on to suggest that adopting a mixed grouping, as I did, can support those children working below AREs as they can feel valued, an argument that my research evidence supports. Blatchford et al (2003) cite social relationships in the classroom as a prerequisite for effective group work, and where this was the case within my workshops, my data supports Blatchford's premise. Therefore, developing positive social relationships across the class is important if children are to be able to involve others and therefore develop their writing. Where involving others positively influenced work was evidenced in children analysing their ideas together, an important creative thinking skill (Robson, 2014).

Figure 6.4 is an illustration of this section of the chapter. Termed '*The writing attainment equation*', it depicts the impact that working within the gaps can have on children's writing and application.

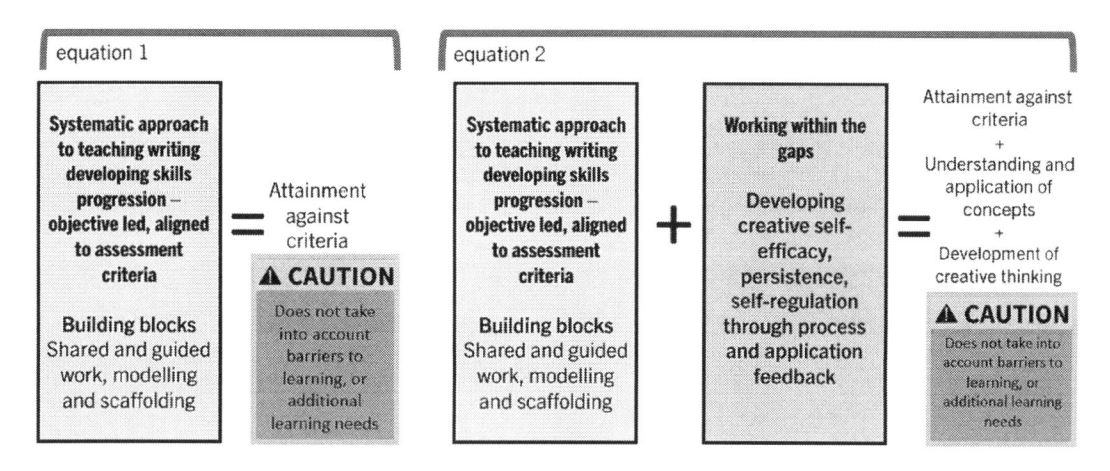

Figure 6.4 'The writing attainment equation'

Chapter summary

This chapter has explored the importance of a teacher working within the gaps of the building blocks of writing to impact positively on learning. Working within the gaps helps the learners make cognitive connections between those building blocks so they can fit them together effectively to enlarge or build mental models (schemata) of writing. This chapter has considered the challenges of making these connections for the novice learner as they don't necessarily have robust schemata to assimilate new knowledge into or the cognitive flexibility to enlarge schemata to accommodate new knowledge. Having presented a rationale for working within the gaps, this chapter has then explored some practical approaches to working within the gaps with a focus on developing creative self-efficacy, persistence and confidence to apply learning from a mentor text and/or teacher modelling and scaffolding. The role that feedback plays in this process has taken centre stage in the creation and use of learning bridges to help achieve this. This chapter has concluded with a focus on the impact that working within the gaps can have on attainment, understanding and application of learning, alongside the more traditional building blocks of writing pedagogy.

Further reading

These three excellent and accessible readings alongside my reflective questions will help develop your thinking from this chapter.

Kirschner, P and Hendrick, C (2020) *How Learning Happens*. London: Routledge.

Chapter 1 of this text develops the idea that a novice learner is not a smaller version of an expert learner. Rooted in understanding how the brain works, this chapter also explores schemata, how they are created and why understanding this is crucial to understanding how children learn. It presents some significant implications for teachers.

Focus question

What might some of the implications be for you as a teacher in understanding how differently a novice learner learns compared to an expert?

National Literacy Trust (2022) Children and Young People's Writing in 2022. [online] Available at: https://literacytrust.org.uk/research-services/research-reports/children-and-young-peoples-writing-in-2022/ (accessed 22 August 2023).

The National Literacy Trust conduct a report on surveys each year on children's reading and writing. This highly informative report provides some interesting insight into what children think and say about writing. Again, there are some implications for teachers to consider.

Focus question

As you read the report, spend some time looking at what the children have said about their motivation for writing. What ideas do you have to harness some of that motivation in your teaching?

OECD (2019) PISA 2021: Creative Thinking Framework (Third Draft). [online] Available at: www.oecd.org/pisa/publications/PISA-2021-Creative-Thinking-Framework.pdf (accessed 22 August 2023).

This is an excellent, highly evidence-informed framework which covers many aspects of creativity and creative thinking. It is quite dense, but the sections individually are quite easy to digest.

Focus question

Read the section starting on page 12: '*individual enablers of creative thinking*'. Consider how some of these can apply to your learning environment and teaching to foster creative thinking.

7 Call the scaffolders: the role of the task

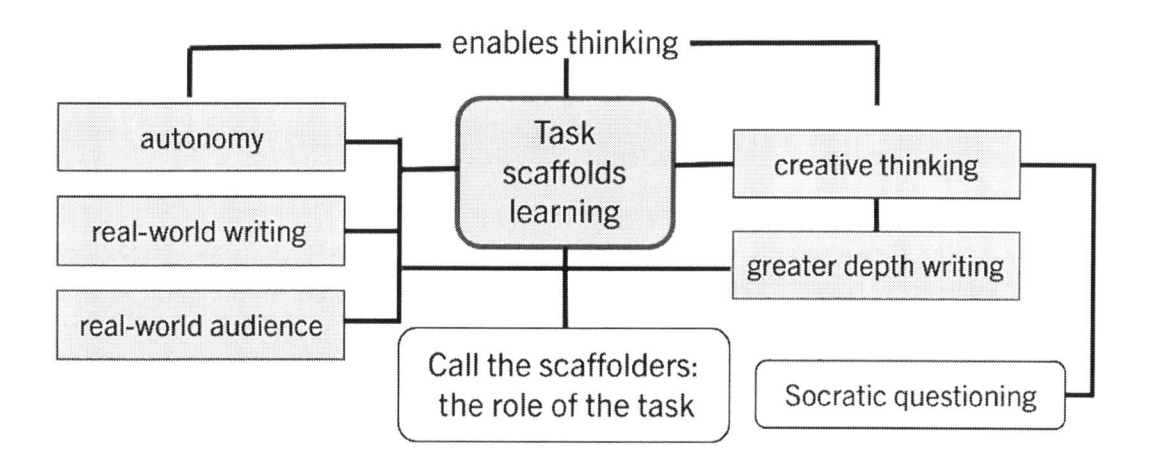

```
                    enables thinking
    ┌─────────────────────┬─────────────────────┐
 autonomy                Task              creative thinking
                      scaffolds
 real-world writing    learning
                                         greater depth writing
 real-world audience
                   Call the scaffolders:
                    the role of the task    Socratic questioning
```

Core Content Framework / Early Career Teacher Framework links

The Department for Education for England and Wales (DfE) provides a framework of minimum entitlement for trainee teachers which is then developed into your Early Career Teacher (ECT) years. This chapter links to the following:

- high expectations (Standard 1) – teacher expectations, high-quality teaching;
- how pupils learn (Standard 2 – Progress) – prior knowledge, purposeful practice, integrating new ideas with existing knowledge;
- subject and curriculum (Standard 3) – knowledge, skills, values, modelling, subject knowledge, thinking critically, mental models (schema);
- classroom practice (Standard 4) – modelling, scaffolds, worked examples, introducing new material in steps, questioning, talk for learning, the role of practice;

→

- adaptive teaching (Standard 5) – not creating distinct tasks, high teacher expectations;
- managing behaviour (Standard 7) – all pupils have opportunity to experience success.

Introduction

I have never worked as a scaffolder, but I have worked on building sites and projects where scaffolding was instrumental to their success. When a building is being renovated or cleaned or work is required high up, it often becomes encased in a carefully created structure, put together with a range of steel clips and boards so that the original building is rarely seen. As parts are completed, the scaffolding is removed and from the steel shell slowly emerges the renovated, cleaned or newly fixed building. In this physical context, scaffolding supports and enables and can be used in a variety of ways to help get the job done.

Transferring the physical steel scaffolding to learning theory, scaffolding (Vygotsky, 1978) can and should lead learners through to task success. Much like its physical counterpart, scaffolding as a pedagogic approach can also support and enable, and be used in a variety of ways to get learning done. Building on his social constructionist beliefs about learning, Vygotsky (1978), cited by Foley, suggests that in order for learning to take place '*appropriate social interactional frameworks must be provided*' (1994, p 101). I am unclear as to what interactional frameworks Foley had in mind here, but I am guessing, based on experience, that this is a reference to such approaches as modelling, talk partners and shared work. However, I want to suggest here that the role of the task is crucial as a scaffold for learning. Tasks set for learners should lead them to learning success, support their learning and enable their learning of key knowledge, skills and concepts, and their understanding. I am therefore considering scaffolding in a less conventional way in this chapter. Instead of seeing the role of scaffolding as a tool to support the task, I suggest that the task is a means of scaffolding learning and can be instrumental in attainment.

This chapter therefore explores the importance of the tasks that children are given and how these in themselves can influence writing attainment. The chapter considers factors such as tasks and activities that simulate real life and provide authenticity and purpose as well as a real audience. It also suggests writing tasks that promote higher-level thinking, such as evaluation and synthesis, and can lead to higher writing attainment, again drawing upon Department for Education Teacher Assessment Framework criteria for writing.

What makes an effective task?

Parr and Limbrick (2010) argue that effective task design is aligned to clear learning goals and provides a clear purpose for writing, which gives clarity for the learners. A pedagogical environment where the writing task is purposeful to the learner is developed by Rothwell (2016) whose work explores blogging to develop writing. Rothwell's (2016) main findings were that blogging increased children's motivation to write. His research found that children publishing their writing to a class blog available to be read on their school's website provided a strong purpose and motivation for quality writing. The blogs received feedback from parents and a wider audience, and this also, according to Rothwell (2016), provided motivation to persist in updating the blogs as they enjoyed the feedback. This is corroborated by Block and Strachan (2019) in the United States through their work with second graders writing. They also found that writing for an external audience also provided motivation for better quality writing. Wiggins (2009) provides further detail as to why authentic tasks often yield greater motivation and writing quality. His work provides evidence for emphasising purpose and audience to develop authentic writing. Authentic writing, as Wiggins states, '*ensures that students have to write for real audiences and real purposes*' (2009, p 30), not just the teacher. Tasks for authentic writing, Wiggins writes, should be '*either real-world or replicas and analogous to the kinds of tasks faced by professionals in the field, adult citizens, and/or consumers*' (2009, p 30). Wiggins' point is that an enabling pedagogical environment is not one where writing tasks are mundane and serve no purpose other than filling time, but tasks that resemble real-world writing tasks where children can see, understand and have a reason for doing.

Wong and Moorhouse (2018), like Rothwell (2016), have also considered the real-life context of blogging as a motivator for writing. They argue that an authentic writing task such as a blog means the writer establishes relationships with their audience. As they establish these relationships with their audience, Wong and Moorhouse argue, the writer '*prioritises content and creativity rather than focusing on accuracy and form alone*' (2018, p 1). Wong and Moorhouse (2018) are making the point that authentic writing tasks force the writer into thinking of their reader and seeing their writing through the lens of the reader, considering whether the reader will want to read it. This argument views writing as a '*social and creative performance*' (Ryan, 2014) where emphasis is not only on getting the technical aspects of writing correct but also engaging creatively with the reader.

Connecting an authentic task to Greater Depth writing

Having considered task effectiveness, this next section explores the relationship between an authentic task and Greater Depth writing. Table 7.1 takes some of the statements from the Department for Education Teacher Assessment Frameworks for Key Stage 2 writing to show how criteria for Greater Depth builds on expected level. This provides a context for looking at a Key Stage 2 case study example that demonstrates how the task influenced writing quality. The full Teacher Assessment Framework for Key Stage 2 writing can be accessed at: www.gov.uk/government/publications/teacher-assessment-frameworks-at-the-end-of-key-stage-2.

Table 7.1 How Greater Depth writing criteria develops from expected level

Working at expected level	Working at Greater Depth
Write effectively for a range of purposes and audiences, selecting language that shows good awareness of the reader	Write effectively for a range of purposes and audiences, selecting the appropriate form and drawing independently on what they have read as models for their own writing
Select vocabulary and grammatical structures that reflect what the writing requires, doing this mostly appropriately	Distinguish between the language of speech and writing and choose the appropriate register; exercise an assured and conscious control over levels of formality, particularly through manipulating grammar and vocabulary to achieve this
Use the range of punctuation taught at Key Stage 2 mostly correctly	Use the range of punctuation taught at Key Stage 2 correctly and, when necessary, use such punctuation precisely to enhance meaning and avoid ambiguity

A key point to notice about the difference between expected level writing and Greater Depth writing at Key Stage 2 is that Greater Depth writing centres much more around authors' decision-making. A Greater Depth writer uses what they have read to inform their writing, and makes conscious choices around formality, manipulating grammar to achieve this. A Greater Depth writer uses punctuation effectively to communicate meaning. Essentially, the writer is also a creative thinker, choosing from a range of possibilities to problem-solve, not looking to just use what has been taught because they should, but to use it to communicate intentionally. It is my belief that the nature of the task given to the learner can help or hinder this process.

In Chapter 3 of this book, I have discussed autonomy as part of an enabling environment for writing. The concept of autonomy is inextricably linked with task design. As discussed in Chapter 3, children need to have the opportunity to be involved in some decision-making around learning tasks as this will increase motivation and persistence (Falconer et al, 2018).

CASE STUDY

Year 5: history inspired playscripts and performance

Caroline, a PGCE student halfway through her course, was planning a unit of work for the first time. Her school-based mentor, Des, had suggested she take on an English unit and try and link it to the class's history topic of monarchy and how the role of monarchy has changed over time. Caroline was stumped; she approached Des for support, and they decided that he would coach her through the process, working with her to both plan and teach it. Figure 7.1 shows a series of questions that Des took Caroline through to think about what the children would learn, what they would produce and how they would get there. Notice how Des focused on the children's learning as well as Caroline's teaching.

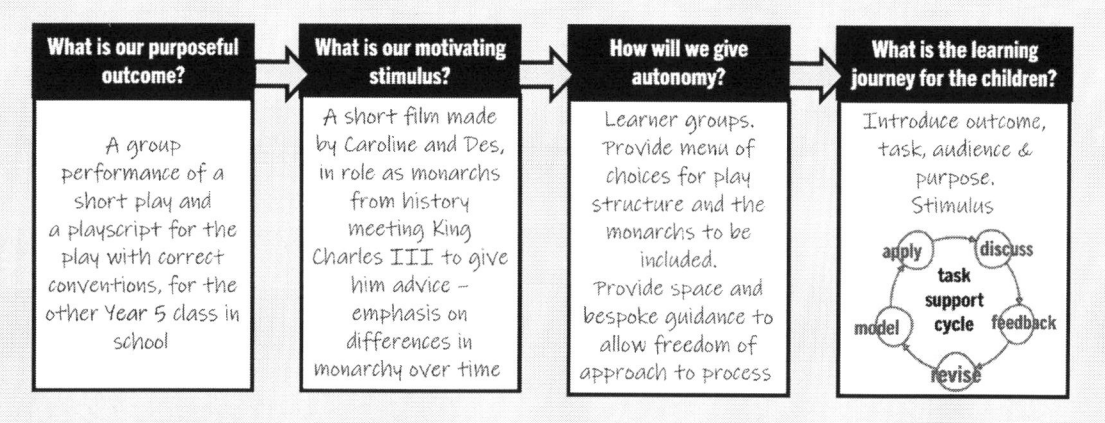

What is our purposeful outcome?	What is our motivating stimulus?	How will we give autonomy?	What is the learning journey for the children?
A group performance of a short play and a playscript for the play with correct conventions, for the other Year 5 class in school	A short film made by Caroline and Des, in role as monarchs from history meeting King Charles III to give him advice – emphasis on differences in monarchy over time	Learner groups. Provide menu of choices for play structure and the monarchs to be included. Provide space and bespoke guidance to allow freedom of approach to process	Introduce outcome, task, audience & purpose. Stimulus. apply – discuss – task support cycle – feedback – model – revise

Figure 7.1 Structuring thinking about children's learning to support planning

Des and Caroline discussed the need for a clear audience and purpose for the learning and how the children could be more involved in making decisions about their learning. Rothwell (2016) links effective task design, including autonomy, through the process with motivation and persistence, particularly meaningful tasks that lead to authentic feedback. In this way the design of the task can effectively enable Greater Depth learning. The thinking frame in Figure 7.1 provided a good starting point for them to plan their unit of work. Des encouraged Caroline to be brave with flexibility in the children's learning journey by employing a cyclical approach to the process. Rather than thinking in discrete lesson-by-lesson steps, Des felt the class would respond well to a less linear approach to the unit, providing a more fluid set of learning steps to achieve the outcomes.

Following the unit, Des and Caroline evaluated the learning the children had engaged with as well as making teacher assessment judgements on their written scripts. The design of the task can either facilitate creative thinking or be more traditional and routine (Church, 2010) and task design also includes group organisation. The task of preparing a performance through script writing and rehearsal proved to be motivating and enjoyable, attitudes connected to creative thinking (Robson, 2014). Children from several learning groups expressed their enjoyment of the task:

> I liked the performance because it was very fun when we were doing the instruments and practising them and the costumes.
>
> (Child A, learning group 1)

Children from another group shared how much they enjoyed the acting, dressing up and performance. One particular comment focused on having an opportunity to demonstrate their skills:

> We get to act stuff out and show what we can do.
>
> (Child B, learning group 3)

The performance element, acting, dressing up and musical instruments were the frontrunners in the race for enjoyment accolades and the script writing a little further back. Des was concerned that the learning focus might have got lost at the expense of the performance. Many of the children had said they would not have enjoyed the task as much without instruments or dressing up.

It could be argued, however, that these *'props'* help make the task more authentic. Wong and Moorhouse (2018) suggest that a real-world writer seeks to establish a relationship with their audience, and when the children knew who their audience was, their discussion of ideas centred upon what their audience would be interested in. One group knew their friends in the other Year 5 class were interested in the books and TV series adaption of *Horrible Histories*, so amended some of the content and incorporated these into their scripts. One group did some research with the other Year 5 class and found an interest in knights and castles, and so used that information in their work. The purpose was to engage their audience, and this provided a motivating context for manipulating punctuation, sentence structure and targeted vocabulary. Figure 7.2 is a typed extract of the opening of one of the group's scripts (no spelling or punctuation has been altered). The group, by their choice, was a group of learners identified previously by Des as working at expected level, according to the Key Stage 2 Teacher Assessment Framework.

Chat with Charles – the new live interview show about monarchy.

Characters

King Charles III – Jonny, Richard the Lionheart – David, Richard's guards – Ellie and Billie, Prompt – Layton.

Scene 1

King Charles is sat on a throne with a sofa to his left. He smiles at the camera.

Charles: Hello and welcome to my new show, chat with Charles *(pauses for applause and smiles broadly, one hand waving regally at the audience).* This is the show where I get advice from Kings and Queens of old on what sort of King I should be. Tonight, my guest is... RICHARD THE LIONHEART. *(Charles leads the applause, standing now. Richard enters from stage left, flanked by serious looking guards. Richard strides in with confidence).*

Charles: *(with a beaming smile).* Welcome Your Grace. Please sit. *(Richard sits and the guards move behind the sofa).*

Richard: *(almost shouting)* Right! What's this all about? Out with it!

Figure 7.2 *Script extract – Chat with Charles*

If you now look back at Table 7.1 you can see some of the authorial decisions the group have made. They have made some detailed stage direction choices that give a suggestion of character. Their use of punctuation – exclamation, ellipsis and short sentences – conveys meaning and provides information as to how the characters should deliver the lines. Their communication of intent is superb. You can decide if you think this piece of writing shows working at Greater Depth. Des and Caroline did not teach exclamation marks or ellipsis; they did not teach sentence structure using a mentor text. They did model the playscript for their stimulus film and explained their choices, they did provide regular process feedback to each group and they did make suggestions for development. However, their design of the task, planned provision of learner choice and flexible approach may well have had an impact on the learning.

Reflective questions

» In what ways do you think the planned autonomy, task design and more fluid plan for the unit contributed to higher quality thinking and therefore writing?

» What did you think of Des's approach to supporting Caroline? What might some advantages of co-constructing a unit of work and co-teaching it with a mentor/student be?

» Wong and Moorhouse (2018) suggest that a real-world writer seeks to establish a relationship with their audience. In what ways can this relationship contribute to higher quality writing?

Activity

The next time you are planning a unit of work for English, think about how you can link it to another curriculum area to connect learning for your class. Is there opportunity for some real-world writing for a real-world audience? How will you design your task to enable Greater Depth thinking and therefore writing? Maybe spend some time as part of your unit building a relationship with the audience and support your learners to use punctuation and grammar intentionally as part of their communication choices. Maybe previous punctuation and grammar learning just needs to be brought back into their working memories rather than being retaught. Perhaps your task design could help there. Table 7.2 suggests some real-world writing tasks and corresponding possible audiences that I have found helpful in task design over the years.

Table 7.2 Real-world writing suggestions

Real-world writing task	Real-world audience
Class blog	Parents, prospective parents and teachers
Evaluation report on a class trip	Trip providers
Invitation	Invitees to an event
Job advert	Potential applicants
Professional email	Headteacher / Staff members
Political manifesto	Potential supporters
Instructions for a supply teacher	Supply teachers
Persuasive letter	Local MP, newspaper
Journalistic article about a charity	Potential donors

The relationship between task, creative thinking and attainment

One of the challenges we know children face when learning is making connections. In earlier chapters, and certainly through my research that provides the basis for this book, I have suggested that children find it difficult connecting different elements of the learning process together.

Cremin (2015) in her work on creative teachers lists connection-making as a key creative thinking skill, and Paul and Elder (2019) refer to this aspect of creative thinking in terms of training, but it gets seemingly little attention in much of the literature on creative thinking. Barr et al (2015), in their work on creative thought, use the term '*creative connections*' to refer to how the mind can unify two apparently disparate elements, as was evident in the work carried out by Des and Caroline in the case study above – children connecting concepts of monarchy 1000 years apart – so the idea of the nature of the task supporting creative thinking and in turn developing Greater Depth attainment does need exploring. Church (2010) agrees that a possible reason for successful connection-making could be to do with the nature of the task. Her work on engagement theory and facilitating higher level thinking suggests that an activity that builds thought, synthesis and evaluation different to traditional routine school activities can help build connections. The devising, composing and performance of a playscript with certain ingredients, as developed by Des and Caroline, could well have been this type of task.

How does creative thinking develop Greater Depth writing?

Figure 7.3 is a developmental aspect of my current thinking for writing framework (Figure 0.8 in the introduction to this book). It emphasises the task as the key enabler to creative thinking and the impact it can have on attainment.

Task design
Simulates real life and develops higher level thinking: synthesis, evaluation, connecting concepts

Creative thinking
connection-making
problem-solving
collaboration

⬇

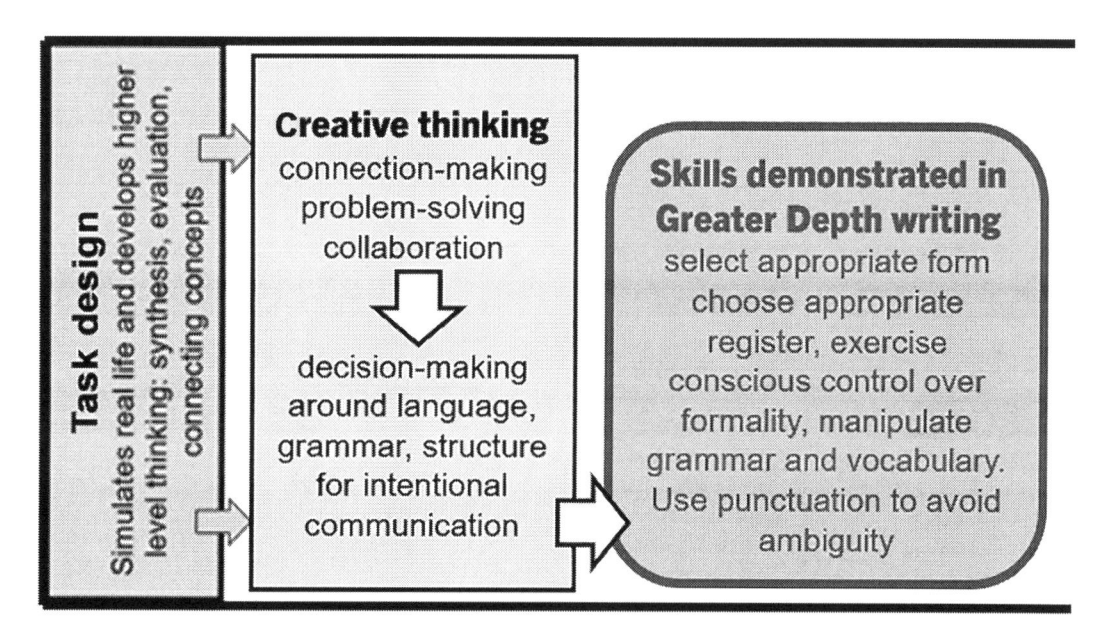

decision-making around language, grammar, structure for intentional communication

Skills demonstrated in Greater Depth writing
select appropriate form, choose appropriate register, exercise conscious control over formality, manipulate grammar and vocabulary. Use punctuation to avoid ambiguity

Figure 7.3 *Relationship between creative thinking and Greater Depth writing within the boundaries of the task*

It is important to note from Figure 7.3 that there is a significant link between creative thinking skills and writing. Task design can either enable or constrain thinking. If the task has enough flexibility to enable thinking, it therefore also enables authorial decision-making, and you will see from Figure 7.3 that the skills demonstrated in Greater Depth writing, taken from Table 7.1, are all about authorial decision-making. However, one can only make authorial decisions if one has the prior knowledge to do so. In the work exemplified by Des and Caroline's case study earlier in this chapter, the children's domain-specific knowledge (Sternberg, 2003) of playscripts and knowledge of their chosen topics through being given freedom to choose impacted upon their written scripts. The children were evidently able to relate their prior knowledge of the writing form and apply their knowledge of their chosen worlds to develop some innovative work. Wang (2012) argues that the primary link between creative thinking and writing is elaboration of ideas, and I would agree. In the children's scripts there was more evidence of specific details, but also genre-specific language, humour and intentional use of punctuation for effect. Having the playscript as a task also allowed the writers to connect with their audience (Rothwell, 2016), which provided further motivation for writing to communicate intentionally more effectively.

So far in this chapter, I have focused on Key Stage 2, and yet this same idea of the task as a key enabler for thinking and Greater Depth writing is also transferable to Key Stage 1.

CASE STUDY

Year 1, part 1: an invitation to a teddy bears' picnic

Maija, in the last term of her first ECT year, was planning a unit of work on information text for her Year 1 task. She wanted to make the writing purposeful for the children so they would be motivated to write for a real-world audience. She had a teddy bears' picnic planned for near the end of term, and felt that presenting information in the form of invitations to give out to parents would provide that motivating real-world opportunity. Maija's thinking and planning is shown in Figure 7.4, using the same frame as Figure 7.1.

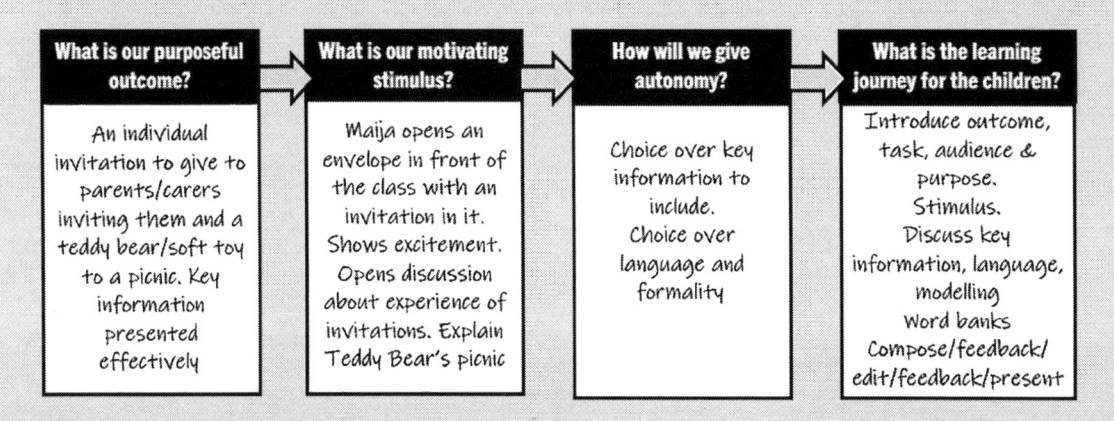

What is our purposeful outcome?	What is our motivating stimulus?	How will we give autonomy?	What is the learning journey for the children?
An individual invitation to give to parents/carers inviting them and a teddy bear/soft toy to a picnic. Key information presented effectively	Maija opens an envelope in front of the class with an invitation in it. Shows excitement. Opens discussion about experience of invitations. Explain Teddy Bear's picnic	Choice over key information to include. Choice over language and formality	Introduce outcome, task, audience & purpose. Stimulus. Discuss key information, language, modelling Word banks Compose/feedback/edit/feedback/present

Figure 7.4 Maija's thinking and planning structure

Maija wanted to give her children every opportunity to write at Greater Depth, and while she felt she was taking a risk by giving more autonomy in the task she believed that, given the children's progress over the year, the risk was worth taking. Table 7.3 takes some of the expected standard criteria and writing at Greater Depth criteria for Key Stage 1 from the Department for Education Teacher Assessment Framework for writing and shows how, similarly to Table 7.1, these are related. The full version of the Department for Education's Teacher Assessment Framework for Key Stage 1 can be accessed here: www.gov.uk/government/publications/teacher-assessment-frameworks-at-the-end-of-key-stage-1.

Table 7.3 How Greater Depth writing criteria develops from expected level at Key Stage 1

Working at expected level	Working at Greater Depth
Write about real events, recording these simply and clearly	Write effectively and coherently for different purposes, drawing on their reading to inform the vocabulary and grammar of their writing

Table 7.3 (Cont.)

Working at expected level	Working at Greater Depth
Demarcate most sentences in their writing with capital letters and full stops, and use question marks correctly when required	Make simple additions, revisions and proofreading corrections to their own writing
Use co-ordination (eg, or/and/but) and some subordination (eg, when/if/that/because) to join clauses	
Spell many common exception words	Spell most common exception words • add suffixes to spell most words correctly in their writing (eg, -ment, -ness, -ful, -less, -ly)

You will notice, much like the relationship between expected and Greater Depth at Key Stage 2, the differences centre on authors' decision-making. Maija was keen for her children to make their own decisions about what key information should be on the invites and how it should be presented. Maija wanted her children to see the range of possibilities that were available and the key concept was the purpose of the invitation. One of the keys to success in the children's understanding was the questioning Maija used. Maija deliberately planned to use Socratic questioning.

Elder and Paul (1998) discuss the importance of Socratic questions to develop thinking and learning. They go on to develop this in a later 2019 work where they discuss the role of the teacher in the process more effectively. Bowman (2017) provides a helpful infographic which identifies six types of Socratic questions. These are questions that:

1. clarify thinking and understanding;
2. challenge assumptions;
3. examine evidence;
4. consider alternatives;
5. consider implications and consequences;
6. are meta questions.

The purpose of this type of questioning is to develop understanding of concepts through the exploration of initial ideas and evaluate them. In an earlier blog, Bowman (2015) suggests that these types of questions develop critical thinking. I would add creative thinking to that, as the processes learners go through in evaluating, refining and seeking alternative possibilities very much align to creative thinking definitions used in earlier chapters in this book.

In an earlier section in this chapter, you will have seen my argument for the connections between creative thinking and Greater Depth writing, and so using these types of questions develops the type of decision-making needed to demonstrate the necessary skills.

CASE STUDY

Year 1, part 2: questions enabling thinking and writing

Having excited the class with her own opening of the invite, Maija showed it to the class. She told them that it might help them when they were creating their invites and they began to explore the content. Maija encouraged thinking about alternatives, challenging their assumptions and thinking about an effective invitation. The children's understanding impressed Maija. They understood the purpose of an invitation and were then able to explore some of the implications. When some of the class suggested the implications for the language and design based on this, she could not believe it. Some of the discussion focused on using capital letters for the date, time and place so they stood out. Others discussed the type of clothing, debating about the weather and implications. One child said that the invitation needed to let them know when it would finish so they knew when they would go home.

As she reflected on the unit, what stood out to Maija most was the way in which the children had been able to connect their learning between the invitation she shared with her class, the discussion and how that directly impacted on writing. It was evident in some of the examples of her children's work that, although some of the transcriptional elements such as spelling, handwriting might not have achieved Greater Depth, much of the decision-making around content and structure had.

In this example from Key Stage 1, you will again see how the design of the task, real-world and open-ended in nature, enabled thinking, which in turn enabled some key elements of Greater Depth writing. Maija did need to provide some additional support through Socratic questioning, but the results were not just good products, but learners who had developed their thinking, problem-solving and understanding of writing purpose.

Chapter summary

In this chapter scaffolding has been considered in a way that is perhaps slightly different to what you might expect. Rather than scaffolding in terms of teaching tools that support learners to get the job done, in this chapter, task design and framing have been considered as enablers of thinking and therefore a scaffold for learning. In this chapter you have also considered the relationship between task design, thinking and Greater Depth writing. Through comparing the criteria for expected level and Greater Depth writing in Tables 7.1 and 7.2 you have seen how writing at Greater Depth requires development of thinking and authorial decision-making. Throughout this chapter, exemplified in the case studies, developing real-world tasks for real-world audiences has been at the centre of task design. These real-world, authentic tasks have demanded a higher level of thinking, problem-solving and evaluation in order to be achieved and have thus developed the necessary cognitive flexibility to make communication choices that make writing Greater Depth. The role that questioning plays, in this chapter, Socratic questioning, as a scaffold to aid creative thinking as part of the task has also been explored. Throughout the examples, however, there have also been the threads of autonomy and choice. Enabling learners to make decisions themselves, have some autonomy in task approach, content, language and structure, rooted in their own decision-making, can be a huge motivator for writing success.

Further reading

These three excellent and accessible readings, alongside my reflective questions, will help develop your thinking from this chapter:

The Writing for Pleasure Centre. [online] Available at: https://writing4pleasure.com/purposeful-and-authentic-class-writing-projects/ (accessed 23 August 2023).

This excellent resource develops some of the thinking outlines in this chapter. The authors emphasise the value of real-world writing and provide some helpful ideas and resources. It is very accessible and informative.

Focus question

Have a read of some of the '*reviewing your practice*' questions on this site. Which ones most challenge you and what action will you take to develop your pedagogy?

Evans, J (2018) Building an Innovative, Socratic Curriculum for Content-heavy Subjects. *Impact*. [online] Available at: https://my.chartered.college/impact_article/building-an-innovative-socratic-curriculum-for-content-heavy-subjects/ (accessed 23 August 2023).

Although this case study is written from a secondary science perspective, the impact of Socratic questioning on critical thinking is very clear. It has a focus on developing understanding not just learning information and factoids.

Focus question

As you read this case study, focus on Table 1. Notice particularly the '*teacher will*' column. Consider how the teacher is using some of the Socratic questions identified in this chapter, and reflect on how you could adapt the approach to your context.

Wong, K and Moorhouse, B (2018) Writing for an Audience: Inciting Creativity among Young English Language Bloggers through Scaffolded Comments. *TESOL Journal*. [online] Available at: https://doi.org/10.1002/tesj.389 (accessed 23 August 2023).

While the research underpinning this article takes place in Hong Kong with English as an additional language learners, the principles of real-world tasks and real-world audiences are highly relevant. The findings around increased motivation to write are very interesting.

Focus question

As you read this article, consider how you can motivate your learners to write with real-world tasks and audiences. Are your reflections on children's motivation to write similar to those of the authors of the article?

8 Here comes the building inspector: assessment and learning

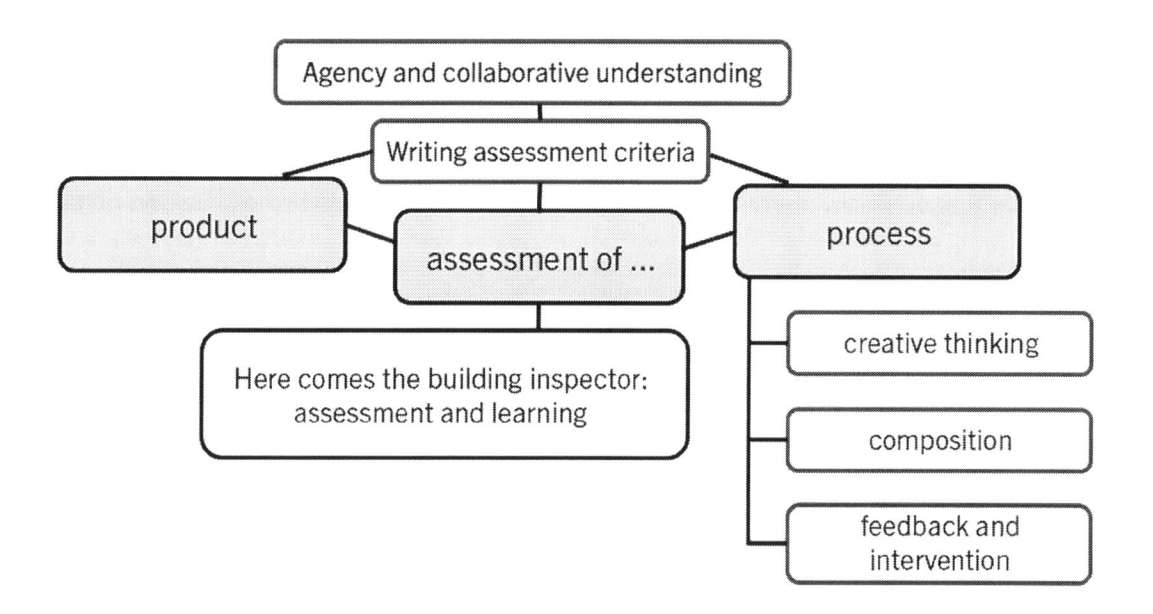

```
                 Agency and collaborative understanding
                              │
                   Writing assessment criteria
     product ─────────────────┤───────────────── process
                      assessment of ...
                              │                  ├── creative thinking
            Here comes the building inspector:   ├── composition
               assessment and learning           └── feedback and
                                                     intervention
```

Core Content Framework / Early Career Teacher Framework links

The Department for Education for England and Wales (DfE) provides a framework of minimum content entitlement for trainee teachers which is then developed in your Early Career Teacher (ECT) years. This chapter links to the following:

- high expectations (Standard 1) – setting clear expectations, a culture of mutual trust;
- classroom practice (Standard 4) – questioning, check-ins;

→

> - assessment (Standard 6) – effective assessment is critical to teaching, high-quality feedback, pupils' regulation of their own learning;
> - managing behaviour (Standard 7) – opportunity for meaningful success, self-regulation, investment in learning through perception of success and failure.

Introduction

Many years ago, at a Year 6 teachers professional development course on Standard Assessment Tests (SATs), I remember being asked a really interesting question. The question was asked by the then head of the Qualifications and Curriculum Authority (QCA). It was this. *'Is it the SATs that are the problem, or their high-stakes nature?'* As a young teacher at the time, this was the first time I had really thought about accountability. Since then, I have heard it said on many occasions over the years that teachers' professional judgement ought to be trusted and external accountability through bodies such as Ofsted or publishing results of high-stakes assessment is diametrically opposed to creativity and creative thinking. But is it?

During my brief spell working on a building site, work always intensified when the arrival of the building inspector was imminent. In order to move onto the next stage of work the inspector had to sign off what had been done. They were accountable for the safety of the work done and their signature meant that the work had met the required standard. This is not a chapter about external accountability, but it is about demonstrating the meeting of externally imposed criteria for meeting or exceeding age-related expectation. The building inspector assesses the work, dialogues with the tradesmen, discusses challenges and processes undertaken to achieve the required standard. The inspector has a document which informs them about what the required standard is and they make a professional judgement. In the same way, you as teachers assess the work, but also dialogue with the learners, discuss the learning process with them and therefore assess progress to achieve outcomes. You do that using a framework for assessment.

In the previous three chapters, and more specifically in the previous chapter, I have referred to the Department for Education Teacher Assessment Frameworks for writing. These are used in England to summatively assess children's writing and facilitate a professional judgement regarding whether the child is writing below, at or above age-related expectations. In this chapter the concept of understanding and working with assessment framework and criteria is explored using Dunsmuir et al's (2015) Writing Assessment Measure (introduced in Chapter 5). This chapter explores the importance of assessing the processes involved in writing as well as the product, and develops into how to evaluate or assess creative thinking as part of that product. The chapter's main premise is that a creative thinking pedagogy for teaching writing is not necessarily opposed to writing assessment criteria and rubrics, as is often perceived. In fact, a creative thinking approach can facilitate a better understanding of such criteria and how to embed them into excellent writing.

It's all a bit back to front!

What I mean by the heading above is that, traditionally, and this process is exacerbated by the DfE frameworks, assessing writing starts with the product. Teachers, myself included, have taken in children's books at the end of a lesson, taken in the final written piece at the end of a unit of work, and used a Teacher Assessment Framework to assess it. A quality judgement has been made about the product. I have argued throughout this book so far that writing is a process, yet assessment of writing traditionally pays little heed to the process. Writing, Dunsmuir et al posit, is a '*complex process that is essential for extending learning, thinking and communicating with others*' (2015, p 2). It would seem therefore more appropriate, more front to back, to pay some heed in assessing writing to the writer's navigation of and engagement with this complex process as well as the product.

What could this look like in practice?

In Chapter 4 of this book, you will have read Maariya's case study where she created a science-fiction writing simulation, '*Galactic Defence*'. Through her teaching, Maariya was able to engage in the writing process with some of her class who, without scaffolded support, would have been identified as working below age-related expectations, due largely to difficulties with the transcription elements of writing. Figure 8.1 is Maariya's scribing verbatim and in situ of one child's verbal story construction. Analysing this using a further adaptation of Dunsmuir et al's (2015, p 15) Writing Assessment Measure (Table 8.1), verbally this child's ideas, organisation and vocabulary use was more effective than many of the children assessed by their teacher as exceeding age-related expectations.

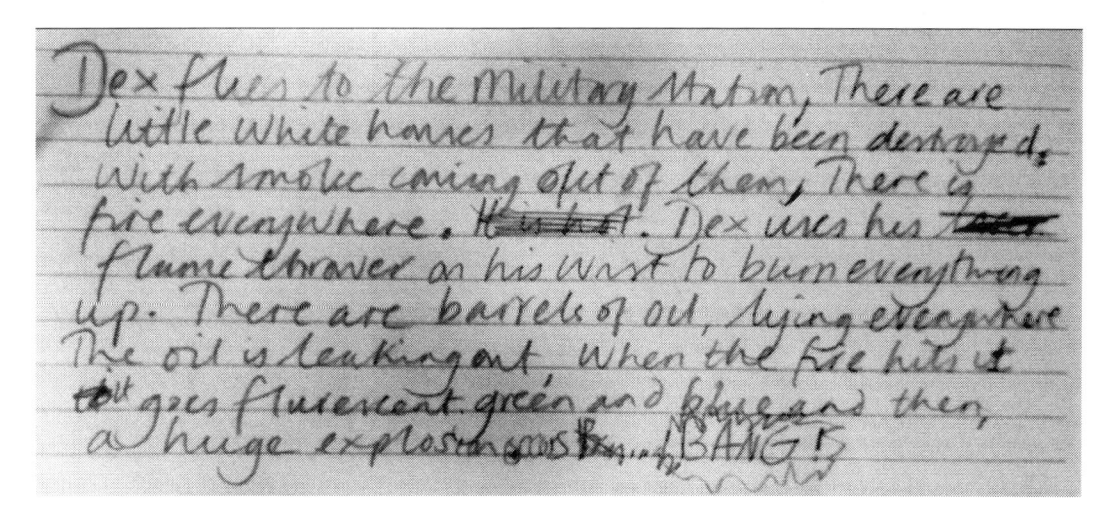

Figure 8.1 Maariya's in situ scribing of a child's composition

Table 8.1 Adaptation and development of Dunsmuir et al's (2015) Writing Assessment Measure

Element	Statements of achievement (against age-related expectations)			
	Working towards	**Expected level**	**Expected level +**	**Exceeding**
Punctuation	Shows awareness of full stops	Accurate use of capital letters and full stops	Secure use of full stops and capital letters	Range of punctuation used for structure and effect
Sentence structure and grammar	Simple sentences used	Conjunctions used to create compound sentences	Extending sentences using subordination	Complex sentences and clauses manipulated for effect
Vocabulary	Uses simple vocabulary appropriate to content	Selects interesting and varied verbs	Varied use of adjectives, verbs, specific nouns	Well-chosen, vivid vocabulary used
Organisation and structure	Communicates meaning but flits from idea to idea	Themes are expanded upon. Logic is apparent	Identifiable structure using cohesive ties	Paragraphs well-organised, based on themes
Ideas	Short sections of repetitive and limited text	Ideas developed and elaborated upon by adding detail	Imaginative and varied with descriptive detail	Creative and interesting. Engages the reader

Using creative thinking to engage with criteria

Ghaffar et al (2020) draw upon the creative thinking skills of collaboration and co-construction to help learners in their study better understand assessment criteria for writing. Understanding the importance of learner agency and autonomy to develop motivation and writing competence, Ghaffar et al's (2020) work showcases teachers' work with pupils, to help them understand and reframe criteria with them to gain greater understanding of competence requirements. Their findings revealed not only an improvement in grades but also enhanced levels of interaction and engagement. Ownership, in the case of this study, led to a greater understanding at the start and throughout the writing process, rather than an externally imposed decontextualised criteria applied at the end. Hattie (2010), in his meta-analysis, would term this approach as making teaching visible to the learner, or not making the learner have to try and guess what success looks like. In a review of Hattie's work, Terhart (2011) explains Hattie's view of education as where there is a need to overcome a self-centred perspective of teaching and learning. In other words, the teacher must be able to view learning as the learner sees it, take a step back and support them to success. This is supported by findings from Xiao and Yang's (2019) study on formative assessment developing self-regulation. Their work developed a range of formative assessment activities, some collaborative that developed agency, a sense of achievement and therefore led to persistence and self-regulation in learning. Self-regulation, as discussed in Chapter 1 of this book, is an essential process in successful writing.

CASE STUDY

Year 3: understanding criteria – learners putting on a teacher's glasses

David, an experienced lower Key Stage 2 teacher, was looking for an approach to engage his class in exploring criteria for what makes effective writing. David wanted to use an approach that helped the children understand and take more ownership of the success criteria from the Department for Education Teacher Frameworks for writing and utilise them in the writing process. David arrived at the idea of enabling his children to see their learning through the lens of a teacher. He provided them with a pair of glasses each. By putting them on, David told them, they would be thinking and seeing like a teacher. First, the children put the glasses on and had some fun, imagining what David might be wanting from them. Some of the answers made mention of learning! Once they were used to the idea, before they began to plan their writing, their first English lesson was looking at and making sense of some of the Year 3 statements for exceeding expectations in writing. David also wanted them to understand why. To each pair of children, he gave a discussion frame. Each frame had a statement from the school's Year 3 writing assessment criteria for exceeding age-related expectations. Table 8.2 shows this assessment criteria.

Table 8.2 David's school's Year 3 'exceeding' writing criteria

At Year 3, children exceeding age-related expectations can
demarcate most sentences with capital letters and full stops, question marks and exclamation marks;
describe settings and characters, including the use of expanded noun phrases and adverbials to specify;
use detailed paragraphs to organise and structure writing;
use a range of co-ordinating and sub-ordinating conjunctions;
use inverted commas for direct speech, including a comma for the reporting clause, a capital letter to start and punctuation inside inverted commas;
correctly in their writing (see Year 3–4 curriculum): • use apostrophes for singular and plural possession; • use commas for fronted adverbials; • spell most words correctly (Year 3 list); • use a range of prefixes and suffixes to spell most words.

David gave each pair of learners a statement from the above table and asked them to put on their teacher glasses and discuss collaboratively what they think the statement meant. Following that they should discuss why their statement was there and why it was important in terms of communication. They each fed back and discussed and edited each one. By the end of the lesson, following a lot of editing, discussion, dealing with misconceptions and heated debate, the whole class, as far as David could tell, understood what was expected and why it was important. David created large versions of each frame and covered one wall of his classroom with them. Figure 8.2 shows one of David's completed discussion frames.

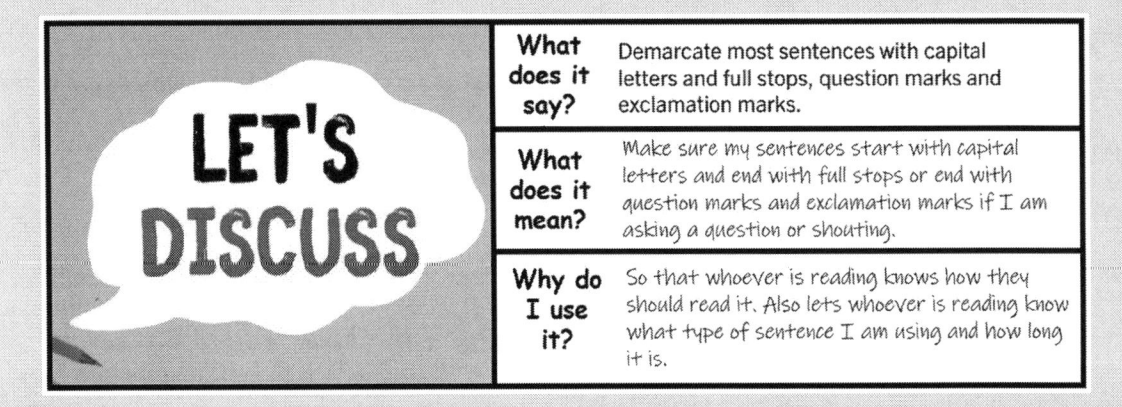

	What does it say?	Demarcate most sentences with capital letters and full stops, question marks and exclamation marks.
LET'S DISCUSS	What does it mean?	Make sure my sentences start with capital letters and end with full stops or end with question marks and exclamation marks if I am asking a question or shouting.
	Why do I use it?	So that whoever is reading knows how they should read it. Also lets whoever is reading know what type of sentence I am using and how long it is.

Figure 8.2 One of David's discussion frames, completed

During subsequent lessons, David was able, as were fellow pupils, to redirect the class to the wall display, helping them remember. David noticed many more children were considering the language and grammatical choices they were making in their quest for effective communication. Following book scrutiny with another school, David was pleased that a greater percentage of his class had many exceeding expectations features in this piece of writing than previously.

> ### Reflective questions (?)
>
> » What do you think about David taking a whole lesson out of his unit of work to explore and make sense of the assessment criteria in a creative way?
>
> » How do you think David might have adapted this activity for those learners in his class for whom exceeding expectations criteria might be too far to stretch?
>
> » Was David's approach of making the learning visible helpful for the learners or should assessment criteria be used by the teacher only after writing?

Teacher learning gains from assessing the process, not just the product

If you have read and engaged with the Introduction to this book and followed some of the threads in other chapters, you will notice that the ideas and thinking put forward are rooted in some research that I have undertaken. To demonstrate what achievement information a teacher can get from assessing the writing process as well as the product, I now return to some of that research evidence more explicitly. This evidence suggests that assessing the process can impact positively on the product.

The context is a Year 6 whole day writing workshop which I facilitated in role as a scientist with a biohazard simulation created in the classroom. The workshop was designed to follow a flexible and recursive structure of stimulus, plan, compose, edit, present. A mentor text was used to model writing with the outcome of producing a strategy for governor approval to bring the school community to safety. Through engagement with the learners during the writing process, some interesting evidence emerged.

The enjoyment and engagement the children displayed did not influence creative thinking and writing for all of the children in the classes. Evidence from observations while working with the class (6D) showed that some of the children found the different approach challenging.

> *It was clear that the different structure and approach was challenging for the back two tables.*
>
> (6D observation extract)

The back two tables in the classroom were occupied by children assessed as working above age-related expectations. Evidence suggested that these children from both classes found the school system safe and predictable. Change for them was challenging, perhaps because of their own confidence in their success with the traditional school system. My workshop design was more open-ended, emphasising possibility thinking, and was perhaps less formulaic than the school's approach. Looking again at Robson's (2014) Analysing Children's Creative Thinking Framework, a tolerance of ambiguity is seen as part of persistence and self-efficacy. McWilliam and Haukka (2008) connect this attitude of a tolerance of ambiguity to flexibility and adaptability which coheres with Meadows' (2006) cognitive attitude of choosing challenges. However, evidence here suggests that these children identified as working above age-related expectations arguably did not demonstrate this attitude associated with creative thinking. It is possible that the structured approach within which the children usually worked, a necessity to meet the demands of high-stakes testing, has facilitated comfort and safety for those working above age-related expectations at the expense of providing challenge and opportunity to apply skills and ideas flexibly.

This confidence in safety was also evident in the writing of those children working above-age-related expectations. MacArthur (1999) suggests that those who struggle with writing struggle with the transcriptional elements such as handwriting, spelling, sentence structure, punctuation. By implication, therefore, those who do not struggle with writing, or arguably those assessed as working at or above age-related expectations (AREs), can juggle the transcriptional elements more successfully. Through analysis of the writing of the eight children

118 • *Thinking for Primary Writing*

working above AREs and the sixteen working at AREs, applying my adaptation of Dunsmuir et al's (2015) assessment measure (see Chapter 5, Table 5.1) the transcriptional elements of their writing were assessed as consistently higher than those working below AREs, whereas their composition was assessed at similar or even occasionally lower. Figure 8.3 is an extract from the opening of a story by a group working above AREs. In this example, transcriptional elements were assessed at a high level, whereas the compositional elements, vocabulary, ideas and structure and organisation were assessed as lower in comparison.

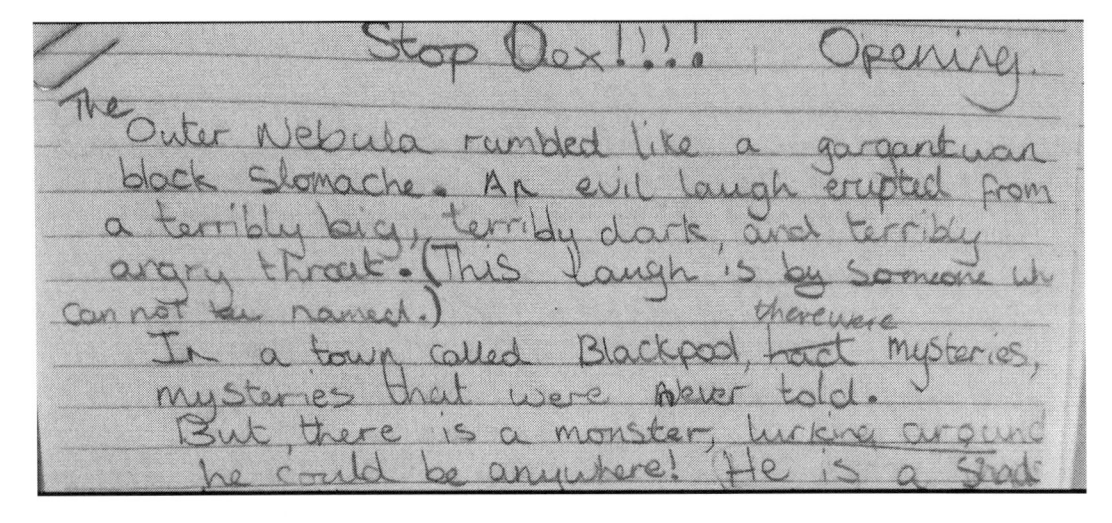

Figure 8.3 Group writing, opening – above AREs

Figure 8.4, written by a group working below AREs, is comparable in terms of assessment of compositional elements, while vocabulary and ideas are arguably more innovative and risky. The transcriptional elements, particularly spelling, punctuation and sentence structure, however, were assessed at a much lower level.

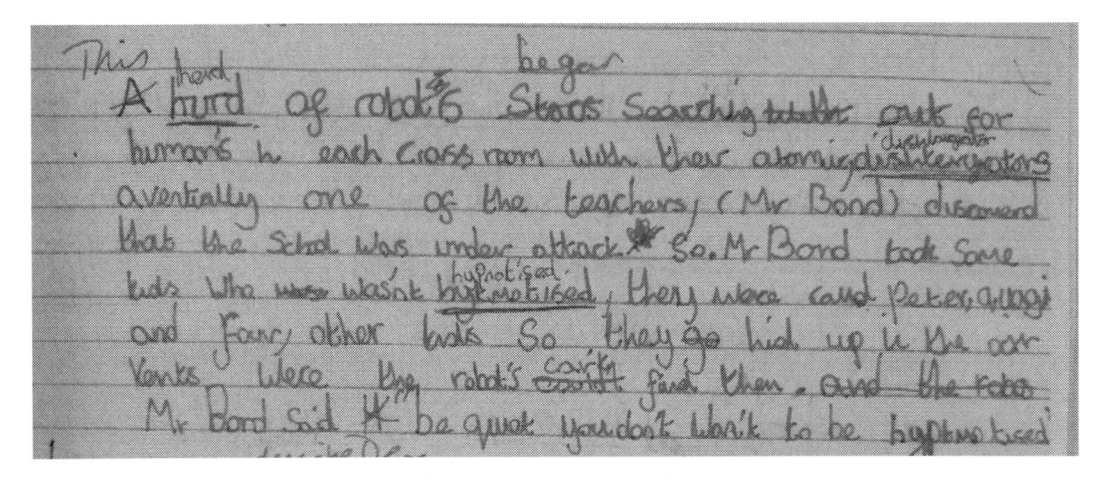

Figure 8.4 Group writing, opening – below AREs

Evidence showing an apparent lack of achievement by those children working above AREs was corroborated by 6D's class teacher who, during interview, stated with regard to her most proficient writers,

> *I don't think his ideas were as innovative as they usually are … I was disappointed by the back table to be honest.*
>
> (6D semi-structured interview)

The challenges of transcription were also evidenced in this data set. Interview data from 6D's class teacher emphasised the difficulty for those working below AREs in writing:

> *It has a big impact on the structure of their sentences because they struggle … quite a lot of the time it goes brain dump on the page.*
>
> (6D semi-structured interview)

However, those children assessed by their teachers at working below AREs or having particular learning or behavioural needs seemed to achieve as highly as the rest of their classes and surprised their teachers with their thinking. 6D's class teacher noted:

> *The vocabulary they used was impressive – xx and xx wouldn't usually stretch themselves to such advanced vocabulary.*
>
> (6D semi-structured interview)

The class teacher was similarly impressed with her children assessed at working below AREs in writing:

> *They wanted to keep writing, especially xx with SEBD (Social and Emotional Behavioural Difficulties), wouldn't normally have done that … my normal low achievers have done some really good work.*
>
> (6D semi-structured interview)

Evidence from writing analysis certainly corroborates this, as demonstrated above with the writing examples. Ten of the 12 pieces of writing from children working below AREs were assessed at the same or higher in composition elements than their above AREs counterparts.

Drawing these threads together

The evidence above, albeit from one context, does provoke some interesting thinking and some interesting questions to impact on practice. First, by just assessing the product after the event, busy teachers with many demands on their time can be hoodwinked by neat writing, accurate spelling and punctuation. Accuracy in these transcriptional elements are often what determines whether a child is deemed to be not yet meeting, expected or exceeding age-related expectations. I am not for one moment suggesting that transcriptional accuracy is a bad thing, it certainly is not. But what I think this evidence shows is that cognitively, and perhaps in creative thinking, those children who may well be deemed to be working at below age-related expectations in terms of product are certainly not in terms of process. Therefore, by not engaging with learners during the writing process, they can be labelled according to their transcriptional skills and their composing skills can be overlooked.

In the Introduction to this book, I have used literature to make the point that high-stakes testing narrows the curriculum, but I would also add that a highly structured approach, where the structure no longer scaffolds and enables, just constrains, also has a narrowing effect. The evidence in the previous section suggests that those learners identified as working above-related expectations had confidence that they could successfully navigate the usual structured and predictable approach to English teaching and had perhaps become complacent. Could it be that the structured scheme had little impact on their learning? As a result, creative thinking skills such as problem-solving, risk-taking, innovation and embracing pretence were not really evident in their work. There could be many reasons for that, of course, but I believe it to be a question worth exploring. To conclude this section, Figure 8.5 represents how assessing and engaging within the process can impact positively on achievement and attainment on the product.

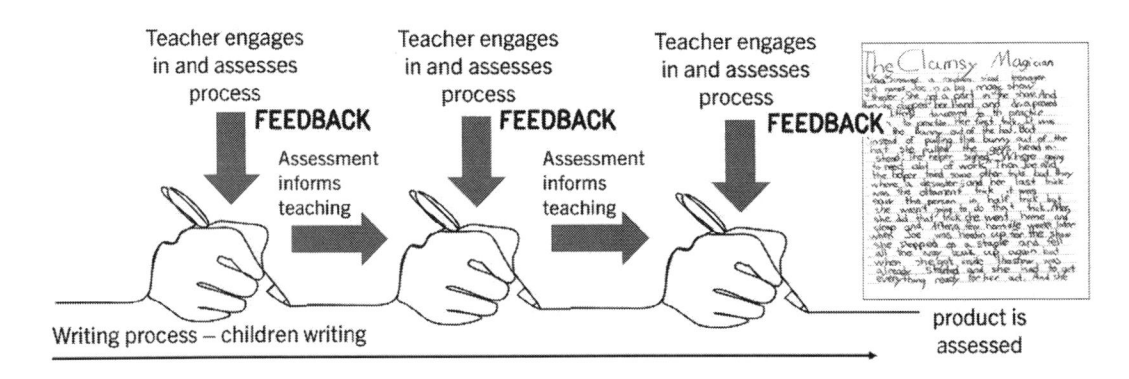

Figure 8.5 *Assessment of process, intervention and impact on product quality*

Assessing creative thinking: observation, not testing

The focus of this chapter so far has been assessing and engaging with the writing process, not just assessing the product. Part of that process, and also alluding to the discussion earlier in this chapter, is the role that creative thinking plays in the composing process. If you return to Table 8.1 towards the start of this chapter and look at the '*exceeding*' column, you will notice many of the criterion statements involve creative decision-making, thinking like authors. There is no mention of specific features to include, instead to manipulate, to choose, to organise and to engage. All of these verbs require creative thinking and authorial decision-making. How, then, can one assess or evaluate creative thinking and the role it plays in writing?

Assessing creativity is fraught with problems, challenges and lack of consensus, and there is clearly a lack of agreement on the most effective tools to use. Said-Metwaly et al (2017) suggest that creativity tests from researchers such as Torrance are seen throughout the literature to be reliable, citing, for example, the work of Cropley (2000), Lemons (2011) and Torrance (2008). However, Said-Metwaly et al (2017) go on to say that the validity of these tests in measuring creativity has been called into question. Here they cite, for example, Baer (2016) and Hennessey and Amabile (2010). Reasons stated for this include the fact that scores only reflect one factor of creativity, in this case divergent thinking. Creativity and creative thinking can also be seen not as a general set of skills that can be objectively tested and replicated but as a cognitive process rooted in a domain-specific context, and it is in that context that creativity should be 'assessed'.

For the reasons outlined above, to achieve a more contextualised assessment of creativity an observation approach to analyse creative thinking may be more effective. The context-embedded approach I took in the research outlined earlier in this chapter is heavily influenced by Robson (2014), who has developed an observation framework called Analysing Children's Creative Thinking (ACCT) to observe, record and analyse evidence of children's creative thinking in their social and cultural contexts. I chose to use her framework as a basis for my own observation to analyse the creative thinking of the learners I worked with as they engaged in the writing workshops I facilitated. The following section explores Robson's (2014) framework in more detail and demonstrates how it will be adapted, from literature for my research.

Robson's Analysing Children's Creative Thinking (ACCT) framework

Before exploring Robson (2014)'s framework in more detail, I first discuss the importance of using a framework more generally to analyse/assess this complex concept. Robson (2014) is not the first creativity researcher to use this type of analytic tool. Earlier creativity researchers, such as Torrance (1966), have developed frameworks with which to assess creativity based upon their own research and definitions of creativity. Guilford (1967), cited by Paraskeva et al (2015) established a creative thinking framework with four criteria: originality (is the thinking novel or suggesting something new?), fluency (can many diverse ideas be developed quickly?), flexibility (can the thinker adapt to new situations, improvise and manoeuvre strategies to meet a range of challenges?) and elaboration (can the thinker provide more detail and information to their initial thoughts?). This framework is seen as the foundation for later frameworks, such as Batey (2012) and Robson (2014), that aim to encapsulate creative thinking. Making any assessment of the products of creative thinking is problematic, but trying to assess or evaluate the process, as in creative thinking itself, is arguably even more so. This is because creative thinking judgements are made based on interpretation of behaviour observed and language heard, and are therefore subjective and based on the conception of creative thinking the judge adheres to. Table 8.3 is a framework for observing and assessing creative thinking that I have developed based on Robson (2014).

Table 8.3 A framework for observing and assessing creative thinking

Observation/assessment of creative thinking record	
Creative thinking attitude/skill	**Notes**
Exploration: • exploring • engaging in a new activity • knowing what you want to do	
Involvement and enjoyment: • trying out new ideas • analysing ideas • speculating • involving others	
Persistence: • persisting • risk-taking • completing challenges	
Observing the attitude with which learners engage	
• embracing complexity • embracing ambiguity and uncertainty • embracing pretence	
Informed by Robson (2014); Sternberg (2003); Meadows (2006)	

Robson (2014)'s first category is '*exploration and engagement*'. Exploration is, according to Robson, an approach to thinking that must embrace new challenges, ambiguity and making a choice to engage in a new way of thinking. This is a characteristic of creative thinking found throughout the literature, notably Sternberg (2003). Reflecting on exploration, I would argue that in the context of writing, exploration and engagement must be combined with specific knowledge of the writing context. Exploration is by nature open-ended and with that comes the need to be tolerant of ambiguity and lack of certainty. In his discussion of creative thinking, Merrotsy recognises that '*the term tolerance of ambiguity ... is found in the creativity literature ... perhaps expressed as tolerance for ambiguity or tolerance toward ambiguity, as a commonly cited trait of the creative personality*' (2013b, p 232). The exploration process therefore requires the attitude of embracing the grey areas of a writing challenge, where the boundaries of the problem are ambiguous, and seeing that as challenging and interesting rather than stressful and too hard.

Robson's (2014) second category is involvement. Involvement and enjoyment align with problematising, or seeing a situation, task or activity as something that needs to be solved, because it encompasses the willingness to try out ideas, analyse them, speculate and also involve others (Robson, 2014). Willingness to try out, speculate and analyse new ideas feature in literature as characteristics of creative thinking. Thinkers displaying these attitudes are happy to break conventional rules. In the context of writing, this may involve children being willing to break traditional grammatical conventions in their writing, being willing to try something different in their work to what they may have normally been taught. It may also involve being willing to introduce characters into their work who would not normally fit the genre. In terms of analysing ideas, learners would be actively involved in the writing process, taking ownership of their ideas and therefore enjoying their learning.

Another element of this second category is '*involving others*'. In their observations of young children engaged in activity, Robson and Rowe found that children working with or alongside one another yielded significant examples of creative thinking. They found that '*interactions between children more often supported thinking in that they were concerned with developing an idea*' (2012, p 360). In other words, creative thinking is a social practice. Plucker et al define creativity as '*the interaction among aptitude, process and environment by which an individual or group produces a perceptible product* that is both *novel and useful*' (2004, p 90). They also discuss the interaction between aptitude for thinking, the process of thinking and the environment, which, dependent on how it is interacted with, can enable or constrain creative thinking.

Robson (2014)'s final category is persistence. Within this category she places risk taking and completing challenges, possibility and divergent thinking. Persistence is required to try out ideas and seek a variety of solutions during problematising. Problematising may require thinking divergently, asking '*what if*' questions, and so, in this context, persistence is required to seek possible solutions, not one solution. This links to self-regulation, a key writing process. Persistence is not just about the willingness to keep going with a task, but the ability to keep thinking around the task, persistence in thinking, trying out new ideas, keeping the thought process going – a process Nijstad et al (2010) term '*cognitive persistence*'. They connect cognitive persistence with cognitive flexibility, a concept already discussed in an earlier chapter. Nijstad et al also outline a persistence pathway as representing '*the possibility of achieving creative ideas, insights, and problem solutions through hard work*' (2010, p 44). This is important to consider as it can often be omitted in creativity research and in thinking about this area. Hard work, persistence and perseverance are not really words associated with creativity. Cropley and Cropley remind us why perseverance and persistence are so important. They state that this thinking process may be '*messy, reiterative, and often involves two steps forwards for one step backwards plus several side-steps*' (2015, p 137). In order to navigate a level of messiness and uncertainty, being able to cope with things not working out in a perfectly straightforward way, persistence is needed.

Chapter summary

This chapter has considered the role that assessment plays throughout the writing process. In it, traditional approaches to assessing writing, marking the final product, have been challenged. The challenge is not that assessing products shouldn't happen, but that this might be more effective if the learning process to achieve the product was also assessed, not necessarily in a summative way but, as Figure 8.5 suggests, in a formative, recursive way to *'meddle in the middle'* (McWilliam, 2009) of learning. This would facilitate feedback to support learner development with the aim of impacting positively on the final product. This chapter has also demonstrated that creative thinking pedagogy and writing criteria can happily coexist. Drawing on Hattie's (2010) work on making learning visible, this chapter suggests that spending time giving children agency and purpose around what they are learning and helping them develop a shared understanding of what success looks like can impact positively on writing. This chapter has concluded with a detailed exploration of an observation approach to assessing creative thinking as part of the writing process. Throughout this chapter, underpinned by a range of literature, there are practical ideas that you can utilise in your practice to develop creative thinking in your learners and in so doing help them achieve more in their writing.

Further reading

The following three excellent and accessible readings, alongside the reflective questions, will help develop your thinking from this chapter.

Robson, S (2014) The Analysing Children's Creative Thinking Framework: Development of an Observation-Led Approach to Identifying and Analysing Young Children's Creative Thinking. *British Educational Research Journal*, 40(1): 121–34.

This excellent and readable article sets out a useful framework for observing creative thinking in young children. The approach to observation is also very clear.

Focus question

As you read this article, what do you think some of the challenges may be presented through using the approach Robson suggests to assessing or analysing creative thinking?

National Association for Teaching English (NATE) (2020) *The Teaching Sequence for Writing*. [online] Available at: www.nate.org.uk/wp-content/uploads/2020/02/Teaching-sequence-for-writing.pdf (accessed 23 August 2023).

This presentation has some very helpful ways into all the different stages of the writing process. It provides theoretical and practical approaches, activities and understanding of writing processes.

Focus question

The second page/slide states that children should be more focused on '*looking at how language works with the purpose of using it in their own writing than labelling word classes and learning rules*'. Do you agree? If so, what might some barriers be?

Cremin, T and Myhill, D (2019) Creative Collaboration: Teachers and Writers Working Together. *Impact*. [online] Available at: https://my.chartered.college/impact_article/creative-collaboration-teachers-and-writers-working-together/ (accessed 23 August 2023).

This brilliant piece of original research is quite inspiring. It explores teachers of English and famous authors collaborating to co-construct and teach some English units. The findings are inspiring.

Focus question

As you read this article, note the power of teachers and writers learning alongside each other. How do you think you might incorporate some of these ideas into your teaching?

9 The big reveal: what they said

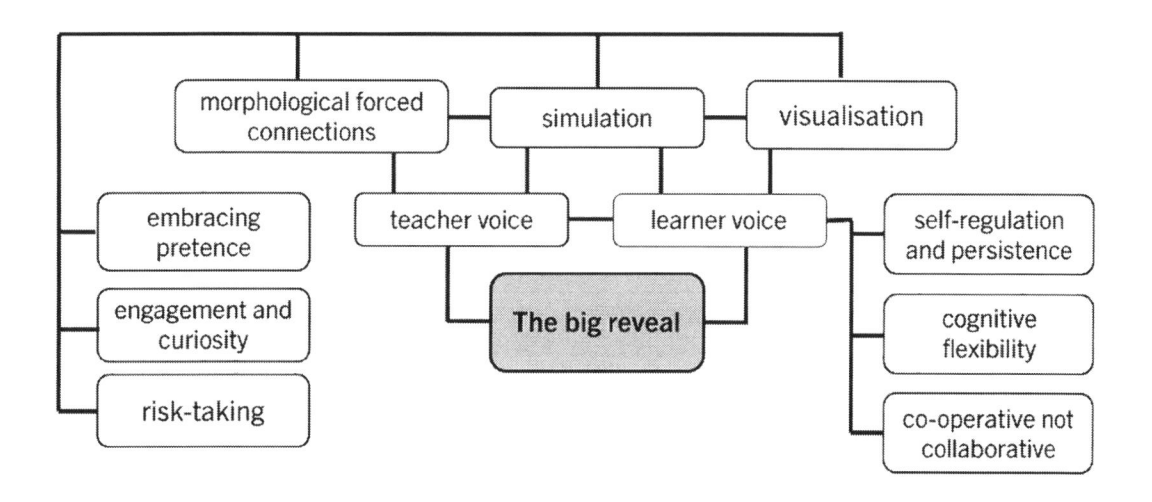

```
                    morphological forced
                        connections              simulation         visualisation

        embracing                       teacher voice    learner voice      self-regulation
         pretence                                                           and persistence

     engagement and                              The big reveal                cognitive
        curiosity                                                              flexibility

        risk-taking                                                        co-operative not
                                                                             collaborative
```

Core Content Framework / Early Career Teacher Framework links

The Department for Education for England and Wales (DfE) provides a framework of minimum content entitlement for trainee teachers which is then developed in your Early Career Teacher (ECT) years. This chapter links to the following:

- high expectations (Standard 1) – teachers affecting motivation, well-being and behaviour;
- how pupils learn (Standard 2) – learning involves a lasting change in pupils' capabilities;
- subject and curriculum (Standard 3) – thinking critically, linking new knowledge to previous knowledge, application and transfer of learning;
- managing behaviour (Standard 7) – relationships, motivation, resilience, learning success;
- professional behaviours (Standard 8) – reflective practice, high-quality professional development to improve practice.

Introduction

I think I may have already admitted in an earlier chapter of this book that I enjoy watching house design, building and renovation television programmes. I enjoy the design and building processes, the practical side of creating an amazing building either from the ruins of a previous one or starting from scratch on a plot of land. However, my favourite part of these shows is the last part, the big reveal. For these intrepid, brave and usually innovative people who are seeking a more workable home for their family, the projects have been high risk, financially and personally. However, many of these programmes also involve local communities coming together, tradespeople giving their time, tools and resources to create something incredible. My favourite part, then, is when the homeowner returns, often in tears, to find a total house transformation, or the couple, sat in their glorious new kitchen, sharing their years of hard work, battling weather, planning laws and inflation to achieve their dream home. It is the big reveal that gets me every time. It is emotional because these projects have required sacrifice, risk and overcoming challenge, and how the homeowners express that is very powerful.

I think there are parallels here with successful creative learning. I would agree the risk is not quite as big, but learning is messy, it is often hard, it does require sacrifice, and so what learners have to say about their learning is powerful and important. This chapter gives voice to the children and teachers who came on the journey with me, engaging in the research that provides the basis for this book and that resulted in my thinking for writing framework. Drawing on data collected, teachers' and children's perspectives on creative thinking approaches to teaching writing will be shared and explored. This chapter not only explores the successes and great writing achievements but also some of the challenges encountered while undertaking these approaches. While there is some learner and participant voice in earlier chapters, this chapter provides greater depth. It takes some of the approaches introduced in earlier chapters, such as creating and using a simulation, morphological forced connections and visualisation, and explores them through the lens of the learners.

Creating and using a simulation

What is a simulation?

A simulation provides real-world learning by putting the learner in an experiential learning environment (Laverie et al, 2020). Research from a range of professional learning disciplines such as nursing and business suggest through their findings that simulation is an effective pedagogical tool to develop progress and attainment (Carson and Harder, 2016; Humpherys et al, 2021). Simulation as a pedagogical tool arises from the belief that learning and doing are inseparable, a theory known as situated cognition (Pankowski and Walker, 2016; Cobb, 2001). Learners should therefore be active in the learning process, actively doing, not just listening, and simulation provides the forum for learners to do that.

In the context of the research that this chapter reports on, the simulation I developed demanded turning the learners' classroom into a science laboratory. Practically, this involved the use of biohazard posters, hazard tape and myself in the role of a professor of astronomical science suitably attired and acting the role. All of this provides an experience for the learners. An experience that encouraged curiosity, enjoyment and problem-solving. This simulation is first introduced in Chapter 4, through Maariya's Year 6 case study '*Galactic Defence*'.

How did the simulation develop creative thinking?

The simulation was designed to engage the children and develop curiosity (Robson, 2014) but it also aimed to facilitate another attitude of creative thinking, embracing pretence. Robson (2014) also discovered through her work that socio-dramatic play, such as a simulation like '*Galactic Defence*', was the most likely of any activity to lead to high levels of creative thinking. How both classes I worked with engaged with the simulation certainly influenced their creative thinking in terms of trying out ideas (Robson, 2014).

The simulation problem-solving context also provided a way to include everyone; every learner had an experience thrust upon them, a drama that engaged the participants, and as Cremin states, '*the lived experience of drama becomes a natural writing frame that is charged with the emotions and experiences of the imagined world*' (2009, p 98). A simulation therefore can allow children to become fully immersed in the context and enrich their work through a deeper experiential engagement with the problem to solve.

Employing the pedagogic tool of teacher-in-role (Prendiville, 2000), as part of the simulation, I facilitated the workshops as a professor for '*Galactic Defence*', engaged the children as junior researchers and used writing in role (Cremin et al, 2006) for the children to bring themselves to the writing process. Robson (2014) cites Donaldson (1978), who states that children perform best in environments and contexts that make sense to them and have meaning for them; they can relate to them from experience. This suggests that a way to discover the extent to which children can think creatively is to do it in their context with tasks that are personally meaningful and context-embedded.

A further element of note to take into consideration with regards to learning through this research into creative thinking and participant voice is the social aspect of thinking and learning.

Robson (2014) suggests that trying out ideas, speculating and analysing ideas is more effective in terms of creative thinking if done with others. In other words, creative thinking is a social practice. Elisondo (2016) states that creative thinking is intrinsically social. This aligns to the work of Plucker et al who define creativity as '*the interaction among aptitude, process and environment by which an individual or group produces a perceptible product that is both novel and useful*' (2004, p 90). The key phrase I am emphasising is '*an individual or group*', demonstrating that the creative process can involve minds thinking together.

Engagement and curiosity

The use of the simulation had a significant impact on the engagement and curiosity of both Year 6 classes (6D and 6H) within which the simulation was set up to provide the context for the writing workshops. Observation of class 6D noted,

> *Children were buzzing and asking questions – the simulation had really piqued their interest.*
>
> (6D observation extract)

This was corroborated by 6D's class teacher in interview, who agreed that the children had been hooked straight away and the stimulus had been vivid. She noted that one of the boys was

> *So into it and he genuinely thought he was a robot.*
>
> (6D semi-structured interview)

This enjoyment and engagement was reflected by children in 6D's focus group. One boy, assessed as working above age-related expectations (AREs), commented on how my being in role really engaged him. He also identified the decorating of the classroom and wearing identification lanyards that made him think it was real.

The simulation certainly stimulated their curiosity and led to a vast range of ideas. Comments prevalent cross the data set, from interviews with both class teachers, observations and notes, such as the example below, illustrate this:

> *They came up with fantastic ideas … some really deep thinking ideas.*
>
> (6D semi-structured interview)

The responses from 6H varied. One of the boys assessed at working above AREs commented in a focus group discussion that he enjoyed pretending it was real, clearly embracing the pretence. However, others in the group were not able to suspend their disbelief. One child commented,

> *It weren't daft or anything like that … it's just a bit of fun … cos robots can't take over your body, that's just stupid.*
>
> (Child F, 6H focus group)

Evidence from the data shows that a majority of those children working above AREs were willing to embrace the pretence of the simulation. I am not for one minute claiming that these children believed it was real, but they wanted to embrace the pretence because it had captured their imagination. For these children who engaged, their ideas went deeper and were more thoughtful, demonstrating a greater ability to analyse those ideas (Robson, 2014). For those that wouldn't allow themselves to embrace the '*Galactic Defence*' pretence, there was limited innovation in thinking, a notable lack of excitement and, consequently, their writing lacked any passion. Cremin et al (2006) argue that this kind of dramatic work provides an effective precursor to writing and that writing in a role, in this case junior researchers, reveals a better understanding of the issues and gives a clearer voice. The challenge, however, is to engage those learners who won't embrace the pretence. Can they

The big reveal • 131

be persuaded into the simulated world you have created? There are a number of strategies I used, some worked with some learners and others worked with others. These were:

- give some choices over how to respond and be involved;
- be enthusiastic yourself about the simulation and the learning involved;
- give the learners a challenge, and challenge them to complete it;
- provide social learning opportunities;
- make the learning purposeful and the outcome important;
- praise the process and thinking, not the product.

Creative thinking

The simulation also had an influence on the children's creative thinking. Observation data from 6D showed that there was

> *lots of vibrant discussion and creative ideas from all groups about how Robot Dax came to infiltrate the senior leaders – liked open-endedness, freedom and flexibility at this point in the process.*
>
> (6D observation extract)

At the beginning of the composition process, the opportunities for creative thinking did appear to influence the children's verbal and ideas-based work.

Areas of challenge

However, where the simulation and ensuing creative thinking became less influential was as the writing process developed from a variety to an agreed idea, confidence to speculate and analyse ideas seemed to disappear. One reason for this could be that with the complexity of writing the cognitive flexibility to juggle '*simultaneous constraints*' (Hayes and Flower, 1980) was too much for my research participants to manage. Trying to keep the balls of spelling, handwriting, sentence structure and punctuation in the air is just too much when the ideas ball is added. This was evidenced during the latter stages of the writing process where children in both classes struggled to maintain focus, yet wanted more time to write. The class teacher of 6D stated in interview,

> *They go off task easily and it's fair enough to say they want more time ... but if they're not doing it then ...*

This is evidence that these writers lacked the self-regulation to keep going. Graham and Harris (2000) argue that the main difference between skilled and novice writers is self-regulation. Zimmerman and Risemberg (1997) say that writing is often self-initiated and self-sustained. Evidence from my data shows that there was a lack of self-sustaining from many of the children in both classes. Robson (2014) terms this persistence, maintaining involvement in the task. The class teacher commented that the children are used to working '*pacily*', doing short, sharp activities through their structured school system. Therefore, it could be that this attitude had not been allowed to be developed.

The impact of taking a different approach

The enjoyment and engagement brought about by the simulation did not influence creative thinking and writing for all the children in the classes. Evidence from observations while working with 6D showed that some of the children found the different approach challenging.

> *It was clear that the different structure and approach was challenging for the back two tables.*
>
> (6D observation extract)

The back two tables in the classroom were occupied by children assessed as working above AREs. Data analysed suggested that these children from both classes found the school system safe and predictable. Change for them was challenging, perhaps because of their own confidence in their success with the traditional school system. My workshop design was more open-ended, emphasising possibility thinking, and was perhaps less formulaic than the school's approach. Looking again at Robson's (2014) Analysing Children's Creative Thinking framework, a tolerance of ambiguity is seen as part of persistence and self-efficacy. McWilliam and Haukka (2008) connect this attitude of a tolerance of ambiguity to flexibility and adaptability which coheres with Meadows' (2006) cognitive attitude of choosing challenges. However, evidence here suggests that these children identified as working above age-related expectations arguably did not demonstrate this attitude associated with creative thinking. It is possible that the structured approach developed by the school, a necessity to meet the demands of high-stakes testing, has facilitated comfort and safety for those working above AREs at the expense of providing challenge and opportunity to apply skills and ideas flexibly.

The challenges of teamwork

It was evident that working in a team for the children in 6D was a barrier to learning rather than a support tool. Their class teacher surmised that this behaviour could be due to stress caused by chaotic home lives. Rybski Beaver (1997), in her work on the role that emotion plays in how children cope with life's stresses, cites anger as an outward sign of life stress. Therefore, the class teacher's surmise could be valid. Adverse experiences in early life affect cognitive function, cognitive flexibility, creative thinking and anger responses to situations (Ji and Wang, 2018; Dahlitz, 2017). The class's emotive response to teamwork as a support was certainly not helpful for them, although different, and neither was 6H's. For 6H, from observation corroborated by interview data, teamwork was an opportunity to allow someone else to do the work. Their class teacher noted,

> *I mean they were engaged but when it was their turn not to write ... If they were all doing their own task it would mean ... they couldn't skive.*
>
> (6H semi-structured interview)

Teamwork therefore became a co-operative activity, each doing their own bit, rather than collaborative where they all support one another to develop their writing. The connection between using each other's ideas and their written pieces was not made. Writing was seen very much as an individual endeavour. Writing together, I observed, seemed to hold no benefits for them. However, the children's perspectives from both classes on how they worked as teams and their understanding of the role that teamwork can have in developing writing belied what was observed. Class 6D's focus group seemed to understand how working together can support the writing process. One after the other, children shared their views:

> ... work hard with my table ... We have to have teamwork to work altogether and that's really important.
>
> Helps us work with ... the people around us.
>
> I like having more people around me with more minds and more knowledge so we can add it all up and make something good out of it.
>
> I could give my ideas to other people so that they can get better than they are now.
> (Child B, C, D, E, 6D focus group)

Class 6H focus group also demonstrated understanding that was not seen in observation:

> It was really fun writing the stories ... like to share my group ... share your own opinions and share ideas together.
> (Child F, 6H focus group)

This is an example of children not making connections between support tools provided (teamwork in this case) to develop writing and using the team for that purpose. However, it is possible that while the children had been taught why teamwork was important, they had not fully connected it to their experience.

Did the simulation work?

The simulation did engage curiosity and interest. It provided a stimulus for thinking and idea generation. It engaged and motivated many of the learners in the class. In fact, for both Year 6 classes involved, many of those assessed as working below AREs by their teachers were more motivated than their above AREs counterparts. Their ideas were more innovative and in general there was a greater willingness to think creatively. Where creative thinking had limited impact was where these ideas needed to be translated into public text. There is a role here for the concept of working in the gaps between the blocks, as identified through my thinking for writing framework. The use of the simulation in this element of the research has certainly identified areas, in this context, for teachers to work with learners to apply their ideas and lay some scaffolding between the great creative and innovative ideas the learners may have and turning those into public text.

The use of simulation has also highlighted the reverse challenge. Those learners identified as working above AREs need some working in the gaps the other way. These learners had developed the fluency to create effective public text, and their cognitive flexibility to juggle the mechanical constraints of the writing process was strong, but, as a result, there was limited capacity for innovation in thinking and developing ideas. Following on from this, the level of cognitive maturity in these young learners was not sufficient to manipulate the skills required for effective teamwork, even if perhaps they had been taught.

> ***Reflective question*** (?)
>
> » If you are considering using a simulation, think about how it will benefit the learning for all the children in your class. Will working differently be a barrier to writing attainment? Will working in groups?

Morphological forced connections

In Chapter 2 of this book, I introduced a case study of Richard working with a class of Year 2 children on superheroes and the Great Fire of London. This is a prime example of children forcing connections between two seemingly unconnectable things – in this case the world of London in 1666 and the world of Marvel superheroes. One of Richard's learners provided the title for the class book they produced, with a brilliant creative question, '*I wonder what would happen if superheroes landed when the Great Fire of London started?*' What does this have to do with creative thinking? Connections of this type are a key element.

Iskander and Nurusholih (2019) report on some comic character design using a morphological forced connection method. They created a matrix showing different elements of a comic character – for example, form, costume and personality – and listed a series of choices. They then randomly connected the choices to create new characters. The creative thinking involved here forces one to make connections that may not have been considered, and thus new ideas are formed.

Richard's case study is taken from part of the research I undertook that foregrounds this book. Initially, the forcing of connections between 1666 London and Marvel superheroes created some incredible theories and ideas from these six-year-old research participants. However, their teachers highlighted a challenge. Elements such as risk-taking, persistence, elaboration of ideas and embracing uncertainty and ambiguity were found to cause difficulty for children from both Year 2 classes (Elm and Birch). For example, both classes struggled with tolerance of risk (Robson, 2014). In interview Elm's class teacher commented,

> At the start they seemed to just focus on the language they knew … no kind of out of the box thinking was there?
>
> (Elm semi-structured interview)

In observation of Elm class, it was noted that there was a huge lack of risk-taking with ideas, and Birch's class teacher commented similarly with children in her class, focusing specifically on some children's strict adherence to a prompt sheet:

> … he followed it to a tee, that's not part of what I was asked … he doesn't like to stray away from that.
>
> (Birch semi-structured interview)

The big reveal • 135

My reflective diary also noted that in their openings the children almost all went for something they knew, scene setting, and there was a lack of willingness to try something else out. Year 2 opening samples below give four examples, two from each class working above and below age-related expectations. The examples in Figure 9.1 demonstrate the use of predictable and known scene-setting openers.

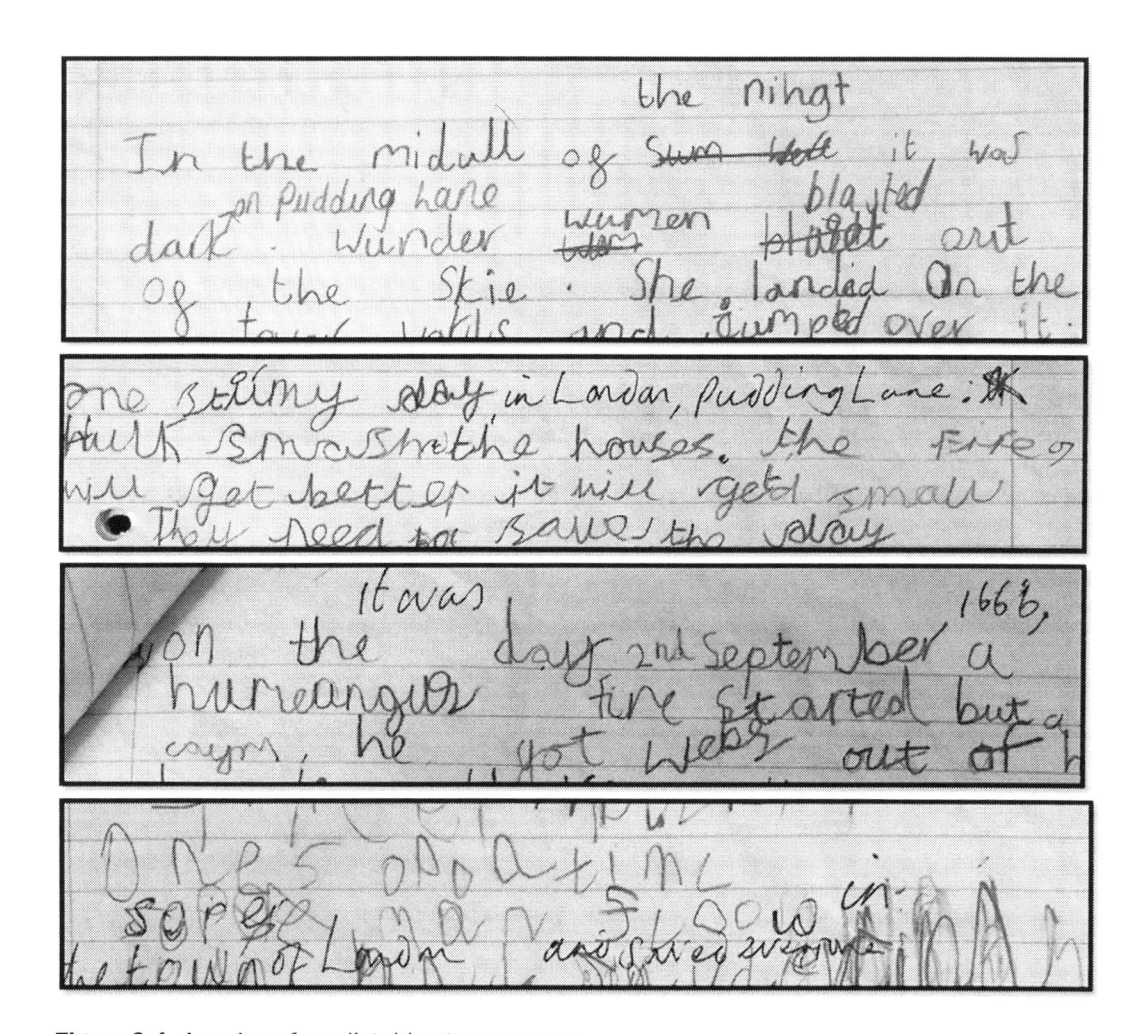

Figure 9.1 A series of predictable story openers

Reflections

'*They are only six!*' This was a comment from one of the Year 2 class teachers as we were discussing the children's engagement. There is so much to explore there around cognitive development, experience, physical development and domain-specific knowledge that the research outcomes can be called into question. Resnick (2007), however, argues that young children do think creatively. He posits the creative approach to learning in kindergarten helps learners develop the creative skills they need in the twenty-first century. Abbasi

(2011) confirms this. Drawing on longitudinal research into divergent thinking that Robinson (RSA, 2010) discusses in his talk 'Changing Paradigms', she reports that in this work 98 per cent of kindergarten children scored at genius level in divergent thinking, yet this had dropped to 50 per cent by the time they were retested five years later. Young children, then, literature shows, are able to think creatively. However, perhaps it is the cognitive processing ability for which age was a factor, not creative thinking? Perhaps the concept of working in the gaps between the blocks, as identified through my thinking for writing framework, is again applicable here. How do teachers support novice writers to turn their creative and risk-taking ideas – in this case developed through morphological forced connections – into risk-taking text?

Visualisation

The final part of this chapter looks at the impact that the creative thinking technique of visualisation had on children's writing. Returning to Richard's case study from Chapter 2 on superheroes and the Great Fire of London, the use of a floor map to develop a sense of place and its impact on writing is considered. The large floor map of London in 1666 with streets and landmarks laid out was intended to facilitate curiosity (Robson, 2014). This tool allowed the children to physically walk through London in 1666, see where the landmarks were and playfully visualise, as a way into composition (Craft et al, 2007).

The map also provided what Foley suggests is a *'social interactional framework'* (1994, p 101). He states that for learning to take place, such a framework needs to be used to provide structure to hang learning upon. The giant floor map of London in 1666 was a tool for children to engage with the Great Fire of London both historically and geographically, and be able to imagine what being there might have been like. Pantaleo (2016) suggests that, to enable thinking and learning, a learner should be actively engaged with their environment, and this is what the floor map sought to do. In interview, Elm's class teacher commented on its success in achieving its aim:

> *I really liked how you set the classroom up at the beginning of the day. I think that was definitely a hook. It helped the reluctant writers give it a go ... they were exploring the pictures of the buildings in London ... they could see it and visualise it.*
> (Elm semi-structured interview)

Part of the purpose of the giant map was to also provide geographical information so children could position their stories and not worry about having to spell street names or names of key landmarks or characters. This floor map was translated into A3 table maps with the same design, landmark pictures and street names, and time was taken to ensure the children made this connection. Birch's class teacher, in interview, was unsure as to whether the children had made the connection:

> *The model bit on the floor was great ... But did they use it? When they had the maps on the table did they use it? Maybe not.*
> (Birch semi-structured interview)

However, in focus group discussion, Birch class demonstrated they certainly understood what the map was for:

> *The big, big map ... cos we knowed where everything was and what everything was called.*
>
> (Child D, Birch focus group)

And this was supported by Elm focus group, who saw the map as a support for their writing:

> *The map ... because it helped me spell the words ... what helped me is the map ... and my brain helped me.*
>
> (Child B, Elm focus group)

This was also evident during the workshop itself. Elm's class teacher observed that the children were exploring the relationship between the pictures of London and their classroom map, visualising the fire from different perspectives. However, when analysing the writing, there was little mention of any of the place names from the map. Where there were characters such as Samuel Pepys and some key landmarks such as the River Thames, there was some evidence that the map had been used, as emphasised in a Year 2 writing sample four in Figure 9.2, from a child in Birch class working below AREs.

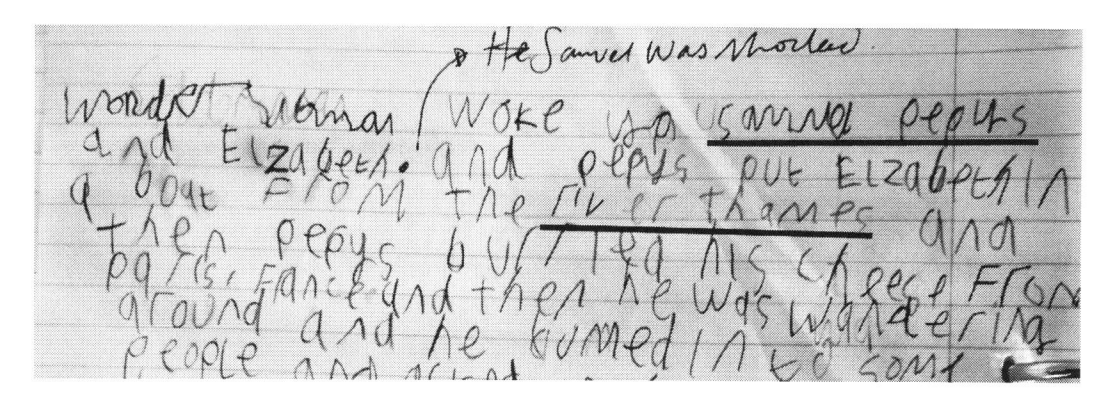

Figure 9.2 Evidence of floor map names applied to writing

It could be argued therefore that Birch's class teacher may have concluded correctly. While the children may have known what the map was for and even been able to articulate it, perhaps in their rush to write their ideas down they were not able to focus on and apply what this support tool offered; perhaps the application element of cognitive function (Kiely, 2014) was a process too far in this case.

Chapter summary

Across the three creative thinking tools explored in some depth in this chapter, there is one clear theme that stands out: connections. This is a theme discussed earlier in the book and often returned to as I think it is crucial to your understanding of how children learn. Through this chapter, from my research participants' perspective, you have seen evidence that while a simulation is an exciting and motivating tool to capture imagination, engender curiosity and be the catalyst for innovative thinking and problem-solving, applying those to creating public text is where the teacher's work should focus. You have also seen that the reverse can also be true. Perhaps those who have the cognitive flexibility to juggle the complex processes of creating public text need some work in the gaps to challenge them to innovate.

Similarly, a creative thinking tool such as morphological forced connections, used to build innovative connections beyond the everyday, is great to excite and create bold new ideas. However, you have seen evidence in this chapter, albeit one context, that demonstrates the need for the teacher to work in the gap between innovative creative thinking and translating that into risk-taking, innovative public text.

Finally, working in the gap between a huge floor map that helps children create a sense of place and their writing can support connection between one and the other, and how the clues and information on one can be used to relieve some working memory space to devote more to keeping the balls of the writing process in the air.

Further reading

These three excellent and accessible readings, alongside my reflective questions, will help develop your thinking from this chapter.

> Resnick, M (2007) All I Really Need to Know (about Creative Thinking) I Learned (by Studying How Children Learn) in Kindergarten. *Proceedings of the 6th ACM SIGCHI Conference on Creativity and Cognition.* [online] Available at: https://dl.acm.org/doi/abs/10.1145/1254960.1254961 (accessed 22 June 2023).
>
> *This insightful paper starts from the perspective that young children are creative thinkers – they naturally design, explore, play and experiment all the time. The paper suggests that these skills are valuable for twenty-first-century life and should be nurtured and developed.*
>
> ### Focus question
>
> Figure 1 on page 2 of the paper presents a diagram for the kindergarten approach to learning. How do you think this can apply to learning and teaching in other contexts?

Copping, A (2015) A Murder Mystery. In Waugh, D, Bushnell, A and Neaum, S (eds) *Beyond Early Writing* (pp 33–46). Northwich: Critical Publishing.

This chapter explores a Victorian murder mystery I created. This was a simulation where I was in role and the children wrote in role. The learning and development of writing is explored in this chapter.

Focus question

What does this chapter say about how the simulation influenced higher writing attainment?

Education Endowment Foundation (2021) Collaborative Learning Approaches. [online] Available at: https://educationendowmentfoundation.org.uk/education-evidence/teaching-learning-toolkit/collaborative-learning-approaches (accessed 23 August 2023).

This paper reports on a research project that explores the purpose and impact of collaborative learning approaches.

Focus question

In what ways do some of the report's findings cohere with perspectives presented in this chapter? Is this your experience, too? What strategies have you used to develop collaborative learning?

10 Changing the landscape

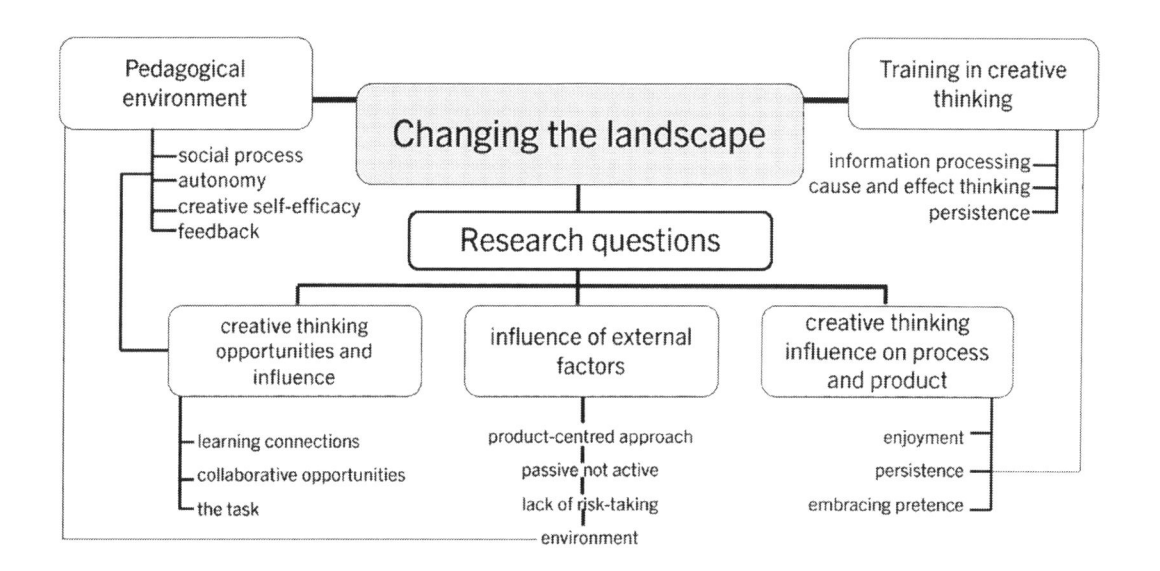

```
Pedagogical                                          Training in creative
environment                                          thinking
         ┌─ Changing the landscape ─┐
         │─social process           │─information processing
         │─autonomy                 │─cause and effect thinking
         │─creative self-efficacy   │─persistence
         │─feedback                 
              Research questions

  creative thinking      influence of external      creative thinking
  opportunities and           factors               influence on process
     influence                                         and product

  ─ learning connections      product-centred approach    enjoyment
  ─ collaborative opportunities    passive not active     persistence
  ─ the task                  lack of risk-taking      embracing pretence
                              environment
```

Core Content Framework / Early Career Teacher Framework links

The Department for Education for England and Wales (DfE) provides a framework of minimum entitlement for trainee teachers which is then developed into your Early Career Teacher (ECT) years. This chapter links to:

- high expectations (Standard 1) – teachers are role-models, changing attitudes, high-quality teaching affects life chances;

- how pupils learn (Standard 2 – progress) – learning involves a lasting change, memory and working memory, worked examples;

- subject and curriculum (Standard 3) – explicitly teaching knowledge and skills within subject areas;

- classroom practice (Standard 4) – effective teaching transforms beliefs and capabilities;

→

- adaptive teaching (Standard 5) – targeted adaptive teaching in a responsive way;
- assessment (Standard 6) – high-quality feedback to encourage effort and identify where to improve;
- managing behaviour (Standard 7) – intrinsic motivation, influencing resilience and success;
- professional behaviours (Standard 8) – reflective practice, engaging in high-quality professional development.

Introduction

One thing I notice as I reflect on the many house design programmes I have watched is that the architects and builders involved often want to make a statement. They want their building to be a talking point, to say something about who they are – and not just add to the landscape but often to change it. Changing an existing architectural landscape can be risky, it provokes debate and it risks creating problems within a community, but it can also be a powerful landmark that forces people to sit up and take notice.

This final chapter acts as a conclusion to the book. It returns to the starting point of the research upon which this book is based, the research questions, and answers them explicitly, creating a summary of the whole book. In the Introduction to this book I laid out the following questions.

1. From teachers' and children's perspectives, to what extent do opportunities to think creatively during the writing process influence children's work?
2. From their viewpoint, to what extent do teachers' perspectives, personal experience and external factors such as school policy, influence their writing pedagogy and the development of children's creative thinking?
3. From the teachers' and children's perspectives, how is creative thinking evidenced and how does this evidence influence writing process and product?

This chapter concludes with some pedagogical suggestions to change the landscape of the current, pervading, product-focused and scheme-led writing pedagogy and help teachers plan and teach in ways they have always wanted to but are hindered by high-stakes assessment and expensive schemes. All of this without compromising on quality writing.

However, before addressing these questions, there were some assumptions I had made about children's thinking. These are evident throughout this book, and, while undertaking the research upon which this book is based, these assumptions were significantly challenged.

Creating an environment for thinking and then training

The first of these assumptions I had made was that children can think creatively. This assumption was based on empirical studies from literature (Craft, 1999; 2003; Resnick, 2007; Craft et al, 2013), my own prior research (Copping, 2016) and my own experience of working as a teacher and consultant in a range of primary settings. However, a key finding from this research is that although all children have the capacity for creative thinking (Paul and Elder, 2019), there are prerequisites that need to be in place for creative thinking to flourish and develop. This is illustrated through the training in thinking foundation to the cognitive writing process and the overarching thinking environment in my final think for writing framework, shown first in the Introduction (Figure 0.8) and repeated in Figure 10.1 below.

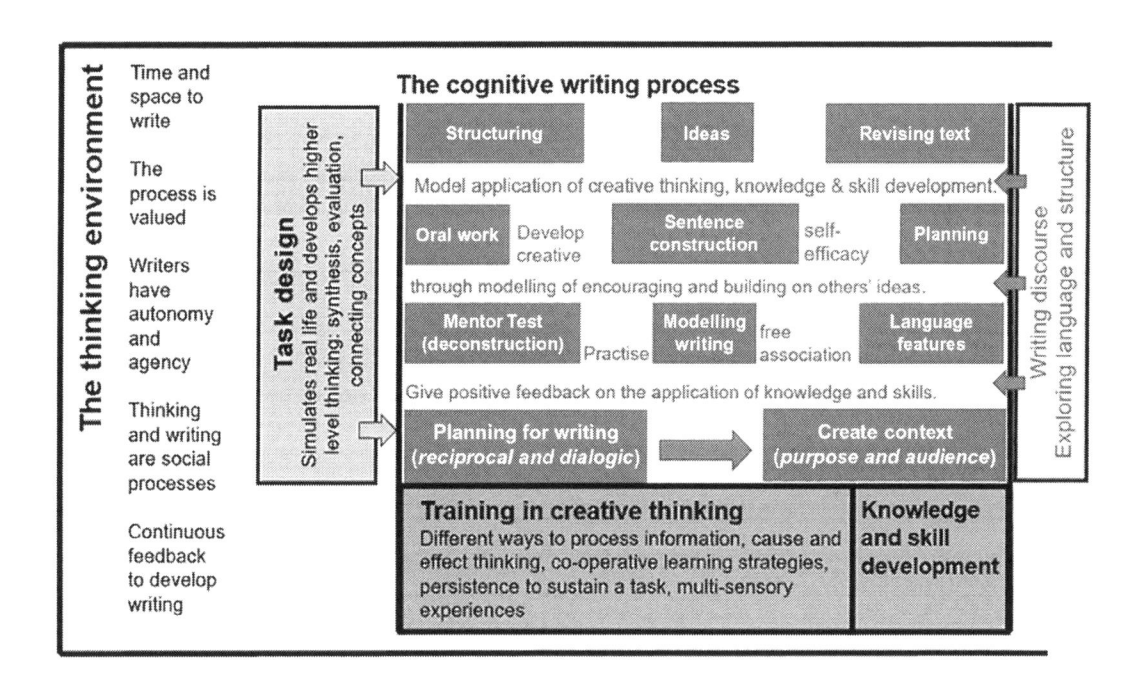

Figure 10.1 Current thinking for writing framework

First, I named the pedagogical environment determined by the class teacher (Cremin, 2006), '*the thinking environment*'. This is the desired context within which the cognitive writing process can take place. Factors of an effective pedagogical environment are prominent in the literature as well as my findings. These are writing as a social process (Pantaleo, 2016), valuing that process (Graves, 1983; Bereiter and Scardamalia, 1993) and writers having freedom, autonomy and agency (Grainger et al, 2003; Gadd and Parr, 2016). However, my findings also suggested that a child's confidence can influence their creative thinking. Confidence to think creatively comes through having developed creative self-efficacy (Tierney and Farmer, 2002), which Farmer and Tierney later define as '*the belief one has the ability to produce creative outcomes*' (2017, p 23). Creative self-efficacy, my research draws out, is not just an innate sense or ability, it is an attitude that needs to be trained and developed to allow creative thinking to flourish. Creative self-efficacy is developed through the self-assurance to apply the knowledge the learner has to the task they are engaged in. This self-assurance is most effectively developed through feedback on learning (Schunk and Rice, 1987).

However, the most effective feedback to develop this self-assurance is not pure praise, as expected, but feedback on application, helping the learner pinpoint how they have applied that knowledge and that this is desired. While feedback is evident in *'the thinking environment'*, where feedback is sought and given is important, feedback to develop self-efficacy through self-assurance needs to be ongoing. *'The cognitive writing process'* element of my thinking for writing model, as shown above, has been designed in the form of a brick wall with gaps the same size as bricks. The text between the bricks is of equal importance as the bricks. This text refers to developing self-efficacy through ongoing feedback on application of knowledge. It has been placed here to illustrate that developing and training children's creative self-efficacy in order to develop their thinking is an ongoing process and should take place throughout the writing process.

As well as training in creative thinking skills such as information processing, cause-and-effect thinking and persistence, my research also found that for writing and thinking as social practices to be maximised, training the children in working together is imperative. Without this, my research showed, working together collaboratively was in many cases a barrier to the children's learning. It was not until time was spent in two of the workshops, explicitly teaching what effective teamwork looks like and introducing a co-operative learning strategy, that teamwork became a support. However, this training did not provide a neat answer, even with the role-giving as a support. Positive social relationships within each team are a prerequisite of effective thinking (Blatchford et al, 2003) and these need training to develop effective team dynamics and therefore effective creative thinking.

The impact of social deprivation on cognitive processing and creative thinking

My thinking for writing framework in Figure 10.1 suggests that, if children are learning in the context of an effective thinking environment, actively engaging in quality creative thinking training and receiving ongoing feedback to build creative efficacy, then they will be able to think creatively and it will influence their writing. However, another significant finding of my research suggests that this is not the case. Mumford et al (2006) argue that limitations in cognitive processing capacity can impair creative thinking. My data suggests that many of the children who took part in my research, especially evident during workshops 3 and 4, did not have the information-processing capacity to deal with the many simultaneous constraints to be juggled within the writing process. Other skills they were also asked to juggle simultaneously, such as working together, problem-solving, risk-taking, deconstructing and using a mentor text, were too much for them. These demands can cause cognitive overload (Sweller, 1988; De Jong, 2009) for the learner and impact upon the brain's ability to complete the tasks set. You may have worked with learners who live in areas of social deprivation and seen first-hand some of the challenges these learners face, and perhaps seen learners frustrated and angry because they are not able to process information like many of their peers. While there are a number of influences on cognitive processing (Ford and Stein, 2016), McManus and Poehlmann (2012) suggest that social deprivation can impact cognitive processing negatively. This is not to say that supporting the development of cognitive processing should be limited to those learners who experience social deprivation. Developing cognitive processing capacity is important for all learners as it develops higher level thinking skills such as evaluation, synthesis, logical argument and application of knowledge to a variety of contexts. Therefore, one important piece of landscape-changing cognitive architecture is that learning and teaching should involve a greater emphasis on the development of effective pedagogic environments and training to help develop creative thinking.

Creative thinking opportunities and their influence on the work

The first research question

1. From teachers' and children's perspectives, to what extent do opportunities to think creatively during the writing process influence children's work?

In this book, case studies are derived from the writing workshops I designed for the research that has formed the foundation of this work. Each of the workshops facilitated a wide variety of creative thinking opportunities, from embracing pretence through writing in role and visualising London in 1666 to creating ideas, analysing them, persisting in ideas and making connections between them. Other opportunities included involving others through team working. Each of the pairs of workshops was designed as a problem-solving approach to writing, from Year 6 saving the school from alien robot force, Dax, to Year 2 exploring how superheroes could have halted the Great Fire of London and Year 4 combining scientific facts about water, a fantasy land and a musical element into a playscript. Evidence from my data suggests that these creative thinking opportunities had limited influence on the children's work. Where my data suggests that the pedagogic environment set by the teacher resulted in passivity through teacher control and a lack of willingness to take risks, creative thinking was not as evident, but the quality of the work was not really impacted. One of the reasons for this, as discussed earlier in this chapter, could have been to do with cognitive load and the complexity of the writing process. Given the links between the juggling of complex simultaneous constraints and cognitive overload discussed in earlier chapters, it is therefore helpful for teachers to understand this complexity and deliberately not overload the learner. Meanwhile, teachers can help learners build cognitive flexibility (Morin, 2020) through some of the training outlined in Figure 10.1.

The significance of making learning connections

Connection-making during the writing process influenced the children's work significantly. Findings from data across all six workshops indicated that children were seemingly unable to make connections in two different ways. First, data showed that children were finding it challenging to make connections between different elements of the writing process across their workshop. There was the occasional piece of evidence that showed children were able to see, for example, how a large map they worked with to visualise London in 1666 helped them with their writing using place names. However, for a significant majority of the children, data from all workshops showed that when each activity (writing process phase) was completed, there was little sense that skills, knowledge and understanding gained supported the next stage. Where the understanding of writing as a process was more evident, the teachers had deliberately made it so.

A lack of connection was also evident in terms of relating reading and writing, a mentor text and their own composition. Even though the learner participants were regularly involved in mentor text deconstruction, data showed that children could not apply their previous knowledge of using a mentor text to the different context of the workshops. It was evident that the learners knew what the building blocks of the writing process were – for example, mentor text, composing and editing text, drawing a comic strip, modelling writing, teamwork – and how to use them discretely. However, the evidence shows they struggled to make connections between them to develop writing.

The lack of connection-making ability perhaps illustrates a lack of creative self-efficacy to apply the knowledge they had. It could also be argued that a systematic and repetitive approach employed by their school, driven by attainment in tests, had become a writing procedure to follow rather than developing application. The impact of the school's system is discussed in more depth later in this chapter in exploring findings relating to research question 2.

Collaborative opportunities: enabler or barrier to learning?

Involving others was also a significant creative thinking opportunity that influenced the children's work. Evidence showed that teamwork was a barrier for some children's learning rather than the support it was intended to be. This manifested itself in frustration and anger, group dynamics and some children misunderstanding what teamwork involved. Even with role-giving and role signifiers in later workshops, self-regulation to sustain those roles through the whole workshop was a real challenge. The influence of this on the work was different for identifiable groups of learners. For those children identified as working above age-related expectations (AREs), involving others proved to be more of a challenge and a barrier for many of them to achieve what was normally expected. Data shows that for these children, many of whom had a high level of attainment using the school's individual approach to writing, giving up control was difficult. Hallam et al (2004) suggest that children working above AREs may get frustrated with group work, particularly when they are working with children who are achieving not as highly as they are. Hallam et al (2004) later suggest that a mixed grouping such as I used can support those children working below AREs as they can feel valued, and my data supported this. Blatchford et al (2003) cite social relationships in the classroom as a prerequisite for effective group work, and where this was the case within my workshops my data supports Blatchford's premise. So, developing positive social relationships across the class is important if children are to be able to involve others and therefore develop their writing. Where involving others positively influenced work was evidenced in children analysing their ideas together.

The significance of the task

The role of the task has been discussed in earlier chapters and is summarised here. Where the task was more open-ended and gave the learners more autonomy and freedom, there was more enjoyment demonstrated and evidence of connecting the purpose of the task with the quality of writing needed. Lambirth (2016) suggests that young writers prefer writing tasks where they are able to express themselves, and Gadd and Parr's (2016) work on effective teachers cites giving pupils more freedom and autonomy as an aspect of their practice. They also suggest that these teachers give children input into decisions around learning activities, giving them more agency in their writing. However, the most significant finding relating to how the task influenced the children's work centred round the thinking that those tasks engender. The playscript task in workshops 5 and 6 required the children to synthesise, evaluate, analyse and apply information, all higher thinking skills, as well as take risks. Data from these workshops showed the greatest influence of the task on the children's work.

External factors influencing pedagogy and children's creative thinking

The second research question

2. From their viewpoint, to what extent do teachers' perspectives, personal experience and external factors such as school policy, influence their writing pedagogy and the development of children's creative thinking?

The predominant external factor present across my whole data set was the highly systematised and product-centred approach to teaching English that the school had developed. The reasons for it were essentially driven by external measures of school effectiveness, such as high-stakes test results and Ofsted expectations. Evidence showed evidence of learners being passive recipients rather than active participants in their learning. With the use of this approach, albeit from my limited observations and limited time working in the school, I did not see the children given opportunity to take risks in their writing and thinking. This was evidenced through the children having difficulty with the open-ended nature of the writing tasks that I set. Permission given for them to think about how they wanted to communicate through writing was very difficult for them to embrace, perhaps because their usual English work is very prescriptive. As a result, the use of the support tool, a mentor, almost became a constraint. Even though mentor texts were used every week with the school's approach to writing, I was using them slightly differently and that seemed to cause problems for the children.

Data from workshops 5 and 6 provided slightly different findings relating to the school's approach to writing pedagogy. Evidence from these workshops showed that the teachers had worked together to adapt the school's approach to align more with their own beliefs of writing as a journey, a process. This understanding was evident in the responses of the children to the workshops, as they were keen to be active in the learning and more comfortable with process writing.

The significance of the pedagogical environment

The pedagogical environment was also significant in influencing writing pedagogy and creative thinking. Each of the teachers who took part in my research had different levels of experience, areas of expertise and preference and different personalities, and my data shows that these influenced the pedagogical environment of their classrooms. Evidence also suggests that the pedagogical environment is influenced by external factors such as an imposed whole-school approach. This whole-school approach did have an effect on the learning environment. First, those children currently assessed as attaining above AREs showed a lack of flexibility in their understanding of writing as a process. There was evidence of frustration at the different challenges posed by working with others in the process. Second, discussion of writing was categorised by what Lambirth (2016) terms a skills discourse. Discussion of what makes better writing, in my data, consisted of handwriting and spelling mainly. Lambirth (2016) also suggests that children articulate the elements of writing they struggle most with and my data certainly supports this, as those transcriptional elements of writing (handwriting, spelling, punctuation, sentence structure) were a big challenge for those children working at or below AREs. However, this was not the case for this group of learners in workshops 5 and 6 where the environment was organised so that the social aspects were an enabler and not a constraint; the writing was part of the process and it had a definite audience and purpose. The task allowed more autonomy for the learners and where higher levels of persistence were needed towards the end of the writing process, a performance was the product. In these workshops, children's transcriptional elements of the process were assessed at a higher level and were used more intentionally to communicate meaning.

Creative thinking and its influence on process and product

The third research question

3. From the teachers' and children's perspectives, how is creative thinking evidenced and how does this evidence influence writing process and product?

Several cognitive attitudes of creative thinking were evidenced during my research workshops. Within this section the three most significant in the data are discussed.

The first, enjoyment, is followed by persistence, significant across my whole data set due to the children being seemingly unable to demonstrate it. Following this, embracing pretence will be discussed in terms of its influence on writing process and product.

Enjoyment

Evidence from my data showed that the children enjoyed each of the workshops they participated in. They were motivated by the contexts and by the tasks set. Their enjoyment of the workshop did influence creation of ideas, enthusiasm and engagement with the process. Observations throughout the day from the class teachers and myself corroborated the belief that generally the children did enjoy the workshops. However, for the first four workshops, the enjoyment, I would argue, did not really influence product. Analysis of writing from the first four workshops did demonstrate some high levels of composition but, overall, the quality of the product did not reflect engagement with the earlier parts of the writing process. Yet during workshops 5 and 6, the enjoyment earlier on was evident in many of the groups' performances of their playscripts, where a finished product was not an individual piece of writing. A possible reason for this could be the complexity of the writing process. Given the analysis of their writing and observation, many of the children engaged in putting ideas into coherent text, a significant number of whom could be termed struggling writers. In earlier chapters, I have discussed literature that suggests the transcriptional process is the aspect that struggling writers find most challenging. This was evident through the analysis of children's writing from workshops 1–4. Editing and revising text (largely transcriptional processes) took place during the latter stages of these workshops; therefore, it could make logical sense that children's enjoyment waned at this point, and this of course influenced their product. However, data from these first four workshops shows that children who were not struggling writers also struggled to maintain enjoyment, due to group work and struggling with a more flexible approach to writing. In workshops 5 and 6, where the writing was part of the process, not product, and there was a clear purpose for effort in transcription, attainment of these children's transcription elements of writing was generally higher.

Persistence

Another reason for enjoyment not being carried through into the latter stages of each workshop is persistence. Persistence, and several synonyms of it, such as perseverance and stamina, appeared across the whole of my data set, and due to it being a creative attitude, it is suggested as a training focus (Figure 10.1 earlier in this chapter). Persistence is connected strongly to self-regulation, which Harris et al (2011) posit that struggling writers find more challenging than more competent writers. It would therefore make sense that the struggling writers taking part in the workshops would find sustaining the management of complex processes difficult and therefore find editing, revising and improving quality of product very challenging. For workshops 5 and 6, a lack of persistence and self-regulation was evident in that rehearsals lost focus, role organisation could not be sustained and more teacher interventions were needed.

Embracing pretence

A creative thinking attitude that the vast majority of the children found easy to demonstrate was embracing pretence. This facet of creative thinking is connected to learning gains in trying out ideas and hypothesising. My data suggests that embracing pretence directly influenced writing process in terms of trying out and developing a wider range of ideas, but these ideas did not always translate into written product. The challenge for the children was, as identified earlier, turning those ideas into text, the same phase in workshops 1–4 where enjoyment waned. During workshops 5 and 6 this did not appear as much of a problem as, for many of the children, these balls seemed to be kept in the air more intuitively; something in the task of writing a playscript meant their prior knowledge was more easily activated – perhaps the lack of pressure of producing a very neat final piece was a factor. Analysis of the 20 scripts from workshops 5 and 6 demonstrates higher achievement in those transcriptional elements than the stories from workshops 1–4, but attainment in the composition elements was not as high.

Thinking for writing framework

My thinking for writing framework developed through this research is intended to provide a theoretical model for teachers to engage with in their planning and design of units of work. It gives elements to remember and a pedagogical approach that adds something different to the writing landscape.

The main contributions my thinking for writing framework makes are through the enablers or prerequisites mentioned above, but also and significantly, through the emphasis of teachers supporting learners to connect parts of the writing process. Helping learners understand how one part builds upon the other through working between the gaps of the bricks develops creative efficacy and applies knowledge to a variety of contexts through feedback.

Teacher focus

The teaching of writing, in my experience, is often focused on creating mentor texts, planning activity, modelling writing and devising scaffolds to support the learners. This is also evidenced by the plethora of published plans available for teachers. My research does not suggest teachers should not focus their time here, but rather that teachers should spend time and energy working with learners to connect those building blocks. The implication for primary practice here is for teachers to develop the skills to work within those gaps: modelling how to apply creative thinking skills and domain-specific knowledge and giving ongoing feedback to the learners about their application to build creative self-efficacy and assurance to apply knowledge and skills across contexts. Teachers also need to focus on process and task design. Is it always effective to ask for a '*published*' piece of writing to mark the end of the process? My research has concluded that having the product as a revised and edited piece of writing may not always yield the most effective learning. Without training and development, struggling and novice writers find self-regulation in writing a challenge and editing and revising are often left to the end of the process at a point where children cannot sustain their writing. They have already juggled lots of different skills to turn thoughts into coherent sentences that communicate meaning, and their brains may well be experiencing cognitive overload. This impacts their ability to complete the task. In order to avoid cognitive overload, teachers need to consider the complexity of the writing process, understand the many constraints novice writers are juggling when writing and consider this in their task design.

The final element for teachers to focus on is their establishment and maintenance of an effective pedagogical environment for thinking. At the time of writing this final section, I have just sent cohorts of PGCE students into their first ECT jobs, and so it is here I will finish with them in mind, with some questions as they start to think about their first classroom and what environment they wish to develop. However, they can also be helpful as a reset if you are an experienced teacher.

- In your planning, how will you ensure your children have time and space to think as part of their writing?
- How will you ensure that the full process of writing is valued in terms of recording attainment, not just the final product?
- How will you provide your learners with some autonomy and agency within the writing tasks you set?
- How will you help social writing practices to be an enabler, not a constraint, to attainment?
- How will you ensure you are providing continual feedback that develops application, thinking and self-efficacy?

Chapter summary

Changing the pedagogical landscape

The process of returning to my three research questions and bringing together some of the key themes identified in this book has engendered some pedagogical architecture to add to the existing landscape of primary English. These are represented in Figure 10.2.

Figure 10.2 Changing the landscape of primary English

The first of these is that for creative thinking to fully impact on writing attainment, creative thinking skills need to be developed as part of a school's curriculum along with skills development, training and development of creative thinking. While all do have the capacity to think creatively (Sternberg, 2003), some attitudes of creative thinking need more training and require creative efficacy, which also needs developing.

The second is that teachers need to not just teach the building blocks of writing but work between the gaps of these blocks. Through analysis of data, it has become apparent to me that many children struggle to make connections between different parts of the writing process, seeing them as separate tasks, rather than parts working towards a whole. This is mainly due, I would argue, to the complex juggling of simultaneous skills needed to produce effective writing and the significant cognitive processing skills needed to manage this.

The third relates to persistence and self-regulation. As writing is such a complex process, requiring significant cognitive processing, brains become overloaded and learners are not able to sustain writing through to the latter stages of the process, typically editing and revising. This affects the quality of work produced.

The fourth, task design, arises from this. Task design has been a significant factor throughout this research. My data shows that where process writing is valued, a tangible audience and purpose for the writing is identified and the actual writing is not at the end of the process, the pressure to produce is off and the quality in terms of author's intent and effective communication rose.

The fifth and final theme links to this: external influences and the pedagogical environment. My findings have highlighted the impact of a product-based approach to writing pedagogy that is necessitated by high-stakes measures of school effectiveness. These high-stakes measures, in my research case, have driven the introduction of a structured system for teaching writing that while doing its job, increasing test scores, has influenced teachers creating pedagogical environments that have not supported learners to develop their cognitive processing and connection-making or engage with writing as a process.

The gap between thinking and writing, my data suggests, can be filled by developing children's creative self-efficacy, which is connected to confidence (Mathisen and Bronnick, 2009; OECD, 2019). Developing children's self-efficacy could be seen therefore as the conceptual glue that holds the fields of creative thinking and writing together. Within this development, children should be coached to make connections between building blocks of the writing process through feedback on their skills at applying their knowledge to other contexts. This may be as a complement to whole-class writing instruction. Development of creative self-efficacy in this way also builds persistence and self-regulation, two important attributes that are cognitive connections between creative thinking and writing pedagogy.

Further reading

The following three excellent and accessible readings, alongside the focus questions, will help develop your thinking from this chapter.

Gadd, M and Parr, J (2016) It's All About Baxter: Task Orientation in the Effective Teaching of Writing. *Literacy*, 50(2): 93–9. [online] Available at: https://onlinelibrary.wiley.com/doi/epdf/10.1111/lit.12072 (accessed 19 July 2023).

This excellent piece of empirical research, based in New Zealand, recognises the need for teacher autonomy in task orientation. It also adds to the discussion in this chapter around freedom and autonomy for the learners.

Focus question

The article connects learning gains to teacher instruction that orientates the learner effectively around the task. As you read it, can you identify implications for your practice?

Mathisen, G and Bronnick, K (2009) Creative Self-Efficacy: An Intervention Study. *International Journal of Education Research*, 48: 21–9. [online] Available at: www.sciencedirect.com/science/article/pii/S0883035509000305 (accessed 19 July 2023).

This excellent article explores the concept of creative self-efficacy. The authors make some strong suggestions around developing and training in self-efficacy and connects to positive creative outcomes.

Focus question

How will you help your learners develop and maintain creative self-efficacy? What impact might this have on all curriculum areas?

Main, P (2023) Thinking Hard Strategies. [online] Available at: www.structural-learning.com/post/thinking-hard-strategies (accessed 20 July 2023).

This interesting, practical and highly accessible blog connects thinking with learning gains. The author provides a range of helpful strategies that can become part of your pedagogy. These ideas are underpinned by cognitive science.

Focus question

How do you think visual strategies such as dual coding and using thinking maps can enhance the teaching and learning in your context?

References

Abbasi, K (2011) A Riot of Divergent Thinking. *Journal of the Royal Society of Medicine*, 104(10): 391. [online] Available at: https://dx.doi.org/10.1258%2Fjrsm.2011.11k038 (accessed 19 June 2023).

Acquah, D (2013) School Accountability in England: Past, Present and Future. *Centre for Education Research and Policy*. [online] Available at: www.aqa.org.uk/about-us/our-research/research-library/paper?path=school-accountability-england-past-present-future (accessed 23 August 2023).

Alborough, J (2014) *Where's My Teddy?* 2nd edition. London: Walker Books.

Alexander, R (2008) *Essays on Pedagogy*. Abingdon: Routledge.

Alvez, R and Limpo, T (2015) Progress in Written Language Bursts, Pauses, Transcription, and Written Composition Across Schooling. *Scientific Studies of Reading*, 19(5): 374–91. [online] Available at: www.tandfonline.com/doi/abs/10.1080/10888438.2015.1059838 (accessed 23 August 2023).

Amabile, T (1996) Creativity and Innovation in Organizations. Harvard Business School Background Note 396–239. [online] Available at: www.hbs.edu/faculty/Pages/item.aspx?num=13672 (accessed 23 August 2023).

Amabile, T (2012) Big C, Little C, Howard and Me: Approaches to Understanding Creativity. Working Paper 12–085. [online] Available at: www.hbs.edu/ris/Publication%20Files/12-085_eb9ecda0-ec0a-4a32-8747-884303f8b4dd.pdf (accessed 23 August 2023).

Andrews, R, Torgerson, C, Beverton, S, Freeman, A, Locke, T, Low, G, Robinson, A and Zhu, D (2006) The Effect of Grammar Teaching on Writing Development. *British Educational Research Journal*, 32(1): 39–55. [online] Available at: www.jstor.org/stable/30032657 (accessed 23 August 2023).

Arrimada, M, Torrance, M and Fidalgo, R (2019) Effects of Teaching Planning Strategies to First Grade Writers. *British Journal of Educational Psychology*, 89: 670–88. [online] Available at: https://bpspsychub.onlinelibrary.wiley.com/doi/full/10.1111/bjep.12251 (accessed 23 August 2023).

Badger, R and White, G (2000) A Process Genre Approach to Teaching Writing. *ELT Journal*, 54(2): 153–60. [online] Available at: www.researchgate.net/profile/Richard_Badger/publication/31211657_A_process_genre_approach_to_teaching_writing/links/5554750508ae6fd2d81f4915.pdf (accessed 23 August 2023).

Baer, J (2016) *Domain Specificity of Creativity*. San Diego, CA: Elsevier Academic Press.

Bailey, M (2002) What Does Research Tell Us About How We Should Be Developing Written Composition? In Fisher, R, Brooks, G and Lewis, M (eds) *Raising Standards in Literacy* (pp 23–38). London: Routledge Falmer.

Bailey-Galreith, A (2015) 'Explain Yourself': A Powerful Strategy for Teaching Children Cause and Effect. [online] Available at: www.learningandthebrain.com/blog/cause-and-effect/ (accessed 22 August 2023).

Bandura, A (1997) *Self-Efficacy: The Exercise of Control.* New York: Freeman.

Barr, N, Pennycook, G, Stolz, J and Fugelsang, J (2015) Reasoned Connections: A Dual-Process Perspective on Creative Thought. *Thinking and Reasoning*, 21(1): 61–75. [online] Available at: www.tandfonline.com/doi/abs/10.1080/13546783.2014.895915 (accessed 23 August 2023).

Batey, M (2012) The Measurement of Creativity: From Definitional Consensus to the Introduction of a New Heuristic Framework. *Creativity Research Journal*, 24(1): 55–65. [online] Available at: https://doi.org/10.1080/10400419.2012.649181 (accessed 23 August 2023).

Beard, R and Burrell, A (2010) Investigating Narrative Writing by 9–11-Year-Olds. *Journal of Research in Reading*, 33(1): 77–93. [online] Available at: https://onlinelibrary.wiley.com/doi/abs/10.1111/j.1467-9817.2009.01433.x (accessed 23 August 2023).

Beghetto, R and Kaufman, J (2007) Toward a Broader Conception of Creativity: A Case for 'Mini-c' Creativity. *Psychology of Aesthetics, Creativity and the Arts*, 1(2): 73–9.

Beghetto, R and Kaufman, J (2010) Broadening Conceptions of Creativity in the Classroom. In Beghetto, R and Kaufman, J (eds) *Nurturing Creativity in the Classroom* (pp 191–205). New York: Cambridge University Press.

Bereiter, C and Scardamalia, M (eds) (1987) *The Psychology of Written Composition.* New York: Routledge.

Bereiter, C and Scardamalia, M (1993) Composing and Writing. In Beard, R (ed) *Teaching Literacy: Balancing Perspectives* (pp 155–75). London: Hodder and Stoughton.

Bereiter, C, Burtis, P and Scardamalia, M (1988) Cognitive Operations in Constructing Main Points in Written Composition. *Journal of Memory and Language*, 27(3): 261–78. [online] Available at: www.sciencedirect.com/science/article/abs/pii/0749596X8890054X (accessed 23 August 2023).

Berninger, V, Vaughan, K, Abbott, R, Begay, K, Byrd Coleman, K, Curtin, G, Minich Hawkins, J and Graham, S (2002) Teaching Spelling and Composition Alone and Together: Implications for the Simple View of Writing. *Journal of Educational Psychology*, 94(2): 291–304. [online] Available at: https://doi.org/10.1037/0022-0663.94.2.291 (accessed 23 August 2023).

Bethell, C, Newacheck, P, Hawes, E and Halfon, N (2014) Adverse Childhood Experiences: Assessing the Impact on Health and School Engagement and the Mitigating Role of Resilience. *Health Affairs*, 33(12): 2106–115. [online] Available at: www.healthaffairs.org/doi/10.1377/hlthaff.2014.0914 (accessed 23 August 2023).

Blatchford, P, Kutnick, P, Baines, E and Galton, M (2003) Towards a Social Pedagogy of Classroom Group Work. *International Journal of Education Research*, 39(1–2): 153–72. [online] Available at: www.sciencedirect.com/science/article/pii/S0883035503000788 (accessed 19 July 2023).

Block, M and Strachan, S (2019) The Impact of External Audience on Second Graders' Writing Quality. *Reading Horizons*, 58: 68–94. [online] Available at: www.proquest.com/docview/2314197810?pq-origsite=gscholar&fromopenview=true (accessed 23 August 2023).

Bowman, J (2015) Socratic Questions. [online] Available at: www.jamesbowman.me/post/socratic-questions/ (accessed 23 August 2023).

Bowman, J (2017) Socratic Questions Revisited. [online] Available at: www.jamesbowman.me/post/socratic-questions-revisited/ (accessed 23 August 2023).

Boyd, P (2022) Teachers Developing Research-Informed Practice in the Post-Truth World. *Research in Teacher Education*, 12(1): 47–52. [online] Available at: www.uel.ac.uk/sites/default/files/rite-may-2022-guest-author-pete-boyd.pdf (accessed 23 August 2023).

Cabeza, R and Nyberg, L (2000) Imaging Cognition II: An Empirical Review of 275 PET and fMRI Studies. *Journal of Cognitive Neuroscience*, 12: 1–47.

Cantor, P, Osher, D, Berg, J, Steyer, L and Rose, T (2019) Malleability, Plasticity, and Individuality: How Children Learn and Develop in Context. *Applied Developmental Science*, 23(4): 307–37. [online] Available at: www.tandfonline.com/doi/epdf/10.1080/10888691.2017.1398649?needAccess=true&role=button (accessed 22 August 2023).

Carson, P and Harder, N (2016) Simulation Use Within the Classroom: Recommendations from the Literature. *Clinical Simulation in Nursing*, 12(10): 429–37. [online] Available at: www.sciencedirect.com/science/article/pii/S1876139916300160 (accessed 20 June 2023).

Cella, H (2022) Why Transcription Is Important in Your Child's Writing and Reading Journey. [online] Available at: www.nwea.org/blog/2022/why-transcription-is-important-in-your-childs-writing-and-reading-journey/ (accessed 23 August 2023).

Church, K (2010) Building Your Own Book Study: Encouraging Higher Level Thinking, Making Connections, and the Ownership of Learning. *The California Reader*, 44(1): 39–45. [online] Available at: http://web.b.ebscohost.com/ehost/pdfviewer/pdfviewer?vid=6&sid=5062730e-5782-4efe-9da4-4e77cb73d497%40pdc-v-sessmgr01 (accessed 13 April 2023).

Cobb, P (2001) Situated Cognition: Origins. In *International Encyclopedia of the Social & Behavioral Sciences*. [online] Available at: www.sciencedirect.com/topics/neuroscience/situated-cognition (accessed 20 June 2023).

Cohen, L (1989) A Continuum of Adaptive Creative Behaviours. *Creativity Research Journal*, 2: 169–83.

Connor, M (2003) Pupil Stress and Standard Assessment Tasks (SATs): An Update. *Emotional and Behavioural Difficulties*, 8(2): 101–7. [online] Available at: www.researchgate.net/publication/247522382_Pupil_Stress_and_Standard_Assessment_Tasks_SATs_An_Update (accessed 23 August 2023).

Copping, A (2016) *Being Creative in Primary English*. London: Sage.

Copping, A (2018) Exploring Connections between Creative Thinking and Higher Attaining Writing. *Education 3–13*, 46(3): 307–16. [online] Available at: www.tandfonline.com/doi/full/10.1080/03004279.2016.1250801 (accessed 19 July 2023).

Corbett, P (2020) Talk for Writing. [online] Available at: www.talk4writing.com/about/ (accessed 23 August 2023).

Craft, A (1999) Creative Development in the Early Years: Some Implications of Policy for Practice. *Curriculum Journal*, 10(1): 135–50.

Craft, A (2003) Creative Thinking in the Early Years of Education. *Early Years*, 23(2): 143–54.

Craft, A (2005) *Creativity in Schools: Tensions and Dilemmas*. London: Routledge.

Craft, A, Cremin, T, Burnard, P and Chappell, K (2007) Teacher Stance in Creative Learning: A Study of Progression. *Thinking Skills and Creativity*, 2: 136–47. [online] Available at: www.sciencedirect.com/science/article/pii/S1871187107000296 (accessed 21 June 2023).

Craft, A, Cremin, T, Burnard, P, Dragovic, T and Chappell, K (2013) Possibility Thinking: Culminative Studies of an Evidence-Based Concept Driving Creativity? *Education 3–13*, 41(5): 538–56. [online] Available at: www.tandfonline.com/doi/full/10.1080/03004279.2012.656671 (accessed 23 August 2023).

Cremin, T (2006) Creativity, Uncertainty and Discomfort: Teachers as Writers. *Cambridge Journal of Education*, 36(3): 415–33.

Cremin, T (2009) *Teaching English Creatively*. London: Routledge

Cremin, T (2015) *Teaching English Creatively*. 2nd edition. London: Routledge.

Cremin, T and Chappell, K (2021) Creative Pedagogies: A Systematic Review. *Research Papers in Education*, 36(3): 299–331. [online] Available at: www.tandfonline.com/doi/epub/10.1080/02671522.2019.1677757?needAccess=true (accessed 23 August 2023).

Cremin, T, Goouch, K, Blakemore, L and Goff, E (2006) Connecting Drama and Writing: Seizing the Moment to Write. *Research in Drama Education*, 11(3): 273–91. [online] Available at: www.tandfonline.com/doi/abs/10.1080/13569780600900636 (accessed 18 June 2023).

Cresswell, J (2003) *Research Design: Qualitative, Quantitative and Mixed Methods Approaches*. Thousand Oaks: Sage.

Cropley, A (2000) Defining and Measuring Creativity: Are Creativity Tests Worth Using? *Roeper Review*, 23: 72–9.

Cropley, A (2006) Creativity: A Social Approach. *Roeper Review*, 28: 125–30.

Cropley, D and Cropley, A (2015) *The Psychology of Innovation in Organizations*. Cambridge, UK: Cambridge University Press.

Csikszentmihalyi, M (1999) Implications of a Systems Perspective for the Study of Creativity. In Sternberg, R (ed) *Handbook of Creativity* (pp 313–36). Cambridge, NY: Cambridge University Press.

Culham, R (2014) *The Writing Thief: Using Mentor Texts to Teach the Craft of Writing*. Newark, NJ: Stenhouse Publishers, International Literacy Association.

Dahlitz, M (2017) Prefrontal Cortex. [online] Available at: www.thescienceofpsychotherapy.com/prefrontal-cortex/ (accessed 20 June 2023).

Damasio, A (2001) Some Notes on Brain, Imagination and Creativity. In Pfenninger, K and Shubik, V (eds) *The Origins of Creativity* (pp 59–68). Oxford: Oxford University Press.

Davies, D, Jindal-Snape, D, Collier, C, Digby, R, Hay, P and Howe, A (2012) Creative Learning Environments in Education – A Systematic Literature Review. *Thinking Skills and Creativity*, 8: 80–91. [online] Available at: https://doi.org/10.1016/j.tsc.2012.07.004 (accessed 23 August 2023).

De Jong, T (2009) Cognitive Load Theory, Educational Research, and Instructional Design: Some Food for Thought. *Instructional Science*, 38: 105–34. [online] Available at: https://link.springer.com/article/10.1007/s11251-009-9110-0 (accessed 19 July 2023).

Deejring, K (2016) The Design of Knowledge Management to Develop Creative Thinking for Higher Education with Project-Based Learning. *Proceedings of the Multi-disciplinary Academic Conference*. [online] Available at: https://books.google.co.uk/books?id=hX-TCwAAQBAJ&printsec=frontcover#v=onepage&q&f=false (accessed 23 August 2023).

DfE (2013) The National Curriculum in England and Wales. [online] Available at: www.gov.uk/government/collections/national-curriculum (accessed 23 August 2023).

DfE (2016) *ITT Core Content Framework*. Crown Copyright.

DfE (2021) The ITT Core Content Framework. [online] Available at: https://assets.publishing.service.gov.uk/government/uploads/system/uploads/attachment_data/file/974307/ITT_core_content_framework_.pdf (accessed 23 August 2023).

Dietrich, A (2004) The Cognitive Neuroscience of Creativity. *Psychonomic Bulletin and Review*, 11(6): 1011–26.

Donaldson, M (1978) *Children's Minds*. Glasgow: Fontana/Collins.

Donnelly, D (2015) Embracing the Learning Paradigm: How Assessment Drives Creative Writing Pedagogy. In Harper, G (ed) *Creative Writing and Education* (pp 46–56). Bristol: Multilingual Matters.

Dunsmuir, S, Kyriacou, M, Batuwitage, S, Hinson, E, Ingram, V and O'Sullivan, S (2015) An Evaluation of the Writing Assessment Measure (WAM) for Children's Narrative Writing. *Assessing Writing*, 23: 1–18. [online] Available at: www.sciencedirect.com/science/article/pii/S1075293514000385 (accessed 23 August 2023).

Durham University and Arts Council England (2021) Durham Commission on Creativity and Education – Second Report. [online] Available at: www.dur.ac.uk/resources/creativitycommission/DurhamCommissionsecondreport-21April.pdf (accessed 23 August 2023).

Elder, L and Paul, R (1998) The Role of Socratic Questioning in Thinking, Teaching, and Learning. *The Clearing House*, 71(5): 297–301. [online] Available at: www.tandfonline.com/doi/pdf/10.1080/00098659809602729 (accessed 23 August 2023).

Elisondo, R (2016) Creativity is Always a Social Process. *Creativity: Theories, Research, Applications*, 3(2): 194–210. [online] Available at: https://sciendo.com/article/%2010.1515/ctra-2016-0013 (accessed 8 October 2023).

Ericsson, K, Roring, R and Nandagopal, K (2007) Giftedness and Evidence for Reproducibly Superior Performance: An Account Based on the Expert-Performance Framework. *High Ability Studies*, 18: 3–56.

Fahrurrozi, Sari Dewi, R and Rachmadtullah, R (2019) Experiential Learning Model based on Creative Thinking in Learning to Write Narrative Texts. *International Journal of Innovation, Creativity and Change*, 5(5): 285–96. [online] Available at: www.ijicc.net/images/vol5iss5/5521_Fahrurrozi_2019_E_R.pdf (accessed 23 August 2023).

Falconer, E, Cropley, D and Dollard, M (2018) An Exploration of Creativity in Primary School Children. *International Journal of Creativity and Problem-Solving*, 28(2): 7–25. [online] Available at: www.researchgate.net/publication/329076263_An_Exploration_of_Creativity_in_Primary_School_Children (accessed 23 August 2023).

Farmer, S and Tierney, P (2017) Considering Creative Self-Efficacy: Its Current State and Ideas for Future Inquiry. In Karwowski, M and Kaufmann, J (eds) *The Creative Self: Effects of Beliefs, Self-Efficacy, Mindset and Identity* (pp 23–47). London: Academic Press.

Fine, A (2007) *Bill's New Frock*. London: Egmont/Harper-Collins.

Fink, A, Benedek, M, Grabner, R, Staudt, B and Neubauer, A (2007) Creativity Meets Neuroscience: Experimental Tasks for the Neuroscientific Study of Creative Thinking. *Methods*, 42: 68–76.

Flyvbjerg, B (2013) Case Study. In Denzin, N and Lincoln, Y (eds) *Strategies of Qualitative Enquiry* (pp 169–203). 4th edition. London: Sage.

Foley, J (1994) Key Concepts in ELT: Scaffolding. *ELT Journal*, 48(1): 101–2. [online] Available at: https://academic.oup.com/eltj/article/48/1/101/3113988 (accessed 23 August 2023).

Ford, N and Stein, A (2016) Risk Factors Affecting Child Cognitive Development: A Summary of Nutrition, Environment, and Maternal-Child Interaction Indicators for Sub-Saharan Africa. *Journal of Developmental Origins of Health and Disease*, 7(2): 197–217. [online] Available at: www.ncbi.nlm.nih.gov/pmc/articles/PMC4800975/ (accessed 19 July 2023).

Gadd, M and Parr, J (2016) It's All About Baxter: Task Orientation in the Effective Teaching of Writing. *Literacy*, 50(2): 93–9. [online] Available at: https://onlinelibrary.wiley.com/doi/epdf/10.1111/lit.12072 (accessed 19 July 2023).

Gardner, H (1991) *The Unschooled Mind: How Children Think and how Schools Should Teach*. New York: Basic Books.

Gardner, P (2014) Becoming a Teacher of Writing: Primary Student Teachers Reviewing Their Relationship with Writing. *English in Education*, 48(2): 128–48. [online] Available at: https://doi.org/10.1111/17548845.2014.11912509 (accessed 23 August 2023).

Ghaffar, M, Khairallah, M and Salloum, S (2020) Co-constructed Rubrics and Assessment *for* Learning: The Impact on Middle School Students' Attitudes and Writing Skills. *Assessing Writing*, 45: 1–15. [online] Available at: www.sciencedirect.com/science/article/pii/S1075293520300295 (accessed 23 August 2023).

Gist, M (1989) The Influence of Training Method on Self-Efficacy and Idea Generation among Managers. *Personnel Psychology*, 42: 787–805.

Graham, S and Harris, K (1997) It Can Be Taught, But It Does Not Develop Naturally: Myths and Realities in Writing Instruction. *School Psychology Review*, 26(3): 414–24. [online] Available at: https://doi.org/10.1080/02796015.1997.12085875 (accessed 23 August 2023).

Graham, S and Harris, K (2000) The Role of Self-Regulation and Transcription Skills in Writing and Writing Development. *Educational Psychologist*, 35(1): 3–12. [online] Available at: https://doi.org/10.1207/S15326985EP3501_2 (accessed 20 June 2023).

Graham, S and Harris, K (2009) Evidence-Based Writing Practices: Drawing Recommendations from Multiple Sources. *BJEP Monograph Series II*, 6: 95–111. [online] Available at: https://doi.org/10.1348/000709909X421928 (accessed 24 August 2023).

Graham, S and Perin, D (2007) *Writing Next: Effective Strategies to Improve Writing of Adolescents in Middle and High Schools. A Report to Carnegie Corporation of New York*. New York: Carnegie Corporation.

Graham, S, McKeown, D, Kiuhara, S and Harris, K (2012) A Meta-analysis of Writing Instruction for Students in the Elementary Grades. *Journal of Educational Psychology*, 104(4): 879–96.

Grainger, T, Goouch, K and Lambirth, A (2003) 'Playing the Game Called Writing': Children's Views and Voices. *English in Education*, 37(2): 4–15.

Graves, D (1983) *Writing: Teachers and Children at Work*. London: Heinemann.

Guilford, J (1967) *The Nature of Human Intelligence*. New York: McGraw-Hill.

Hallam, S, Ireson, J and Davies, J (2004) Primary Pupils' Experiences of Different Types of Grouping in School. *British Educational Research Journal*, 30(4): 515–33. [online] Available at: https://bera-journals.onlinelibrary.wiley.com/doi/epdf/10.1080/0141192042000237211?saml_referrer (accessed 19 July 2023).

Hanscombe, K, Haworth, C, Davis, O, Jaffee, S and Plomin, R (2011) Chaotic Homes and School Achievement: A Twin Study. *Journal of Applied Psychology and Psychiatry and Allied Disciplines*, 52(11): 1212–20. [online] Available at: www.ncbi.nlm.nih.gov/pmc/articles/PMC3175268/ (accessed 23 August 2023).

Harmey, S, D'Agostino, J and Rodgers, E (2019) Developing and Observational Rubric of Writing: Preliminary Reliability and Validity Evidence. *Journal of Early Childhood Literacy*, 19(3): 316–48. [online] Available at: https://journals.sagepub.com/doi/10.1177/1468798417724862 (accessed 23 August 2023).

Harris, K, Graham, S, MacArthur, C, Reid, R and Mason, L (2011) Self-Regulated Learning Processes and Learners' Writing. In Schunk, D and Zimmerman, B (eds) *Handbook of Self-Regulation of Learning and Performance* (pp 187–202). New York: Routledge.

Hattie, J (2010) *Visible Learning: A Synthesis of Over 800 Meta-analyses Relating to Achievement.* Abingdon: Routledge.

Hayes, J and Flower, L (1980) Identifying the Organisation of Writing Process. In Gregg, L and Steinberg, E (eds) *Cognitive Processes in Writing* (pp 3–30). Hillsdale, NJ: Lawrence Erlbaum Associates.

Hayes, J and Flower, L (1981) A Cognitive Process Theory of Writing. *College Composition and Communication*, 32(4): 365–87. [online] Available at: www.jstor.org/stable/356600 (accessed 23 August 2023).

Hennessey, B and Amabile, T (2010) Creativity. *Annual Review of Psychology*, 61: 569–98. [online] Available at: https://doi.org/10.1146/annurev.psych.093008.100416 (accessed 23 August 2023).

Hiatt, K and Rooke, J (2002) *Creativity and Writing Skills: Finding a Balance in the Primary Classroom.* Abingdon: Routledge.

Higgins, S (2015) Research-based Approaches to Teaching Writing. In Waugh, D, Bushnell, A and Neum, S (eds) *Beyond Early Writing* (pp 5–18). Northwich: Critical Publishing.

Humpherys, S, Bakir, N and Babb, J (2021) Experiential Learning to Foster Tacit Knowledge through a Role Play, Business Simulation. *Journal of Education for Business*, 97: 119–25. [online] Available at: www.tandfonline.com/doi/full/10.1080/08832323.2021.1896461?src=recsys (accessed 20 June 2023).

Hutchings, M (2015) The Impact of Accountability Measures on Children and Young People: Emerging Findings. [online] Available at: www.testconfident.com/cms/wp-content/uploads/2016/04/nut-accountability-findings-30-march-_final-mh.pdf (accessed 24 August 2023).

Ionescu, T (2011) Exploring the Nature of Cognitive Flexibility. *New Ideas in Psychology*, 30(2): 190–200. [online] Available at: https://doi.org/10.1016/j.newideapsych.2011.11.001 (accessed 24 August 2023).

Iskander, M and Nurusholih, S (2019) 'Lacerman' Comic Character Design with Morphological Forced Connection Method. *Balong International Journal of Design*, 2(2). [online] Available at: https://doi.org/10.25134/balong.v2i2.2422 (accessed 21 June 2023).

Ivanic, R (2004) Discourses of Writing and Learning to Write. *Language and Education*, 18(3): 220–45. [online] Available at: www.tandfonline.com/doi/abs/10.1080/09500780408666877 (accessed 24 August 2023).

Ji, S and Wang, H (2018) A Study of the Relationship between Adverse Childhood Experiences, Life Events, and Executive Function among College Students in China. *Psicologia: Reflexão e Crítica*, 31(28): 1–9. [online] Available at: www.scielo.br/pdf/prc/v31/1678-7153-prc-31-28.pdf (accessed 21 June 2023).

Kagan, L, Kagan, S and Kagan, M (1997) *Co-operative Learning Structures for Team-Building*. San Clemente: Kagan Co-operative Learning.

Kaufman, J and Beghetto, R (2009) Beyond Big and Little: The Four C Model of Creativity. *Review of General Psychology*, 13(1): 1–12.

Kellogg, R (1999) *The Psychology of Writing*. Oxford: Oxford University Press.

Khatri, D (2014) Effectiveness of Guided Writing in Teaching Composition. *Journal of Nelta Surkhet*.

Kiely, K (2014) Cognitive Function. In Michalos, A (ed) *Encyclopaedia of Quality of Life and Well-Being Research* (pp 974–8). Dordrecht: Springer. [online] Available at: https://link.springer.com/referenceworkentry/10.1007%2F978-94-007-0753-5_426 (accessed 18 June 2023).

Kim, K (2011) The Creativity Crisis: The Decrease in Creative Thinking Scores on the Torrance Tests of Creative Thinking. *Creativity Research Journal*, 23(4): 285–95.

Kirschner, P and Hendrick, C (2020) *How Learning Happens*. London: Routledge.

Lambirth, A (2016) Exploring Children's Discourses of Writing. *English in Education*, 50(3): 215–32. [online] Available at: www.tandfonline.com/doi/abs/10.1111/eie.12111 (accessed 24 August 2023).

Lantolf, J and Pavlenko, A (2001) Second Language Activity theory: Understanding Second Language Learners as People. In Breen, M (ed) *Learner Contributions to Language Learning* (pp 141–58). Harlow: Pearson Education.

Laverie, D, Hass, A and Mitchell, C (2020) Experiential Learning: A Study of Simulations as a Pedagogical Tool. *Marketing and Education Review*, 32(2): 1–14. [online] Available at: www.researchgate.net/publication/347626537_Experiential_Learning_A_Study_of_Simulations_as_a_Pedagogical_Tool (accessed 20 June 2023).

Lemons, G (2011) Diverse Perspectives of Creativity Testing: Controversial Issues when Used for Inclusion into Gifted Programs. *Journal for the Education of the Gifted*, 34: 742–72. [online] Available at: https://doi.org/10.1177/0162353211417221 (accessed 24 August 2023).

Limpo, T, Filipe, M, Magalhaes, S, Cordeiro, C, Veloso, A, Castro, S and Graham, S (2020) Development and Validation of Instruments to Measure Portuguese Third Graders' Reasons to Write and Self-Efficacy. *Reading and Writing*, 33: 2173–204.

MacArthur, C (1999) Overcoming Barriers to Writing: Computer Support for Basic Writing Skills. *Reading and Writing Quarterly*, 15(2): 169–92. [online] Available at: https://doi.org/10.1080/105735699278251 (accessed 24 August 2023).

MacDonald, B and Walker, R (1975) Case Study and the Social Philosophy of Educational Research. In Hamilton, D (ed) *Beyond the Numbers Game: A Reader in Educational Evaluation* (pp 2–11). Basingstoke: MacMillan.

Magorian, M (1981) *Goodnight Mister Tom.* Harmondsworth: Kestrel.

Marshall, B (2017) The Politics of Testing. *English in Education*, 5(1): 27–43.

Maslow, A (1943) A Theory of Human Motivation. *Psychological Review*, 50: 370–96.

Mathisen, G and Bronnick, K (2009) Creative Self-Efficacy: An Intervention Study. *International Journal of Education Research*, 48: 21–9. [online] Available at: www.sciencedirect.com/science/articlc/pii/S0883035509000305 (accessed 19 July 2023).

McManus, B and Poehlmann, J (2012) Parent–Child Interaction, Maternal Depressive Symptoms and Preterm Infant Cognitive Function. *Infant Behavior and Development*, 35(3): 489–98. [online] Available at: https://pubmed.ncbi.nlm.nih.gov/22721747/ (accessed 19 July 2023).

McWilliam, E (2009) Teaching for Creativity: From Sage to Guide to Meddler. *Asia Pacific Journal of Education*, 29(3): 281–93.

McWilliam, E and Haukka, S (2008) Educating the Creative Workforce: New Directions for 21st Century Schooling. *British Educational Research Journal*, 34(5): 651–66.

Meadows, S (2006) *The Child as Thinker.* 2nd edition. London: Routledge.

McGill, R (2023) The Five Minute Lesson Plan. [online] Available at: www.5minutelessonplan.co.uk/ (accessed 20 January 2023).

Medfouni, K, Benyahia, A and Ounis, A (2021) The Importance of Guided Writing Technique to Enhance Students' Writing Skill. [online] Available at: http://hdl.handle.net/123456789/11736 (accessed 8 October 2023).

Merrotsy, P (2013a) A Note on Big-C and Little-c Creativity. *Creativity Research Journal*, 25(4): 474–6. [online] Available at: www.tandfonline.com/doi/full/10.1080/10400419.2013.843921 (accessed 24 August 2023).

Merrotsy, P (2013b) Tolerance of Ambiguity: A Trait of the Creative Personality? *Creativity Research Journal*, 25(2): 232–7. [online] Available at: https://doi.org/10.1080/10400419.2013.783762 (accessed 24 August 2023).

Morin, A (2020) How Kids Develop Thinking and Learning Skills. [online] Available at: www.understood.org/en/learning-thinking-differences/signs-symptoms/developmental-milestones/how-kids-develop-thinking-and-learning-skills (accessed 19 July 2023).

Mumford, M, Blair, C, Dailey, L, Leritz, L and Osborn, H (2006) Errors in Creative Thought? Cognitive Biases in a Complex Processing Activity. *Journal of Creative Behavior*, 40(2): 75–109. [online] Available at: https://onlinelibrary.wiley.com/toc/21626057/2006/40/2 (accessed 18 July 2023).

Myhill, D (2001) Writing: Crafting and Creating. *English in Education,* 35(3): 13–20.

Myhill, D (2009) From Talking to Writing: Linguistic Development in Writing. Teaching and Learning Writing: Psychological Aspects of Education – Current Trends. *British Journal of Educational Psychology*, Monograph Series II (6): 27–44.

Myhill, D, Jones, S and Watson, S (2013) Grammar Matters: How Teachers' Grammatical Knowledge Impacts on the Teaching of Writing. *Teaching and Teacher Education*, 36: 77–91.

National Literacy Trust (2022) Children and Young People's Writing in 2022. [online] Available at: https://literacytrust.org.uk/research-services/research-reports/children-and-young-peoples-writing-in-2022/ (accessed 24 August 2023).

Nijstad, B, De Dreu, C, Rietzschel, E and Baas, M (2010) The Dual Pathway to Creativity Model: Creative Ideation as a Function of Flexibility and Persistence. *European Review of Social Psychology*, 21(1): 34–77. [online] Available at: www.tandfonline.com/doi/abs/10.1080/10463281003765323 (accessed 24 August 2023).

Niu, W and Sternberg, R (2006) The Philosophical Roots of Western and Eastern Conceptions of Creativity. *Journal of Theoretical and Philosophical Psychology*, 26: 18–38.

Nordin, S and Mohammed, N (2017) The Best of Two Approaches: Process/Genre Based Approach to Teaching Writing. *The English Teacher* (XXXV): 75–85. [online] Available at: http://journals.melta.org.my/index.php/tet/article/view/315/211 (accessed 22 June 2023).

Oddsdóttir, R, Ragnarsdóttir, H and Skúlason, S (2021) The Effect of Transcription Skills, Text Generation and Self-Regulation on Icelandic Children's Text Writing. *Reading and Writing*, 34(2): 391–416. [online] Available at: https://link.springer.com/article/10.1007/s11145-020-10074-w (accessed 10 February 2023).

OECD (2019) PISA 2021: Creative Thinking Framework (Third Draft). [online] Available at: www.oecd.org/pisa/publications/PISA-2021-Creative-Thinking-Framework.pdf (accessed 22 August 2023).

Ofsted (2022) Research Review Series: English. [online] Available at: www.gov.uk/government/publications/curriculum-research-review-series-english/curriculum-research-review-series-english (accessed 24 August 2023).

Pankowski, J and Walker J (2016) Using Simulation to Support Novice Teachers' Classroom Management Skills: Comparing Traditional and Alternative Certification Groups. *Journal of the National Association for Alternative Certification*, 11(1): 3–20. [online] Available at: https://eric.ed.gov/?id=EJ1100871 (accessed 20 June 2023).

Pantaleo, S (2016) Teacher Expectations and Student Literacy Engagement and Achievement. *Literacy*, 50: 83–92. [online] Available at: https://doi.org/10.1111/lit.12074 (accessed 19 July 2023).

Paraskeva, F et al (2015) The Development of Creative Thinking through Six Thinking Hats and Web 2.0 Technologies. *International Journal of Technologies and Learning*, 22(2): 15–29.

Parr, J and Limbrick, L (2010) Contextualising Practice: Hallmarks of Effective Teachers of Writing. *Teacher and Teacher Education*, 26: 583–90. [online] Available at: https://doi.org/10.1016/j.tate.2009.09.004 (accessed 24 August 2023).

Paul, R and Elder, L (2019) *The Nature and Functions of Critical and Creative Thinking*. 3rd edition. Tomales, California: Foundation for Critical Thinking Press.

Piaget, J (1952) *The Origins of Intelligence in Children*. New York: International University Press.

Pincas, A (1982) *Writing in English 1*. London: Macmillan.

Plucker, J, Beghetto, R and Dow, G (2004) Why Isn't Creativity More Important to Educational Psychologists? Potential, Pitfalls and Future Directions in Creativity Research. *Educational Psychologist*, 39: 83–96.

Polesel, J, Rice, S and Dulfer, N (2014) The Impact of High-Stakes Testing on Curriculum and Pedagogy: A Teacher Perspective from Australia. *Journal of Education Policy*, 29(5): 640–57.

Prendiville, F (2000) 'Teacher-in-Role': The Undercover Agent in the Classroom. *Education 3–13*, 28(2): 9–14. [online] Available at: www.tandfonline.com/doi/pdf/10.1080/03004270085200141 (accessed 18 June 2023).

Resnick, M (2007) All I Really Need to Know (About Creative Thinking) I Learned (by Studying How Children Learn) in Kindergarten. *Proceedings of the 6th ACM SIGCHI Conference on Creativity and Cognition* (pp 1–6). [online] Available at: https://dl.acm.org/doi/abs/10.1145/1254960.1254961 (accessed 19 July 2023).

Rice, T (nd) AZQuotes.com. [online] Available at: www.azquotes.com/quote/642372 (accessed 24 October 2023).

Richards, R (2007) Everyday Creativity: Our Hidden Potential. In Richards, R (ed) *Everyday Creativity and New Views of Human Nature* (pp 25–53). Washington, DC: American Psychological Association.

Rigsbee, P and Keith, L (2023) Learning Styles and Information Processing. [online] Available at: https://edp304.wordpress.ncsu.edu/processing-with-technology/ (accessed 22 August 2023).

Robinson, K (1999) *All Our Futures: Creativity, Culture and Education*. National Advisory Committee on Creative and Cultural Education. [online] Available at: http://sirkenrobinson.com/pdf/allourfutures.pdf (accessed 24 August 2023).

Robson, S (2014) The Analysing Children's Creative Thinking Framework: Development of an Observation-Led Approach to Identifying and Analysing Young Children's Creative Thinking. *British Educational Research Journal*, 40(1): 121–34.

Robson, S and Rowe, V (2012) Observing Young Children's Creative Thinking: Engagement, Involvement and Persistence. *International Journal of Early Years Education*, 20(4): 349–64. [online] Available at: https://doi.org/10.1080/09669760.2012.743098 (accessed 24 August 2023).

Rossetti, C (1862) A Birthday. In *Goblin Market and Other Poems*. London: Macmillan.

Rothwell, D (2016) Using Blogging to Develop Learners' Writing. *English 4–11*, 56: 9–10.

RSA (2010) Sir Ken Robinson – Changing Paradigms. [online] Available at: www.youtube.com/watch?v=mCbdS4hSa0s (accessed 24 August 2023).

Runco, M (1996) Personal Creativity: Definition and Developmental Issues. *New Directions for Child Development*, 72: 3–30.

Ryan, M (2014) Writers as Performers: Developing Reflexive and Creative Writing Identities. *English Teaching: Practice and Critique*, 13(1): 130–48. [online] Available at: http://education.waikato.ac.nz/research/files/etpc/files/2014v13n3art7.pdf (accessed 24 August 2023).

Rybski Beaver, B (1997) The Role of Emotion in Children's Selection of Strategies for Coping with Daily Stresses. *Merrill-Palmer Quarterly*, 43(1): 129–47. [online] Available at: www.jstor.org/stable/23093731?seq=1#metadata_info_tab_contents (accessed 19 June 2023).

Said-Metwaly, S, Van den Noortgate, W and Kyndt, E (2017) Approaches to Measuring Creativity: A Systematic Literature Review. *Creativity: Theories, Research, Applications*, 4(2): 238–75. [online] Available at: https://content.sciendo.com/view/journals/ctra/4/2/article-p238.xml (accessed 24 August 2023).

Savin-Baden, M and Howell-Major, C (2013) *Qualitative Research. The Essential Guide to Theory and Practice*. London: Routledge.

Schunk, D and Rice, J (1987) Enhancing Comprehension Skill and Self-Efficacy with Strategy Value Information. *Journal of Reading Behavior*, 19: 285–302. [online] Available at: https://journals.sagepub.com/doi/pdf/10.1080/10862968709547605 (accessed 19 July 2023).

Seow, A (2002) The Writing Process and Process Writing. In Richards, J and Renandya, W (eds) *Methodology in Language Teaching: An Anthology of Current Practice* (pp 315–20). New York: Cambridge University Press.

Simonton, D (2011) Big C Creativity in the Big City. In Andersson, D, Andersson, A and Mellander, C (eds) *Handbook of Creative Cities* (pp 72–84). Northampton, MA: Edward Elgar Publishing.

Skidmore, D (2006) Pedagogy and Dialogue. *Cambridge Journal of Education*, 36(4): 503–14. [online] Available at: www.tandfonline.com/doi/pdf/10.1080/03057640601048407?needAccess=true (accessed 24 August 2023).

Smagorinsky, P (2013) What Does Vygotsky Provide for the 21st-Century Language Arts Teacher? *Language Arts*, 90(3): 192–204. [online] Available at: www.jstor.org/stable/41804393?seq=1#metadata_info_tab_contents (accessed 24 August 2023).

Stark, S and Torrance, H (2005) Case Study. In Somekh, B and Lewin, C (eds) *Research Methods in the Social Sciences* (pp 33–40). London: Sage.

Steele, L, Johnson, G and Mederios, K (2018) Looking Beyond the Generation of Creative Ideas: Confidence in Evaluating Ideas Predicts Creative Outcomes. *Personality and Individual Differences*, 125: 21–9. [online] Available at: www.sciencedirect.com/science/article/abs/pii/S0191886917307420 (accessed 24 August 2023).

Sternberg, R (1999) A Propulsion Model of types of Creative Contributions. *Review of General Psychology*, 3(2): 83–100.

Sternberg, R (2003) Creative Thinking in the Classroom. *Scandinavian Journal of Educational Research*, 47(3): 325–38.

Sternberg, R and Lubart, T (1995) *Defying the Crowd: Simple Solutions to the Most Common Relationship Problems.* New York: The Free Press.

Sweller, J (1988) Cognitive Load During Problem-Solving: Effects on Learning. *Cognitive Science*, 12: 257–85. [online] Available at: https://onlinelibrary.wiley.com/doi/pdf/10.1207/s15516709cog1202_4 (accessed 24 August 2023).

Terhart, E (2011) Has John Hattie Really Found the Holy Grail of Research on Teaching? An Extended Review of *Visible Learning*. *Journal of Curriculum Studies*, 43(3): 425–38. [online] Available at: www.tandfonline.com/doi/full/10.1080/00220272.2011.576774 (accessed 24 August 2023).

Thomas, G (2011) *How to Do Your Case Study: A Guide for Students and Researchers*. London: Sage.

Tierney, P and Farmer, S (2002) Creative Self-Efficacy: Its Potential Antecedents and Relationship to Creative Performance over Time. *Academy of Management Journal*, 45(6): 1137–48. [online] Available at: www.jstor.org/stable/3069429?seq=1#metadata_info_tab_contents (accessed 18 July 2023).

Torrance, E (1966) *Torrance Tests of Creative Thinking*. Bensenville, IL: Scholastic Testing Service.

Torrance, E (2008) *The Torrance Tests of Creative Thinking Norms—Technical Manual Figural (Streamlined) Forms A and B*. Bensenville, IL: Scholastic Testing Service.

Van Wynsberghe, R and Khan, S (2007) Redefining Case Study. *International Journal of Qualitative Methods*, 6(2): 1–11. [online] Available at: https://journals.sagepub.com/doi/pdf/10.1177/160940690700600208 (accessed 24 August 2023).

Vass, E, Littleton, K, Miell, D and Jones, A (2008) The Discourse of Collaborative Creative Writing: Peer Collaboration as a Context for Mutual Inspiration. *Thinking Skills and Creativity*, 3: 192–202. [online] Available at: https://doi.org/10.1016/j.tsc.2008.09.001 (accessed 24 August 2023).

Vygotsky, L (1978) *Mind in Society*. Cambridge, MA: Harvard University Press.

Waitman, G and Plucker, J (2009) Teaching Writing by Demythologizing Creativity. In Kaufman, S and Kaufman, J (eds) *The Psychology of Creative Writing* (pp 287–315). Cambridge: Cambridge University Press.

Wang, A (2012) Exploring the Relationship of Creative Thinking to Reading and Writing. *Thinking Skills and Creativity*, 7: 38–47.

Ward, T (2007) Creative Cognition as a Window on Creativity. *Methods*, 42(1): 28–37.

Weisberg, R (1993) *Creativity: Beyond the Myth of Genius*. New York: W H Freeman & Co.

Wiggins, G (2009) Real-World Writing: Making Purpose and Audience Matter. *The English Journal*, 98(5): 29–37. [online] Available at: www.jstor.com/stable/40503292 (accessed 24 August 2023).

Wong, K and Moorhouse, B (2018) Writing for an Audience: Inciting Creativity among Young English Language Bloggers through Scaffolded Comments. *TESOL Journal*, 9(4). [online] Available at: https://doi.org/10.1002/tesj.389 (accessed 11 April 2023).

Wyse, D and Torgerson, C (2017) Experimental Trials and 'What Works?' in Education: The Case of Grammar for Writing. *British Educational Research Journal*, 43(6): 1019–47.

Xiao, Y and Yang, M (2019) Formative Assessment and Self-Regulated Learning: How Formative Assessment Supports Students' Self-Regulation in English Language Learning. *System*, 81: 39–49. [online] Available at: www.sciencedirect.com/science/article/pii/S0346251X18301076 (accessed 24 August 2023).

Zimmerman, B and Risemberg, R (1997) Becoming a Self-Regulated Writer: A Social Cognitive Perspective. *Contemporary Educational Psychology*, 22: 73–101. [online] Available at: https://doi.org/10.1006/ceps.1997.0919 (accessed 20 June 2023).

Index

Note: Page numbers in **bold** denote tables.

accommodation process, 88
adverse childhood experiences (ACEs), 45–6
age-related expectations (AREs), 94, 112, 119
   working above, 7, 113, **115**, 132, 146
   working below, 7, 113, 135
Analysing Children's Creative Thinking (ACCT)
     framework, 121–3
   exploration and engagement, 122–3
   involvement, 123
   persistence, 123
assessment, 112
   ACCT framework. See Analysing Children's Creative Thinking (ACCT) framework
   context-embedded approach, 121
   criteria, 114–15
   and observation, 120–1
   in practice, 113–14
   of process, 117–19
   of product, 113–14
   and quality, 119–20
assimilation process, 88
attainment, 151
   and creative thinking, 94
   equation, 95
   and self-regulation, 78–81
   and writing task, 104–8
author's intent, 67, 82
autonomous multi-sensory writing, 10–13
autonomy in writing, 51–2, 59–60

Big C creativity, 31–2, 44
blogs, 59, 99
brain functions, 74

case studies
   adverse childhood experiences (ACEs) and cognitive overload, 45–6
   assessment criteria, 115–16
   cognitive flexibility, 75–6
   creating images in poetry, 89
   Galactic Defence. See Galactic Defence
   Great Fire of London. See Great Fire of London
   history inspired playscripts and performance, 100–3
   invitation to a teddy bears' picnic, 106–7
   learning environment, 49–51
   possibility thinking, 92–3
   revising and editing text, 19–20
   scaffolding the text production, 39–41
   science-inspired writing, 60–2
   self-regulation and writing attainment, 78–81
   Socratic questions, 108
   visualisation and collaboration, 36–9
   writing a missing chapter, 72
   writing for purpose, 24–5
cause-and-effect thinking, 53–4, 144
challenges, choosing, 73
class web pages, 24–5
cognitive attitudes, 73
   embracing pretence, 149–50
   enjoyment, 148–9
   persistence, 149
cognitive flexibility, 7, 52, 72, 74, 82
   development of, 75–6
   impact on attainment, 77
   and self-regulation, 78
cognitive overload, 16, 44, 45–6, 54, 77
cognitive persistence, 123
cognitive processes
   modelling, 64
   writing as, 17
collaboration, 3, 38, 39, 146
collaborative learning, 49
composition, 16, 17–18, 23
concrete case knowledge, 2
connection-making, 62–6, 72, 74, 104–5
   and author's intent, 82
   cognitive flexibility, 75–6
   purpose of, 72
   and self-regulation, 77–8
   significance of, 145–6
context creation, 59–60
   autonomy in, 59–60
   real world, 59
creative connections, 8–10. See connection-making

creative self-efficacy. *See* self-efficacy, creative
creative thinking, 30, 33–4
   barriers to, 45
   brain functions in, 74
   capability of, 44–5
   and curriculum, 47–8
   definitions and characteristics of, 72–4
   embedding, 46–7
   and Greater Depth writing, 105
   influence on process and product, 148–50
   and teaching approaches, 48–52
   and training in thinking excellence, 45
   training for, 52–4
creative thinking opportunities,
      impact of, 145–7
creativity discourse, 22, 23
curriculum, 44, 47–8

dialogue, 59–60
divergent thinking, 36, 74, 121, 136
domain-specific, 121
domain-specific knowledge, 73–4, 88,
      105, 150
drafting, 17

editing, 17, 19–20, 77
embracing pretence, 3, 38, 145, 149–50
enjoyment, 148–9
exploration, 122–3
external influences, 147–8, 152

feedback on self-efficacy, 143–4
fit mind, 34, 44, 47, 52
Four C Model of Creativity, 31, 47
   Big C, 31–2, 44
   Little C, 32
   Mini C, 33, 62
   Pro C, 33

Galactic Defence, 6, 64–5, 129
genre discourse, 22
grammar writing, 66
Great Fire of London, 8, 34–6, 134, 145
Greater Depth writing, 99–100, 105,
      106–7
group writing, 117
guided writing, 66–8

high-stakes testing, 47–8, 120

ideas
   elaboration of, 105
   organisation of, 21
immersion, 36–9
information gathering, 21
information processing, 53–4, 144
involvement, assessment of, 123
involving others, assessment of, 123

judgement of propriety, 74

knowledge telling, 18
knowledge transformation, 18, 21

learner agency, 52, 114
learning environments, 48–51, 128
lifestyle challenges, 44
linguistic symbols, 18
Little C creativity, 32

marketisation of learning, 5
mentor text, 6, 62–3, 64, 86–8, 93, 117,
      144, 146, 150
mind maps, 35
Mini C creativity, 33, 62
missing chapter, writing a, 72
modelling writing
   and cognitive process, 64
   and creative self-efficacy, 91
Morgan, Nicky, 4
morphological forced connection, 134–7
   reflections, 135–6
   visualisation, 136–7

national curriculum, 4, 47

observation, assessment through, 120–1
Ofsted, 93

pedagogical environment, 48–51, 143, 152
   and autonomy in writing, 51–2
   significance of, 148
persistence, 123, 131, 144, 149, 152
PISA Creative Thinking Assessment, 89
planning, 17, 21, 23–5, 59
playscripts, 10–12, 105, 147
poetry, creating images in, 89
possibility thinking, 74
pretence, embracing, 3, 38, 145, 149–50
Pro C creativity, 33
problem-solving, 36, 73
problem-setting, 73
process discourse, 22, 23
product-centred approach, 48, 147, 152
purpose of writing, 5
purpose, writing for, 23–5

'raindrops keep falling on my head' theme, 10, 60
real-world writing
   and audience, 102–4
   contexts of, 59
reciprocity, 59–60
revising, 17, 19–20, 21, 77

scaffolding learning, 98
scaffolding the text production, 39–41
science-inspired writing, 60–2

self-assurance, 88
self-efficacy, creative, 69, 90
    development of, 88–9, 152
    feedback on, 143–4
    and modelling, 91
self-evaluation, 21, 23
self-monitoring, 21
self-regulation, 18, 19, 21, 63, 69, 77–8, 115, 131, 149, 152
simulation, 3, 6–8
    challenging experiences, 132
    and creative thinking, 131
    and creative thinking development, 129
    definition of, 128–9
    impact on engagement and curiosity, 130–1
    success of, 133–4
    teamwork, challenges of, 132–3
    and writing process difficulties, 131
skills discourse, 22–3
social deprivation, 144–5
social interactional framework, 136
social practices discourse, 22
social relationships, 146
socio-cultural theoretical approach, 49
socio-political discourse, 22
Socratic questions, 107–8
Standard Assessment Tests (SATs), 112
sustained attention, 74

task design. See writing task
Teacher Assessment Frameworks, 4, 72, 86, 98, 99, 112
teacher focus, 150–1
teaching approaches, 44, 48
    enabling autonomy, 51–2
    learning environments, 48–51
teamwork, 146
thinking environment, 143
thinking for writing, 1, 7, 53, 143, 150
    cognitive writing, 144
    and creative thinking, 33–4, 144–5
    teacher focus, 150–1

Torrance Tests of Creative Thinking, 91
training, 52–3, 144
    cause-and-effect thinking, 58
    information processing, 53–4
training in thinking excellence, lack of, 45
transcription, 17, 18–19, 23–4, 81, 119
translation, 17

uncertainty and complexity, managing, 73

visual timetable, 75
visualisation, 3, 8–10, 36–9, 136–7, 145, 146

wall display, 116
What A Good One Looks Like (WAGOLL), 6, 62–3, 64, 86–8, 93, 117, 144, 146, 150
working memory, 74
working wall, 79
working within the gaps, 86, 151
    and attainment in writing, 93
    creative self-efficacy development, 88–9
    modelling, 91
    rationale for, 86–8
Writing Assessment Measure (Dunsmuir et al), 72, **79–80**, 112–13, **114**
writing attainment. See attainment
writing discourses, 21–3
writing process, 5, 16–17
    challenges in, 21–3
    and cognition, 17
    composition, 17–18
    self-regulation, 21
    transcription, 18–19
writing task, 98–9, 152
    connection with creative thinking and attainment, 104–8
    and Greater Depth writing, 99–100
    significance of, 147
written composition, 18